Presented by

J. M Kelsey

- 1984 -

TEACHER'S TREASURY OF CLASSROOM READING ACTIVITIES

by Mary Jo Lass-Kayser

Here at last is the biggest, most comprehensive source of fresh ideas and activities you can use to improve dramatically the reading abilities of all your students.

Brimming with over 3,100 classroom-tested activities, this time-and-work-saving guide will help you get across the vitally important concepts in 11 important reading skill areas— no matter what grade you teach . . . no matter what your students' competency level . . . and no matter what basic reading program you're already using.

OVER 3,100 ACTIVITIES COVER EVERY ASPECT OF READING INSTRUCTION

These activities, which include sparkling games, puzzles, quizzes, imaginative exercises and to-the-point questions, are conveniently arranged so you can select the right ones to solve the particular reading problems your class may be having.

Best of all, these activities have been especially created to help you spark student enthusiasm and participation in all your lessons!

With this valuable treasury of reading skill activities at your side, you'll discover:

- **406 comprehension activities** to give your students a better understanding of what they read
- **195 critical reading activities** to reduce your students' gullibility to the written word
- **171 literature appreciation** activities to stretch your students' imaginations and emotions
- **217 vocabulary building activities** to help your students appreciate the excitement of language
- **206 word perception activities** to teach your students phonic cues, sight cues and structural analysis cues
- **106 auditory perception cues** to show your students how to read new words more easily
- **131 perception activities** to help your students better interpret what they read

PARKER PUBLISHING CO., INC.
West Nyack, New York 10994

TEACHER'S TREASURY
OF
CLASSROOM READING
ACTIVITIES

Mary Jo Lass–Kayser

Parker Publishing Company, Inc.

West Nyack, New York

© 1979 by

PARKER PUBLISHING COMPANY, INC.

West Nyack, New York

Library of Congress Cataloging in Publication Data

Lass-Kayser, Mary Jo
    Teacher's treasury of classroom reading activities.

    Includes index.
    1. Reading—Handbooks, manuals, etc. 2. Activity
programs in education—Handbooks, manuals, etc.
3. Reading games—Handbooks, manuals, etc. I. Title.
LB1050.L368   428'.4'07   79-11720
ISBN 0-13-891135-5

Printed in the United States of America

Dedication

For

David,

Mother,

Mike,

and Enid D

How This Book
Will Help You

Here are just a few of the ways this book will help you teach reading more effectively. . . .

- It compiles creative reading ideas in a compact, easily read outline.
- It will accomplish more with these creative ideas by indicating the basic reading skills these ideas teach.
- It gives you an overall view of these basic reading skills.
- It gives you a checklist of ideas for those times when you can't seem to think of anything new.
- It gives you ideas that are not limited in depth or scope; that work as well with Henry who can interpret Tolstoi, as with Jane who enrolled last week after attending four other 'schools this year.
- It gives you activities for the broad range of abilities characteristic of the typical classroom; a range from beginning reading to post-high school levels.
- It gives you the opportunity to get away from old ideas, get out of a rut, and move in new directions.
- It gives you a way to use creative arts in several subject areas to make reading instruction more effective.
- It gives you activities to broaden a reading program that may otherwise be limited by the use of a specific *kind* of reading program or a specific basal reading text.
- It gives you and the children a chance to have *fun* with reading.

HOW TO USE THIS BOOK

The activities suggested in this book are not tied to a particular reading series, grade level, or classroom organizational pattern. They work, with modifications, for every age, intelligence level, and socioeconomic stratum.

To use this book, let your imagination wander; think of all the possibilities; dream a little. Don't box your thinking into set patterns; don't feel you have to explore in minute detail every little possibility.

For example, you might want a suggestion for developing prediction skills. The first idea you read might be:

"Choose three different occupations referred to in a story. Write why the main characters in the story would or would not be qualified for these jobs."

Think of various ways you can use this idea. Avoid thoughts like: "Good Heavens, that's high school. My second graders can't write; don't even know what the word *occupation* means; and besides I don't have time for all that today." Think a moment. Maybe all you need do is ask a discussion question such as, "Do you think John would make a good mechanic?"

As you look at the hundreds of ideas this book lists, consider these questions:

• Can I use another medium of expression; e.g. drawing for writing, talking for drawing, movement for talking?
• Would this work better with a small group? The whole class? One student?
• Do I want to do a small part of this activity? All of it? More than is described?
• What other activities does this suggestion bring to mind?

* * * * * * * * * * * *

The best part of teaching is growing and having fun *while* you teach. These activities will enrich your classroom and your students' experiences in reading. While a significant scope of skills is included, there is no need to follow any special sequence; no need to feel you "have to cover all the material."

Enjoy yourself, feeling secure that as you and your students have fun, they are gaining basic reading skills.

Mary Jo Lass-Kayser

TEACHER'S TREASURY OF CLASSROOM READING ACTIVITIES

by Mary Jo Lass-Kayser

Brimming with over 3,100 stimulating activities, unique ideas and helpful checklists, this all-inclusive handbook will enable you to spark student participation and add zest to your every reading lesson. Easily supplemental to all the different basic reading programs, this guide is a virtual treasure chest of ideas you can use again and again to save hours of preparation time!

PARTIAL OUTLINE OF CONTENTS

COMPREHENSION SKILLS—406 activities including: Recall • Selecting Main Ideas • Identifying Story Elements • Interpreting Figurative Language • Understanding Cause and Effect

CRITICAL READING SKILLS—195 activities covering: Author Bias and Values • Separating Fact From Opinion • Recognizing Propaganda • Indentifying stereotypes • Comparing two or more sources

CREATIVE READING SKILLS—223 activities covering: Creation of Original Material • Developing Problem Solving Skills • Formulating Questions • Developing Recreational Reading Skills

LITERATURE APPRECIATION SKILLS—171 activities including: Story Elements • Cultural Analysis Through Literature • Different Literary Forms • Famous Writings and Authors

VOCABULARY DEVELOPMENT SKILLS—217 activities including: Vocabulary Patterning • Technical and Specialized Vocabulary • Special Relationships Among Words • Figurative or Idiomatic Language

WORD PERCEPTION SKILLS—206 activities including Etymological Cues • Cues from Word Similarities and Differences • Structural Analysis • Syllable Analysis • Encoding, Decoding or Phonic Cues

AUDITORY PERCEPTION SKILLS—106 activities covering: Memory Skills • Auditory Closure Skills • Auditory Discrimination •

Blending • Oral Language Skills • Listening Skills

VISUAL PERCEPTION SKILLS—126 activities including: Visual Memory Skills • Sequence Skills • Visual Closure Skills • Form Perception • Visual Tracking • Eye Movement

PERCEPTION SKILLS—131 activities including: Multi-Sensory Perception Skils • Hand-Eye Coordination Skills • Body Awareness Skills • Spatial Relationship Skills

WORK-STUDY SKILLS—231 activities covering: Map and Globe Skills • Reading Technique • Note Taking • Outlining • Self-Improvement • Oral Reading • Research • Group Work

REFERENCE SKILLS—127 activities covering: Skills in Using Parts of Books • Dictionary and Other Word Reference Skills • Standard Reference Skills • Library Skills • Bibliography Skills

TEACHING READING THROUGH VISUAL THINKING—318 activities to help teach the 11 basic reading skill areas through visual thinking

TEACHING READING THROUGH INTERPERSONAL READING PROCESS—511 activities to teach the 11 basic reading skills through the interpersonal reading process.

NEW WAYS WITH BOOK REVIEWS—214 activities to teach the 11 basic reading skills through book reviews.

ABOUT THE AUTHOR

MARY JO LASS-KAYSER, a leading educator and consultant in the field of reading instruction, brings to this fully comprehensive volume a teaching background that ranges from elementary to university levels. Currently a professor of education at California State University at Long Beach, she has conducted numerous Reading Skill seminars and has written articles for many leading educational journals.

0-13-891135

Contents

Chapter 3 * Creative Reading Skills * 69

Developing Authors' Skills (69) * Creation of Original Material (78) * Designing Games, Puzzles, Anagrams, and the Like (80) * Developing Creative Thinking Skills; Convergent, Divergent and Evaluative Thinking (80) * Developing Problem-Solving Skills (84) * Developing Planning Skills (84) * Formulating Questions (85) * Understanding the Relation of Reading to Other Media (86) * Evaluating One's Own Written Work (87) * Improving Self-Concept and Self-Development Through Reading (88) * Developing Reader Purpose Skills (88) * Developing Recreational Reading Skills (89) * Developing Reader Emotional Response (90) * A Final Word About Creative Reading (91)

Chapter 4 * Literature Appreciation Skills * 93

Value of Reading (93) * Story Elements: Mood, Style, Plot, Theme, Characterization (95) * Different Literary Forms (97) * Cultural Analysis Through Literature (99) * Bibliotherapy (101) * Famous Writings and Authors (102) * Selecting Appropriate Materials for Self and Others (103) * A Final Word About Literature Appreciation (104)

Chapter 5 * Vocabulary Development Skills * 105

Vocabulary Patterning (105) * New Vocabulary (107) * Technical and Specialized Vocabulary (108) * Special Relationships Among Words: Synonyms, Antonyms, Homonyms, and Homographs (109) * Variations of Vocabulary Due to Regional Differences, Age, Area and the Like (111) * Developing Appropriateness of Vocabulary (112) * Vocabulary Development Through the Study of Etymology (113) * Figurative or Idiomatic Language: Hyperbole, Metaphor, Simile, Personification, Analogy, Malapropism, Palindromes, Onomatopoetic Words or Phrases, Alliteration and Puns (114) * Relating Word Stress, Pitch, and Intonation to Word Meaning (118) * Word Meanings (119) * Nonverbal Vocabulary Development (120) * Word Enrichment (121) * A Final Word About Vocabulary Development (124)

Chapter 6 * Word Perception Skills * 125

Chapter 7 * Auditory Perception Skills * 145

Chapter 8 * Visual Perception Skills * 157

Chapter 9 * Perception Skills * 171

Chapter 14 * New Ways With Book Reviews * 297

1

Comprehension Skills

* * * * * * * * * * * *

To understand *what* is read is the most important part of reading for our students. Understanding what is read opens whole, fresh worlds to them: worlds of new ideas and customs and people; worlds of unfamiliar words and language and descriptions; worlds of sensory impressions and feelings and awareness; worlds of wonder and beauty and excitement.

What greater gift could we teachers give?

RECALL SKILLS

Sample Activities for Discussion, Task Cards, Learning Centers, and Reading Contracts

1. Describe an object or a character from the story, using as few words as possible and being as accurate as you can,
2. How many of the objects, tools, and furniture described in the story are no longer in use? How many occupations are out of date?
3. Newspaper stories usually start with *who, what, where, when, why,* and sometimes *how.* Write a lead paragraph including these details as if you were reporting the events in the story for a newspaper.
4. Write the answers to the following for your story: *who, where, what, when, why,* and *how.*
5. Make a list of five facts that you think were important to the story and five facts in the story that you felt were not so important.

6. Make up a test of ten questions on the story that a person would have to read the story to answer.

7. Make up a crossword puzzle based on the details of this story (poem, article, chapter).

8. Write five incomplete sentences about the story for someone else to complete after he or she reads the story.

9. Write the names of the characters in the story across the top of a piece of paper. Under each character's name, write the things he or she did in the story.

10. Teachers: Play a comprehension game with a group of students who have read the same story. The first student asks a question about the story. Whoever answers it gets to ask a question about the story. (Or go similarly around a circle or down a line in having students ask and answer questions.)

11. Teachers: Make up two sets of cards, one containing questions about details of the story, the other containing the answers. Pass out the answer cards. Read a question (or have a student read a question) and have the student with the correct answer read it.

12. Teachers: Ask questions about story details that can be answered by yes or no. Give each student a card with *Yes* written on one side and *No* written on the other. Have them show the answer by holding up the correct side of the card toward you.

13. Have a *Story Mystery Hour.* Ask students to make up ten clues, each progressively easier, about a favorite book many have read (books should be considered for *Mystery Hour* only when at least five in the class have read them.) Play individually or in teams. Give progressively fewer points for each additional clue until the story title is guessed.

14. Quote some statements made by a story character and ask the children to identify him or her.

SKILLS OF SELECTING MAIN IDEAS

Sample Activities for Discussion, Task Cards, Learning Centers, and Reading Contracts

1. Find or take a picture that could be used for an advertisement or illustration for this story.

2. Make a design or designs for postcards that tourists could buy when they visit this setting.
3. Sell your book to the class by making up a commercial about the most important parts.
4. Preview the story for students who haven't yet read it by sharing some of the important features.
5. What do you think of the title of this story? Can you think of at least five alternatives?
6. Summarize the main idea of your story in one sentence. (Alternates: in one paragraph or one word.)
7. Prepare a radio or TV newscast as if you were reporting on the events that took place in your story.
8. What is the most important sentence in this paragraph? In each paragraph on this page? Etc.
9. Prepare a TV show or a movie about the story for our roller "movie" box. Use shelf paper to draw on or paste together pictures you drew of the most important scenes.
10. Prepare a slide show, a film strip, or a movie about the main ideas in the story.
11. Write a classified ad for one of the characters in the story.
12. Was the title for this story a good one? Explain your answer.
13. Design an advertisement to sell this book through newspapers or magazines.
14. Record a commercial on tape or videotape to sell the story to someone who has never read it before. Include the most important part or parts of the story.
15. Select a picture from a magazine that best fits the story.
16. Copy a paragraph that you particularly liked in the story. Underline the sentence that tells the main idea of the paragraph. Check your choice with the teacher.
17. Teachers: Read a poem to the class and ask the students to write as many titles as they can for the poem. Compare the ideas given and discuss why the author titled the poem as he or she did. (Alternate: Read a story aloud and have students make up titles for it in a similar fashion.)
18. Teachers: Ask students to match newspaper headlines and stories that have been cut apart. (Alternate: Cut out titled paragraphs from old books—science books, readers, etc. Paste the paragraphs on one set of cards and their titles on another set. Have students match titles and paragraphs.)

19. Teachers: Duplicate paragraphs from the story or reading selection and have students draw a line under or circle the main idea in each.
20. Teachers: Look at paragraphs in the story with students and have them make up a title for each.
21. Teachers: Have students give each illustration in the story, chapter, or article; first a one word title, then a two or three word title.
22. Teachers: Give students recipes without a title. See if the students can guess what the recipe is for. Or paste titles of recipes and recipes on different cards and have the students match them correctly.
23. Teachers: Cut the dialogue out of a cartoon strip. Have students write their own dialogue to fit the actions.
24. Teachers: Have students write stories to go with headlines cut from newspapers.
25. Teachers: Reproduce copies of chapters, articles, and the like. Delete the headings. Have students write headings, then compare what they wrote to the author's headings.

SKILLS OF LOCATING DETAILS

Sample Activities for Discussion, Task Cards, Learning Centers, and Reading Contracts

1. Locate a place in the story where someone jumped to a wrong conclusion.
2. Locate and be ready to read the parts of the story that tell *who, what, where, when, why,* and *how*.
3. Look up information in the encyclopedia or in other reference materials about where this story took place.
4. Be ready to locate on a map or a globe where this story took place.
5. On what page of the story did you first meet the main character?
6. How many *e's* are there on page 79?
7. How many *and's* are on page 50?
8. Teachers: Ask students to make up a series of questions from the story that could be used on TV game shows (e.g., *Hollywood Squares, Concentration,* etc.).
9. Teachers: Give questions for which students can locate an-

swers in their readers. Then ask them to find the exact words in the story that prove their answer.

10. Teachers: Have students locate a word (or words) in the story to complete a sentence.
11. Teachers: Have students answer questions similar to the following: Why did Sam run away (page 13, line 2)? What would you have done (page 27, line 4)?

SEQUENCE SKILLS

Sample Activities for Discussion, Task Cards, Learning Centers, and Learning Contracts

1. Write eight sentences, in sequence, about the story. Cut them apart. Give them to someone else. See what sequence he or she makes. Is it the same or different? Could a story be made using the sequence, if it is different?
2. Add an event at some point in the story (Christmas, unexpected arrivals, etc.). Discuss how this would change the story.
3. What would you expect to happen next? See if it does.
4. Make a schedule of your weekend, showing the order in which you did things.
5. If you were to take a bicycle trip from the house where one character lives to that of another, what would you pass first, second, etc.?
6. What happened first in the story? Second? How many more events can you list from the story?
7. Which story character did you meet first? Second? Etc.
8. List the events that led to the climax of this story.
9. Plan a mural that shows the sequence of events in the story or in the life of a character from the story.
10. Write or retell the story from the point of view of some object or pet in the story.
11. Make a time line for the story.
12. Over how long a time did the entire story take place?
13. Make a cartoon strip from the story.
14. Teachers: Set up learning centers where students have to follow instructions in sequence to make or do something. Examples: Origami, cooking, crafts, and art projects.
15. Teachers: Give a number of endings to a story so students will have to read to discover the correct one.

16. Teachers: Make sentence strips for each sentence in a paragraph from the story. Have students put the paragraph together in correct sequence and check their work with the story. Discuss the reasons for any differences between the two.

17. Teachers: Have students make trifolds of stories they read by taping three sheets of cardboard together and illustrating the beginning, middle, and end of the story on the sections.

18. Teachers: Have students write chain poems where each student writes a separate verse or stanza. (Alternate: Write chain stories.)

19. Teachers: Give a certain incident in the story and have students recall what happened just before and just after it.

20. Teachers: Have students write or tell about something they usually do in a sequence, such as getting up in the morning, coming to school, making a paper airplane, and the like.

21. Teachers: Ask students to find sentences in the story that indicate that two events were happening simultaneously, that one event was happening before another, that an event was happening after another, and the like.

22. Teachers: Give students the middle of a story; ask them to write or draw a beginning, write or draw an ending; and then compare their work with other students' efforts. Discuss similarities and differences in perception.

23. Teachers: Take a familiar story; ask the students to illustrate some part of the story on a transparency, using crayons or felt tip pens. As the pictures are projected, ask the class to identify which part of the story is being viewed.

24. Teachers: Ask students to put the lines of a poem in sequence. Compare the different results they get with the author's.

CHARACTERIZATION AND EMPATHY SKILLS

Sample Activities for Discussion, Task Cards, Learning Centers, and Reading Contracts

1. Write three riddles about the characters in the story.
2. List ways in which each character was important to the story.

3. What do you think could have happened previously in one character's life to cause her or him to act the way he or she did?
4. Select a picture that you think a story character would like to have in his home. Explain.
5. If you were to meet one of the story characters, what questions would you like to ask him or her?
6. If the character were an animal, what animal would he or she be?
7. From a box of scrap materials, choose cloth remnants in patterns and textures that you think your favorite character in the story would like. Explain.
8. Look through magazines to find different features that show how you think your favorite character looks (lips, hands, hair, etc.).
9. Which character would you like to be and why?
10. Write a job resumé for a story character.
11. Write a story titled, "A Day in the Life of ____." Choose a story character for your subject.
12. Write an autobiography for a story character.
13. Who was the main character in the story? Who were the subsidiary characters? What are your reasons for your choices?
14. Write a letter as if you were a story character. Do not use the character's name. See if anyone can guess who you are.
15. What five words would best describe how you felt about the actions of your favorite character(s) in the story?
16. For what political office do you think the main character in the book would be suited? Support your choices with logical reasons.
17. What did the author do or what words did he or she use that helped you know what kind of person one of the story characters was?
18. What do you think the main character will be like in ten years? What kind of life will he or she lead? Where will he or she live? Etc.
19. Prepare a dramatic sketch, a monologue, a pantomime, or a shadow play using one of the characters in the story as the subject.
20. Select words beginning with each letter of his or her name that describe your favorite character from the story.

21. Tell which character in the story you liked most and why. (Or which you disliked most and why.)
22. What kind of a person was each of the characters in the story?
23. Make a collage that explains what your favorite character in the story is like.
24. Make a paper bag mask using one character in the story as a model.
25. Make a greeting card that one story character could send to another.
26. Which TV or film stars would you like to see play the characters in the story if it were made into a TV show or a film?
27. If one of the characters in the book had $100, how would he or she spend it?
28. Write a poem or limerick about one of the story characters.
29. Write up an interview with one of the story characters for your favorite TV talk shows or for a newspaper or magazine article.
30. Rewrite or tell the story from the point of view of one of the characters.
31. Which character do you feel behaved most admirably? Give reasons.
32. What three presents do you think each character in the story would like for his or her birthday? Explain your choices.
33. List each character in your story. Was each "good," or "bad," or a combination? Give your reasons.
34. Find examples of stories where objects or animals speak or act as if they were human (personification).
35. Pretend you are an object (or an animal) in our schoolroom. Describe (write or tell) how you feel, what things make you feel certain ways, what you would say if you could.
36. Teachers: Play *Who Said It?* with the class. Speak or show a line of dialogue and have students tell you who said it.
37. Teachers: Have students practice reading aloud the dialogue of one of the story characters until they feel they have the proper interpretation of his or her speech patterns; then, share what they practiced with the class.
38. Teachers: Have a student or groups of students dress a friend as one of the story characters, using newspapers or

scraps of material. See if other students can guess which character it is.

39. Teachers: Have a costume day when all students come dressed as their favorite story book character.

40. Teachers: Give a word or phrase from the story that indicates an emotional reaction of a story character. Have students tell you which story character you are describing.

41. Teachers: For younger students, set up a Hat Box Center; include many kinds of hats characterizing the roles people play in our culture; e.g., police officer, engineer, farmer, cowboy, etc.

SKILLS OF IDENTIFYING LITERARY DEVICE

Sample Activities for Discussion, Task Cards, Learning Centers, and Reading Contracts

1. What was funny in the story? (Sad? Unexpected? Exciting?)
2. Which part of the story did you like best?
3. How would you classify this selection? (Hint: mystery, science fiction, etc.)
4. What techniques did the author use to make you like or dislike the character?
5. Is this selection called prose or poetry? Explain.
6. Where in the library would you look for other stories similar to this one?
7. Did the dialogue passages seem realistic to you? Do people really talk that way? Does anyone you know?
8. What did the author do to make the story (or article, chapter, selection) more interesting?
9. What did you think of the author's opening sentence? (The closing sentence? How effective was the author's opening scene? His or her closing scene?)
10. Sometimes an author has a character think back to a former time or the author writes about a former time as part of the present story. This is called "flashback." Locate examples in your reader or in library books.
11. List the three types of books you most like to read.
12. Teachers: Have students sort stories from a reader into the proper headings for literary forms (e.g., mystery, flashback, humor, sarcasm, etc.).

13. Teachers: Have students make lists of their favorite mystery stories, adventure stories, and the like.
14. Teachers: Have students make a display of book jackets or of books of a similar type (science fiction, etc.) or that use similar literary devices (humor, dialogue, flashbacks, and the like).
15. Teachers: Have students make a display of various opening sentences that they find especially effective and well done.

SKILLS OF IDENTIFYING STORY ELEMENTS

Sample Activities for Discussion, Task Cards, Learning Centers, and Reading Contracts

1. What was the most exciting part of the story for you?
2. Fill in the blanks:
   (a) The title of the story is _____.
   (b) The time of the story _____.
   (c) The setting of the story _____.
   (d) The characters of the story are _____.
   (e) The main events of the story are _____.
   (f) The plot of the story is _____.
   (g) The mood of the story is _____.
3. Write six words that describe the time of the story.
4. Make a list of the words from the story that tell about time.
5. Make up six questions about the setting of your story that someone would have to read the story to answer.
6. Make a map of the story setting.
7. Make a list of words from the article or story that have to do with weather.
8. Fill out this chart with words from your story that tell about each heading:

Time	Place	Characters	Actions

9. What would happen if you changed one of the story elements (mood, plot, setting, theme, and so on) in the story?
10. The climax of the story is usually the time of highest interest. What was the climax of this story?
11. Write five mood words about the story.
12. When did you first realize what the mood of the story (article, poem) was going to be? Be ready to show where in the story (article, poem).
13. Select some music that would create the proper background mood for a favorite book or for the book you are reading.
14. Was the story believable?
15. Teachers: Cut out stories from old readers or magazines. Paste the first parts of the stories on one card, the conclusions on another. Have students match the endings to the beginnings.
16. Teachers: Have students write stories using flip books, wheels, or suggestions drawn from separate boxes labeled *setting, time, mood, characters*, and *type of story*.
17. Teachers: Ask students to think of a possible story from their own lives and tell or outline the mood, setting, theme, plot, characters, and tone for that story.
18. Teachers: Have students locate passages that set the mood of the story and that continue the mood throughout the story.
20. Teachers: Ask students to make lists of words that the author used to set the mood of the story.

SKILLS OF IDENTIFYING REALITY VS. FANTASY

Sample Activities for Discussion, Task Cards, Learning Centers, or Reading Contracts

1. What parts of this story could really have happened? Couldn't really have happened?
2. Is this story fantasy or reality? Explain.
3. Is this story fiction or nonfiction? Explain.
4. What past experiences have you had that would make an interesting nonfiction story? An interesting fiction story?
5. Plan a trip for the class, for your family, or for yourself to the site of one of your favorite stories.

6. Pretend you are one of the story characters. How would your life change?
7. Could you really do in real life what the characters in this story did?
8. Make up five statements from your story that we can use to play *Believe It or Not*. Indicate whether each is true or false.

SKILLS OF UNDERSTANDING HUMOR

Sample Activities for Discussion, Task Cards, Learning Centers, or Reading Contracts

1. Find and be prepared to read aloud a humorous situation, description, or use of words in the story.
2. Find and cut out a picture that you consider funny in a magazine. Be ready to tell us what you found funny in it.
3. Did anything in this story remind you of something funny that happened to you or to someone you know?
4. Make up a "knock-knock" joke about the story.
5. What is the funniest thing that ever happened to you?
6. Where would you rate the humor in this story on a scale of one to ten, with one being the funniest thing you ever read and ten being the least funny?
7. Teachers: Have students write "daffynitions" of words and phrases from the story and share with the class.
8. Teachers: Have students write captions for cartoons and other humorous pictures you or they have collected.
9. Teachers: Ask students to write sentences that contain an adverb that matches up with another word in the sentence to make a funny pattern. Examples: "I'll have the lamb roast," said Sam sheepishly; "Fill 'er up," said Joan emptily.
10. Teachers: Ask students to make a humor scrapbook or bulletin board display of funny things they read, of funny events that happen in the classroom, or of favorite cartoons.

SKILLS OF SELECTING
APPROPRIATE MEANINGS FOR WORDS

Sample Activities for Discussion, Task Cards, Learning Centers, and Reading Contracts

1. Stressing different words in a sentence can change the meaning. Find a sentence in the reading assignment and read it several times, stressing a different word each time. How did that change the meaning?
2. Write down all the emotions the main character felt in the story. How many different words did you use?
3. Make a list of ten to fifteen words that a reader would have to know to understand this story (article, chapter, or book).
4. Choose fifteen words from the story. See how many sentences you can write using just these fifteen words.
5. Which words did the author use in this story that you would like to add to your vocabulary?
6. Pick out all the words and phrases that make a good word picture of an event in the story.
7. In your own words, tell what five words from the story mean. Check your work with the dictionary.
8. Some words represent (or have a connotation of) feelings that may have nothing whatsoever to do with what the word actually means. *Home*, for example, can have a pleasant connotation for some people and an unpleasant one for others. Make a list of pleasant and unpleasant connotations you give five words from the story.
9. Make a list of words from the story that refer to sounds (motion, taste, smell, texture, size, color, and the like).
10. Be ready to pantomime five words from the story. Choose the five and prepare the pantomime so well that everyone will be able to guess what you are showing.
11. Make up a word (or words) that could fit in the story. Explain how your new word fits.
12. Put two or more words together to form a new word or words that fit in the story (e.g., she was a flutter-your-hands kind of person. He was a jumpup).

13. Select one word to describe each character in the story. Explain your choice of words.
14. Write five action and five descriptive words used in the story.
15. Teachers: Select sentences from the reader (or design or have students design groups of sentences) where the meaning of one or several words is ambiguous. Have the class tell as many meanings for the sentence as possible. Example: The *strike* was good. It *struck* him.
16. Teachers: Have students make a mobile representing the multiple meanings of new words.
17. Teachers: Play *Mystery Word* with the class. Example: What word is it?It begins with *y* and ends with *w* and it is a color. Have students make up other mystery words. Vary the difficulty by ability level.
18. Teachers: Have students write their own definitions of new words in the story, then compare them with each other and choose the best definitions, using a dictionary as resource.
19. Teachers: Have students write sentences using words in the story that have more than one meaning.
20. Teachers: Have students list words in the story that have different meanings in different parts of the country.
21. Teachers: Make up cloze exercises (where every fifth word is deleted) from the story or comparable stories and ask students to fill in the appropriate words.

PARAPHRASING SKILLS

Sample Activities for Discussion, Task Cards, Learning Centers, and Reading Contracts

1. Select a story to learn and retell during our next Story Hour. Choose one that the class will enjoy. (Or select a story to learn and retell it to students in lower grades.)
2. What proverb is this? Action with a needle at the correct moment prevents much more action with a needle. (Variation: Take a common proverb. State it in different words. See if anyone recognizes it.)
3. Translate a passage of this story into another language.
4. Find a familiar book that has been translated into another language. Find someone who can translate it for you or

translate it yourself. Compare the stories and the word patterns in the two languages.

5. Write a play using this story as a basis for the plot or for characters.
6. Take a story from a primary basal reader. Using only the word list at the end of the book, rewrite the story so that the text reads more naturally, the way people really talk.
7. Find examples of awkward dialogue in basal readers and rewrite the dialogue in more normal speech patterns.
8. Read the directions (of an assignment, of a recipe, and the like) silently, then be ready to tell me in your own words what you are going to do.
9. Make up a parody (look it up if you don't know what it is) of a Mother Goose rhyme.
10. Find an ad for a product in a foreign language newspaper or magazine. Compare it to an ad for the same product in an English language publication.

SKILLS OF INTERPRETING FIGURATIVE LANGUAGE

Sample Activities for Discussion, Task Cards, Learning Centers, and Reading Contracts

1. Make a collage of the figurative language the author used in this story.
2. Draw a picture of the literal and figurative meaning of a sentence from the story. Examples: "Three cheers for the red, white and blue." "Lightning gun . . . Rose red sunset . . ."
3. Sometimes a picture can help the reader understand a story better. Make one or more illustrations for the story that helps readers see the story action more clearly.
4. What parts of the story caused you to see pictures in your mind? Be ready to read them aloud to us.
5. Make a rebus sentence of one of the sentences in the story.
6. Draw five of the words from the story in a shape that shows their meaning. (Hint: Make the word *horse* look like a horse.)
7. Write a poem in the shape of the thing it describes. (Hint: shapes of a girl, a cloud, the sun, a tree, and the like.)

8. What does the phrase (insert any figurative expression from the story) really mean?

9. Why did the author use the phrase (insert figurative expression) to explain _____ .
   (character, event)

10. What words or phrases helped you get a better idea of what one of the story characters was really like?

11. Pick out some particularly vivid word pictures from the story. Be ready to read them to us.

12. Make a display of books that illustrate common sayings; e.g., history repeats itself.

13. Make up names for a new pop music group.

14. List ten words you would consider "sticky" words; funny words; happy words; exciting words; tiring words, etc.

15. Make a list of expressions in the story that do not mean literally what is said. (Example: crazy as a fox.) Write down what each expression means in reality.

16. Be ready to share words, phrases, or sentences in the story that you felt described things, actions, or people well.

17. Share the color words you found in your story.

18. Make a list or a chain of words that begin with each letter of the alphabet that describes one of the story characters.

19. What words, phrases, or sentences in the story do you think would make a good title for a poem? A TV show? A movie? A song? Any other titles for things you can find?

20. What things described in the book did you find especially beautiful? Hideous? Calming? Sad? What other feeling words can you think of that describe something in the story?

21. Make a list of words from the story that you especially enjoyed or want to use in your own vocabulary.

22. What words, phrases, or sentences that the author used did you especially like or wish you had written?

23. Write a poem using only words or phrases you have selected from the story. (Hint: Write a haiku, cinquain, couplet, limerick, or other type of poem using the words. Add some words of your own if you want.)

24. Teachers: Have students cut out examples of figurative language from newspaper or magazine ads. Use the examples to make displays, collages, or booklets of figurative language examples.

25. Teachers: Discuss with students the meaning of proverbs they see in their reading.
26. Teachers: Have students take a list of words and phrases describing story characters and list them under the characters they describe.
27. Teachers: Ask students to make up nonsense titles for the story.

INFERENCE AND CONCLUSION SKILLS

Sample Activities for Discussion, Task Cards, Learning Centers, and Reading Contracts

1. Would you like to live in the particular place or time of the story? Explain.
2. What would you expect to find in the shopping cart of one of the story characters if he or she went to the grocery store?
3. What would you expect one of the main characters to collect? What hobbies, other than those listed in the story, do you think he or she has?
4. What makes this story different from others like it?
5. Based on what we learned about a character from the story, what do you think he or she will do in later life? (Alternate: What do you think he or she will be like in later life?)
6. Draw an FBI-type mug shot of the villain of the story.
7. How would you expect the story characters to view men? Women? Boys? Girls? With whom would you agree? Disagree?
8. Write a letter to Dear Abby that one of the story characters might have written. Answer for her.
9. Play the "If-then" game. (If this had happened, then _____.)
10. Play the "Good News-Bad News" game. (First the good news, then the bad news.): (a) for a story character, (b) for a historical character, (c) for a personage currently in the news, and so on.
11. Suppose you were a Martian who was sent by your government to observe the customs of the people in the story. What would you report?
12. How many reasons can you think of to explain why

_____ (the leading character) acted as he or she did?

13. Play *You Are There*. Write how you would feel if you actually took part in the action of the story.

14. What decisions did the main character make that you thought were wise? Unwise?

15. Stage a mock trial to prove this story guilty or not guilty of being a good story. Choose some friends to help you, if you wish.

16. If this story took place in your area, how would the plot have to be changed?

17. How do you know what each character was like? Make up other questions about the story that begin with *How do you know*.

18. Make up a play about what went on before this story began.

19. Make one list of all the wise and one of all the foolish things the characters did in your story.

20. What characters in the story showed these traits? Unreliable? Unselfish? Brave? Loyal? Truthful? Give examples of action that prove your point. Make a list of other traits, the characters who displayed them, and the actions that prove your point.

21. Write or tell five true and five false statements about the story.

22. Write six good questions about the story that, while they aren't answered word for word in the story, students should be able to answer from reading it.

23. Take an imaginary walk through the setting of this book. Describe what you experience.

24. Select a classified ad from the newspaper and write a story about it.

25. What three questions is the teacher sure to ask about this story?

26. You are the main story character. Explain to the group how you felt during the events of the story.

27. Write up or tape an interview or a conversation between you and one of the story characters about why things happened as they did.

28. Authors often give direct or hidden clues that help you

know about the kind of person the main character was. Make a list of the clues this author gives about the main character of this story.

29. Teachers: Seal an object in a sack or in a box. Have students try to guess by feel, by shaking, by weight and the like, what the object is.

30. Teachers: Set up a learning center with a selection of books about magic. Encourage students to learn and perform magic tricks. See if other students can guess how the tricks were done.

31. Teachers: Set up a riddle learning center with a selection of books and a variety of riddles and puzzles to be solved. Have students write riddles about stories they read, make collections of favorite riddles, and the like.

32. Teachers: Have students make a list of *why* or *because* sentences or words from the story.

33. Teachers: Play *What's the Question?* with the class. Give an answer from the story and have students tell or write all the questions they can think of that the answer fits.

34. Teachers: Have students cook and serve a meal that would be appropriate for the story characters.

35. Teachers: Have students tape a simulated interview with the author about the book, story, or article.

36. Teachers: Have students play *Twenty Questions* using authors or titles of books as subjects.

37. Teachers: Have students pretend to be one of the story characters. Select a panel of five students. The panel may ask five questions of each student to see if it can guess which story character each is.

38. Teachers: Have a riddle time sometime during each week.

39. Teachers: Set up a riddle learning center where students collect old riddles, read riddle books, and invent new riddles.

40. Teachers: Have students write anonymous autobiographies, then ask the class to guess who wrote each.

41. Teachers: Interpretive questions you can use for any story or story segment: Where are they? What are they doing? What are they getting ready to do? What might they have said? What happened before? After?

SYNTHESIS SKILLS

Sample Activities for Discussion, Task Cards, Learning Centers, and Reading Contracts

1. Teachers: Using the cloze technique, drop out all the verbs from a reading selection. See how the students change the meaning of the whole by the use of different verbs. (Variation: Do a similar exercise by dropping out all the nouns.)
2. Teachers: Have the class make a police identikit for identifying faces or figures. (Alternates: (a) Ask a police officer to demonstrate his or her kit. (b) Get flip books from the library. These books combine various features, faces, bodies, and the like to put together to make interesting characters.)
3. Teachers: Have students list the series of clues in a mystery story that led to solving the mystery.
4. Teachers: Have students give opinions on whether or not a book should be purchased for the library or for their classroom.
5. Teachers: Have students write or tell parallel stories where the original plot is followed but either the characters, the setting, or the time of the original story is changed.
6. Teachers: Ask students to write or tell a story in which a minor character in the original story becomes the main character.
7. Teachers: Ask students to design a game board that could be used to play several different games.
8. Teachers: Ask students if they learned anything from this story that is new, that changed their mind about something, or that showed them they need to learn more about anything.
9. Teachers: Cut apart each sentence from a paragraph out of some reading material. Ask students to see how many ways they can put the sentences together to form a paragraph that makes sense.
10. Teachers: Cut apart each word from a sentence. Ask students to put the words together in as many ways as they can to form new sentences. (Primary students can each hold one word from a sentence and rearrange themselves

in as many different ways as they can to make a new sentence.)

ANALYSIS SKILLS

Sample Activities for Discussion, Task Cards, Learning Centers, and Reading Contracts

1. What new ideas or information did you get from the book (article, story)?
2. Choose a story, an article, or a book and use it to make a reading kit for a learning center that includes:
   (a) Questions (and answers) about the story;
   (b) Something to draw;
   (c) Something to see.
   (d) Make up five questions about the story that would cause readers to have to know something about: (1) the main idea of the story, (2) the details of the story (dates, etc.), (3) the sequence of events or the words the author used.
   (e) Make up one question that requires students to follow directions, scan, skim outline, summarize, or use the dictionary.
   (f) Make up questions about: synonyms or antonyms, word meaning, figurative language and the like.
3. Which parts of this story could not have really happened?
4. What five words would you use to describe this story?
5. What kind of person would enjoy this story?
6. What kind of person would have written this story?
7. Teachers: Using the cloze technique (leaving a blank space to take the place of a word every so often; for example, for every fifth word), give the students paragraphs from a story they are reading or from new material to see how they would fill in the blanks. Example: The girl looked at the ＿＿ as it rushed past ＿＿ on its way to ＿＿. The engineer sounded the ＿＿ as the train faded ＿＿ the distance.
8. Teachers: Cut out one facial feature from a picture of a person. Have several other pictures of that feature available. Ask the children to choose the best one for that par-

ticular face. (Which eyes, lips, or nose, etc., completes the picture best?)

9. Teachers: Have students make up a game based on the story.

10. Teachers: Read a poem to the class, leaving out the last line. Have students make up appropriate last lines. Compare the various last lines with each other and with what the author wrote. Stress originality; talk about differing perceptions that students have of the poem.

11. Teachers: Ask students to tell or list what this piece of writing reveals about its author.

12. Teachers: Have students discuss the first thing they think this writer had to do to write this story (article, etc.); or have students make a list of the steps the author probably followed to complete this piece of writing.

13. Teachers: Play *What's the Question?* with the class. Give an answer and ask the class to come up with the questions to match.

14. Teachers: Ask students to list the elements or parts that make up a good book: (a) to read aloud; (b) to take on a vacation; (c) to make them think, etc.

15. Teachers: Discuss how students go about choosing a good story for themselves to read. Talk about ways different students know a story will be good to read before they read it. (Example: Do they look at the illustrations, read the first paragraph, or what?)

PREDICTION SKILLS

Sample Activities for Discussion, Task Cards, Reading Centers, and Reading Contracts

1. Can you guess how this story will end?
2. What would you do if you were a character in this story?
3. What is another way the author could have ended the story?
4. If you were a fortune teller, what future would you predict for _____ (insert story character)?
5. What do you think _____ (story character) will be doing a year from the end of the story? Five years? Ten years?

6 Write the main character a letter suggesting what might have happened if he/she had acted another way.

7. Write or tell an epilogue (look it up if you don't know what it means) for your story for ten years after it ends. What happened to everyone?

8. If the main character in the story were in our class, what do you think would happen?

9. Predict a future for each of the characters in the story.

10 Write a prediction of the kind of adult each of the younger story characters will make.

11. If one of the story characters lived to be 200 years old, what would he or she be like?

12. What do you predict other readers will feel about this story?

13. Predict how you would react to this book if you were 21 years old.

14. Create another story using the same characters that were in this story.

15. Write or tape record a dialogue of a conversation between one of the characters from this book and one from another book.

16. Teachers: Read part of a story aloud or have students read part of a story silently. Close the book and have the students predict what will happen next

17 Teachers: Show a film strip or film without turning on the sound. Have students predict what it was about and check their predictions with the sound track.

18. Teachers: Have students look at the illustrations for a story and predict what the plot is. Predictions can be checked by reading the book.

19 Teachers: Have students predict what the plot of a story is by hearing (or seeing) only the story title and the names of story characters.

20. Teachers: Cut a page of print from a book, or from a newspaper column, in half vertically. Have students predict and tell or write what was on the missing half.

21 Teachers: Read aloud a portion of the middle of a story and have students try to predict the beginning and/or the end. (Alternate: Show the middle of a film and ask students to try to predict the beginning and/or ending.)

SKILLS OF UNDERSTANDING CAUSE AND EFFECT

Sample Activities for Discussion, Task Cards, Learning Centers, or Reading Contracts

1   What caused _____ (story event or situation) to happen? What other causes not listed in the book might there have been?

2. List as many reasons as you can think of why the author wrote this selection.

3. If all reading materials should suddenly disappear from our lives, what would happen? How would life be different?

4. If one character were removed from the story, how would this cause the plot to be different?

5. Add another character to the story. How would this cause the story to be different?

6. If this story were set in a different time or setting, how would this cause the story to be different?

7. If you lived in this story setting, how would your life be changed? How would you have to change?

8. What do you think caused _____ (story character) to act the way he or she did?

9. You are one of the story characters. Tell the group why you acted as you did in the story.

10. Make a before and after chart of how life was for one story character before and after one event in this story or before and after the entire story.

11. How did each of the story characters affect the plot of the story?

12. Make a time line of story events.

13. Teachers: Discuss with the class why story characters did what they did or why they thought or reacted in a certain way.

14. Teachers: Ask students to look up the words *cause* and *effect* in their dictionaries.

15. Teachers: Have students write "If . . , then . . ." sentences. If all cars were red, then _____.

16. Teachers: Have students give as many causes as they can for a particular effect. Examples: What are all the reasons you can give: If reading were forbidden? If all printed let-

ters were a foot high? If a character in your story called the fire department?

CLASSIFICATION OR CATEGORIZATION SKILLS

Sample Activities for Discussion, Task Cards, Learning Centers, and Reading Contracts

1. Seldom are we in the same mood all the time. Make a chart of moods for your favorite character. What percentage of the time was he/she/it: generous? productive? happy? troubled? friendly? (Alternates: What percentage of the time are you in these moods? In comparison with your favorite character, make a chart showing the degree to which the character and you shared the same moods.) (Judging degree of classification)
2. In a mystery story, what were the false clues the author provided? The real clues? (Judging degree of classification)
3. Make a scrapbook of pictures or lists of things you like, grouped under headings such as *Extremely Liked, Very Much Liked, Average Degree of Liking, Rather Liked, Liked in a Lukewarm Way*. (Or make up your own categories from best-liked to least.) (Judging degree of classification)
4. Make a list of the items your favorite character could see from his bedroom window. (Locational classification)
5. What fiction books have been written about Southern California (Texas, Ohio, etc.). (Locational classification)
6. Make a map of the action of this story. (Locational classification)
7. What kinds of plants would you expect to see if you could take a trip to this story location? (Locational classification)
8. What kinds of transportation could you expect to see outside the classroom window or door? (Locational classification)
9. Make a list of things that you would put in a time capsule for the time setting of this story. (Temporal classification)
10. Make a time capsule for the current year. (Temporal classification)
11. Interview classmates about what they were doing at 2:30 p.m. on Sunday. Write a story or make a chart of the results. (Temporal classification)

12. Make a time line of story events. (Temporal classification)
13. Make a display of books published in the same year. (Temporal classification)
14. Make a display of books written about the same time period. (Temporal classification)
15. Make a list of all the ways your life would be different and all the ways it would be the same if you lived at the time and in the setting of the story. (Functional classification)
16. Make a list of all the nouns in your story. (Functional classification)
17. List five nouns, five verbs, and five adjectives from your story. (Functional classification)
18. Make a family tree for one of the story characters. (Functional classification)
19. Make a scrapbook of pictures of ways of transportation or of clothing for different climates or time eras. (Functional classification)
20. Set up and display collections of favorite recipes, favorite songs, favorite actresses, or stamp collections of class members. (Functional classification)
21. Set up and display individual collections belonging to students, parents, and/or teachers. Choose friends to help you, if you like. (Functional classification)
22. Make a collage of all the things that *red* represents for you. (Descriptive classification)
23. How many things in the story had sharp edges? Were brittle? Were rough? What other categories can you think of that tell how things in the story looked? (Descriptive classification)
24. How many words can you list that describe how the main character looked? (Descriptive classification)
25. Make a list of everything you can think of that comes in hard covers. That is plastic. That is square. What other descriptive words can you think of? List five things that each word describes. (Descriptive classification)
26. Cut pictures from magazines that show each of the following: Hope; Anticipation; Excitement. (Inferential classification)
27. Find many pictures that show different kinds of workers. Group your pictures under three different headings. (Inferential classification)

28. Give two or three Dewey Decimal numbers. How are books with these numbers related? (Inferential classification)
29. Choose five words from your story. Make a list of all the ways these words are alike. (Inferential classification)
30. Make a scrapbook of pictures of things you wish you had. (Inferential classification)
31. How do you think the story would have been different if the transportation were different (e.g., space ship for a stage coach, etc.)? (Inferential classification)
32. What would happen if all forms of transportation (except bicycles) were banned? (Inferential classification)
33. How many words would you use to describe your favorite story character? (Classification by a variety of characteristics)
34. How many different pictures can you draw from one squiggle? (Classification by a variety of characteristics)
35. How many ways are your two favorite story characters alike? (Classification by a variety of characteristics)
36. What are the three most important ways two characters in the story are alike? Different? (Classification by a variety of characteristics)
37. Teachers: Have students search the story for similar elements (e.g., (a) List all things that are green in the story. (b) Which events happened in the city? In the country? (c) Name at least two ways that two story characters are alike.) (Classification by a variety of characteristics)
38. Teachers: Play *20 Questions* using story characters or objects. (Alternate: play *20 Questions*, not restricting content to stories.) (Classification by a variety of characteristics)
39. Teachers: Play guessing games, each time adding another attribute (e.g., How many different things can you think of that are round? White and round? White, soft, and round? White, soft, round, and edible? Etc.). (Classification by a variety of characteristics)
40. Teachers: Give students a group of news stories. Sample activities: How many ways are they alike? Different? What sections of the newspaper would you put them in? (Classification by a variety of characteristics)
41. Teachers: Have students make a list of different categories of the Dewey decimal system. (Functional classification)

42. Teachers: List the characters from a group of stories the students have read. Ask the students to group the characters into as many patterns or categories as they can (e.g., boys, heroes, foolish, etc.). (Classification by a variety of characteristics.)

43. Teachers: Have students make charts showing more and more specific detail. (Judging degree of classification) Example:

General	boy	rock
	red haired boy	hard rock
	red haired cousin	hard, black rock
	red haired, ten-year-old-cousin	hard, black igneous rock
Specific	My red haired, ten-year-old cousin, John	lava

44. Teachers: Give children five objects, words, or pictures, Ask them how many ways these items are related and have students support each of their decisions. (Classification by a variety of characteristics)

45. Ask students to write down all the words they can think of or find that indicate something is not large (tiny, minute, and so on). (Alternates: large, heavy, sharp.) Ask students to think of a label for these groups of words. (Judging degree of classification)

SKILLS OF NOTING
SIMILARITIES AND DIFFERENCES;
COMPARING AND CONTRASTING

Sample Activities for Discussion, Task Cards, Learning Centers, or Reading Contracts

1. How are two characters in the story alike? How are they different?
2. How are you like your favorite character? How are you different?

3. How are these occupations alike? How are they different? Police officer, teacher, fire fighter.
4. Select a partner, then each, separately, write down how you are different and how you are alike. Compare the lists. Save the lists and look at them again a month or two later. Do you still feel the same way?
5. If the main character in the story were in our class, how would things be different? How would they be the same?
6. If we held our class in the time and setting of the story, how would things be the same? Different?
7. Have you ever read a story that was similar to this one? How was it similar?
8. In what ways are the characters similar to people you know? In what ways are they different?
9. Which of the story characters was wiser? Faster? Older? Happier? Smarter? Less tactful? Make five other comparisons between characters.
10. What was the best book you have ever read? The worst? On what do you base your answers?
11. Make a time line comparing the events for three different stories.
12. Teachers: Have students describe how various characters would view the events in the story.
13. Teachers: Ask students to compare how two stories are alike and how they are different.
14. Teachers: Ask students to compare how the culture in the story is like their own and how it is different.
15. Teachers: Since similes, analogies, and metaphors are ways to compare and contrast, ask students to find them in the story, or make up examples of each, for events, characters, setting, and the like.

SUMMARY SKILLS

Sample Activities for Discussion, Task Cards, Learning Centers, or Reading Contracts

1. Why were these particular colors used in the design of the cover or jacket for this book?
2. Make a "pleat" book about the story (fold the paper in accordion fashion and draw a picture on each fold, or tape together pictures you have drawn about the story).

3. Retell favorite stories to classmates or join our Storytelling Club to present stories to younger children.
4. What folk sayings or proverbs do you feel sum up this story best? (Alternate: sum up a story character?)
5. Plan an advertising campaign to promote a book you have read or a book you wrote.
6. Design a car bumper sticker that would be appropriate for the time and setting of the story.
7. Which sentence in the story describes the story best?
8. Was this a book you wish you had written? Why or why not? Summarize your answer.
9. Is this a book you would recommend to a friend? Summarize why or why not.
10. Write a poem about this story.
11. Design a book jacket for your book.
12. Write a one paragraph or one page biography of one of the story characters.
13. Summarize the story out loud in as few words as possible.
14. Tell the highlights of the story in five short sentences.
15. Can you tell the highlights of the story in one brief sentence?
16. Divide the story into three main parts—introduction, plot and ending.
17. Teachers: Play *Title Jury.* Select four students as jurors. Read aloud a short story or excerpt from a story. Have groups of students decide on which title they want to submit to the jury. The jury then chooses the winner from those submitted. (Alternate: titles are submitted by individuals.)

A FINAL WORD ABOUT COMPREHENSION

For our students to be able to comprehend what an author is saying and to relate it to their own lives is all-important to their becoming good readers, as well as to their developing into caring, thoughtful people. Reading offers possibilities for escape from the humdrum, for adventure, for mind-stretching images, for sensory newness, and for glimpses of the world that could be, or, perhaps, the world that should be; all processes that help young people look beyond the obvious, the too pat, or the too quick answer. For our students to learn to analyze, empathize with, and understand the characters and events they read about is possibly the most personally satisfying and fulfilling of all the reading skills we can help them develop. This brings them enrichment, newness, and role models, helping them develop creativity, introducing them to new concepts, and aiding them in increasing the breadth and scope of their thinking and living.

2

Critical Reading Skills

* * * * * * * * * * * *

Teachers' actions make a difference in how well a young reader can evaluate what he or she reads. The teacher who includes critical reading skills as part of the reading curriculum; who asks students questions that promote thinking about the effectiveness and accuracy of what they are reading; who models behavior indicating to children that everything they see in print is not necessarily so; and who remembers that the purpose of teaching any reading skill is to encourage *reading* will be more successful in tempering his or her students' blind acceptance of the written word.

Critical reading does not mean failing to enjoy what one is reading. Examining an author's skills, biases, assumptions, and organizational patterns can become as exciting as a detective story as evidence is pieced together to give students a look at how the author views the world. Evaluating one's own growth, prejudices, and goals through the mirror of what one reads can be uplifting.

EVALUATING THE READING PROCESS

**Sample Activities for Discussion, Task Cards,
Learning Centers, and Reading Contracts**

1. Teachers: Have students draw, write, or discuss their ideas about the topic, *What Is Reading*? Discuss differences and similarities in perceptions. Alternate: Interview adults, other students regarding their ideas.

2. Teachers: Discuss or have students discuss or write about such topics as:
   (a) Why was this lesson assigned?
   (b) Why were you asked to read this book?
   (c) How have books affected your parents? Your community?
   (d) What is the thing you do best in reading?
   (e) What is the thing you do worst in reading?
   (f) What do you need to work on to become a better reader?
   (g) Whom would you rather work with during reading time? Why?
   (h) Which students in the class have helped you become a better reader? Why?
   (i) Which teacher (aside from me) helped you most to become a better reader? What did he or she do?
3. Teachers: Have pupils draw a road map that shows what happened to them "on the way" to learning to read and what will happen to them in the future as they continue to grow in reading skills. (Alternates: Have pupils make a collage, paint, use tinker toys, make a sculpture, use torn paper, etc., to illustrate their growth.) Share these with the class.

EVALUATING THE AUTHOR'S SKILLS

Sample Activities for Discussion, Task Cards, Learning Centers, and Reading Contracts

1. Discuss books that you have chosen to read more than one time. Why? What made you want to reread them?
2. Make a list of articles that one newspaper reporter writes for a newspaper in a month. Can you judge how well he or she writes? What does the list tell you about the reporter? Does the reporter follow a pattern in the way he/she writes a story? Does the reporter tend to use the same words over and over? If the newspaper ran another article by the same reporter without a byline, how could you tell the article was written by him/her? Did you find out anything else about the reporter? If there are no bylines, call the paper and ask a reporter to help you keep track of his/her articles

for a week or ask to see a scrapbook of his/her work. (The string.)

3. Make up a checklist with which to evaluate the author as a writer.
4. Is the author qualified to write on this subject? Give reasons.
5. What did you find out about the author's personality from the book?
6. What five questions would you like to ask the author?
7. Does the story hold your interest?
8. Do the characters seem believable to you?
9. Do people really talk this way? Do you? Do any friends you know? Does any other person?
10. Does the title fit the story? Can you think of an alternate title?
11. Do the illustrations fit the story?
12. Write a sentence (paragraph, story) using this author's style.
13. Did you feel lack of interest in any part of the story?
14. Did the author use too many words, too few, or just enough, in your opinion?
15. How did the book leave you feeling? Satisfied? Unsettled? Incomplete? Other feelings?
16. If you were going to give an award for the worst book(s) you ever read, which would you choose? What are your reasons?
17. Write either a fan letter or a letter of complaint to this author about his/her writing style.
18. List an author's books in the sequence in which they were written. What differences do you see in writing skills over his/her career?
19. Write a letter to an author whose book(s) you have especially enjoyed.
20. Invite an author to your school to talk about his/her writing.
21. What was the season of the year in the story? What was the weather like? Does the author let you know this?
22. Does the dialogue fit the types of persons the characters are supposed to be? Does it fit their backgrounds, personalities, ages, and/or ways of life? Is it current? Does it fit

the time in which the story is set? Is it appropriate? Is it real and lifelike?
23. Evaluate or rate your own writing or that of a friend.

ANALYZING AN AUTHOR'S BIAS, POINT OF VIEW, OR VALUES

Sample Activities for Discussion, Task Cards, Learning Centers, and Reading Contracts

1. What would this author value most:
   (a) A cow or a car?
   (b) A wife or a child?
   (c) Church or fishing?
   (d) Red or blue?
   (e) Sugar or salt?
   (f) Arguing or peacemaking?
   (g) Winning or losing?
   (h) A trip by plane or a trip by boat?
   Does everyone in the class who has read the book agree with you? Can you think of similar questions about this author?
2. Give a direct quote(s) from the book (article, story) to answer:
   (a) One thing the author thinks beautiful.
   (b) One thing the author thinks funny.
   (c) One thing the author thinks right.
   (d) One word the author enjoys.
   Did everyone agree with you?
3. How does the author handle controversial issues in this book? What controversial issue(s) does he/she include?
4. Does the author belong to any group that might influence his/her writing? In what ways?
5. Does the author know what he/she is talking about? How do you know?
6. Which of the author's biases were most like your own? Least like your own? How do you feel about this?
7. Would you want this author for a friend? Explain.
8. Did this author use emotion-laden words? Give examples. What do you think the author's opinion is of each of these topics? How does this affect his/her writing? Change some

words in each of the examples to give an entirely different feeling.

9. If you were a librarian, what other books by other authors who see the subject differently could you choose to balance the views of this author? If you don't know of any, personally, interview a librarian (or several) to see what he or she would suggest.

10. For whom is this magazine (book, etc.) published? Does this affect the opinions it presents?

11. What does the name tell you about the magazine (book, etc.)?

12. Think up as many other suitable names as you can for the magazine (book, etc.) that you are reviewing in view of the opinions expressed in the contents.

13. Pretend that you are a book reviewer for *Ms.* magazine. Write a review of this book from the feminist point of view. Alternates: Write a review of this book for *Jet* magazine, *Rolling Stone, Sports Illustrated, Modern Maturity, Playboy,* etc.

14. Be a magazine writer. *Ms.* magazine has a regular feature called, "No Comment." Look at the last three write-ups, then check the magazines and newspapers in our classroom for similar items. If you find one, write a letter to *Ms.* and try to get your item published.

15. Reread the story, paying special attention to how people talk.
    (a) Is there a difference in the way the author has boys and girls speak?
    (b) If you are a boy, do you talk like the boys in this story? If you are a girl, do you talk like the girls?
    (c) Which speech patterns in the story seem true to life to you?
    (d) Which seem awkward, unreal, or stilted? What do all these things tell you about the author's beliefs?

16. Give all girl characters boys' names; give all boy characters girls' names; do the same for all male and female characters in the story. Read the story again using reversed roles. (Alternate: Reverse ages.)
    (a) How does it sound to you?
    (b) What does this tell you about the author's feelings?
    (c) Do you agree with the author's feelings? Explain.

    (d) Do most people agree with the author about female and
        male characteristics? Explain.

17. Write a letter to the editor of *Ms.* magazine about some of
    your feelings about articles you read in the latest issue.
    (Alternates: *Modern Maturity, Ebony, Seventeen.*)

18. Count the number of pictures of the following in your
    book: boys, girls, men, women, older people, office work-
    ers, blue collar workers, children, adults. What guesses
    would you make about the author's beliefs from this infor-
    mation? How would you feel about reading the book if you
    belonged in another category—for example, if you were a
    boy instead of a girl, old instead of young?

19. List these values from one to ten in the order you feel the
    author would find them important. Support your choices:
    equal rights, women's rights, independence, honesty,
    freedom, humor, intelligence, creativity, home, economics.

20. Make a list of words or phrases that indicate this particular
    author's biases and prejudices; e.g., hateful voice, trampy
    starlet, selfish men.

DISCOVERING THE AUTHOR'S HIDDEN ASSUMPTIONS

Sample Activities for Discussion, Task Cards, Learning Centers, and Reading Contracts

1. What does the author believe are good things? Bad things?
2. What does the author believe to be success? What do his/
    her characters have to do to be successful?
3. Which occupations seem most important to this writer?
    Would everyone agree? Do you?
4. What assumptions about natural resources does the author
    make?
5. What other assumptions does the author make about the
    world?
6. Authors often make assumptions that they may not be con-
    scious of.
    (a) What does the author assume about you?
    (b) What does he or she assume about our government?
    (c) What does he or she assume about men? Women? Boys?
        Girls?

DISCOVERING THE AUTHOR'S PURPOSE

Sample Activities for Discussion, Task Cards, Learning Centers, and Reading Contracts

1. Why do you think the author wrote this book? (Some reasons for writing a book might be: (a) for fun; (b) to expound a viewpoint; (c) for therapy; (d) for money; and the like.) Do you think the reader would have the same reason(s) for reading it as the author did for writing it? Does everyone agree with you? (Alternate: Why do you think the author wrote this particular poem, article, editorial, etc.?)
2. How can we find out the real reasons why this selection was written?
3. What values do you think the author holds that influenced him or her to write this?
4. Would you like to meet the person who wrote this? Why?
5. In your opinion, do you feel the author's reasons for writing this were worthwhile or not? Does everyone agree with you?
6. In your life, are there circumstances that might cause you to write something similar?
7. How could writing something make your life better?

ANALYZING THE AUTHOR'S ORGANIZATIONAL PATTERNS

Sample Activities for Discussion, Task Cards, Learning Centers, and Reading Contracts

1. How do the words the author uses compare with the words your family or friends use?
2. Do you know anyone who talks as this author writes?
3. What kind of a book are you reading? (Fiction, nonfiction, mystery, myth, etc.)
4. Do you feel that this author would listen to you? How did the way he/she organized the story influence your answer? What do you think you could talk about to this author?
5. Does this story read well out loud? Make a recording and see.
6. What did the author include in the story that made it interesting to you:

(a) In the way the book looks?
(b) In content?
(c) In words or phrases?
(d) In the way the story was organized?
7. Make a list of words or phrases that the author used that made you feel happy. (Optimistic, sad, amused, depressed, excited, etc.)
8. Do you think this author believes herself/himself to be better than you? What makes you feel that way?
9. What devices did the author use to cause you to like or dislike a story character?
10. Find and list the *who, what, where, when, why* for a story, an article, a book, and/or a newspaper feature. (Younger readers: discuss each for a particular selection.)
11. Take a field trip to a newspaper office, magazine publisher, and/or a television station to see how they organize their materials.
12. Discuss the writer's use of punctuation marks, and how they affect his/her writing.
13. Did the ending make sense?
14. Did the beginning catch your interest?
15. In your opinion, did the story end at the right time? Too late; too soon?
16. Did you get lost at any place in the story (article, chapter, book, etc.)? Why do you think this was?
17. Would the story (article, etc.) have been easier for you to understand if it had begun in a different way?
18. Make a collection of beginning sentences in fiction writing that you particularly enjoy. (Alternate: A collection of opening sentences for nonfiction writing.)

SEPARATING FACT FROM OPINION

Sample Activities for Discussion, Task Cards, Learning Centers, or Contracts

1. Make a chart of fact vs. fiction in your story.
2. Have a Liar's Club Meeting. See who can tell fact from fiction. See who is best at confusing listeners.
3. List three things from the story that are fact and three that are opinion.

4. Is this story real or make-believe? Can you back up your answer?
5. Collect newspaper editorials. Underline the parts that are opinions in red and the facts in green.
6. Choose a controversial topic. Write down your opinions on the subject, then research various viewpoints. Did your opinions change?
7. Could what happened in the story really happen?
8. All of these answers are true. Which ones do you think are the best reasons why _____ ? (List statements for student choice based on the story.)

RECOGNIZING PROPAGANDA

Sample Activities for Discussion, Task Cards, Learning Centers, and Reading Contracts

1. Did the author try to influence you to do or to believe something? What?
2. Give examples of things that you consider good propaganda in the book. Bad propaganda?
3. Does the author write in an emotional or in an objective manner?
4. Research the standard propaganda techniques. Does the author use any of these? Have you ever used them?
5. Can the reader of this book come to believe something that the author doesn't exactly state but that he/she wants the reader to believe? Give examples.
6. Underline all the words or sentences on a page (or in a chapter) that are opinion. Do other people agree with you?
7. Make a propaganda bulletin board and label each example correctly.
8. Compare a newspaper (or magazine) ad for a product with a television ad for the same product. What are the differences? The similarities?
9. The hardest propaganda to detect is that with which you agree. Find examples to share with us.
10. Write a defense of and/or a rebuttal to the statement, "Propaganda is bad."
11. Which products are not allowed to be advertised on television? Which are restricted to certain hours? Compare with

similar restrictions in your local newspaper. With a national newspaper. With a magazine.

12. Write an ad, a news story, or a fiction paragraph illustrating a propaganda technique.

13. Cut out an ad that appeals to you and one that does not. Analyze your reactions.

14. Try to write a story or other selection to try to "fool" someone.

15. Research some of the famous historical propagandists— e.g., Tokyo Rose, Goebbels, etc.

16. Look at an ad for a food product. Buy the product. Compare your reactions to the ad.

17. Collect newspaper editorials. Underline all the words that describe something in a derogatory manner.

18. Try to sell an idea. Examples: _____ should be president; school should be held only in the mornings; a shower is better than a bath. What problems did you have? What techniques did you use?

19. Keep a word or phrase list of stock phrases that advertisers use to influence thinking.

20. Take a sample of your classmates' opinions on a controversial subject. Plan a presentation designed for balanced coverage of the topic (or a presentation designed to present a particular viewpoint.) Afterwards, take another opinion sampling. Did they change their minds? Should they have?

21. Is anything exaggerated in your book?

22. Make a collection of food products that use various propaganda or persuasive techniques on wrappers, boxes, cans, labels, and the like.

23. Cut out an advertisement from a newspaper and remove all writing or reading material. Show the picture to some classmates. See if they can guess what is being advertised. Write a letter to the advertiser on the basis of your interviews.

24. Keep a class propaganda diary for a week. Record all propaganda techniques used by any person in the classroom and discuss them each day. See if more or less are used by the end of the week.

25. Teachers: Discuss and have students find examples of the use of the following propaganda techniques:

(a) The use of unpopular or unattractive epithets for people who disagree with you; for example, such names as *kindergarten baby*, *frigid*, *uninformed*, *Fascist*, and the like.

(b) The use of large, undefined areas of debate, usually those which have some emotionally loaded connotation for the reader, instead of citing specific facts relative to the case at hand; for example, the identifying of such issues as *peace*, *motherhood*, *sanctity*, *piousness* with the issue, idea, or person being advocated.

(c) The use of symbols, words, or ideas having positive emotional connotations with unrelated issues; for example, the use of American flags, the peace sign, pictures of famous people to promote causes, products or candidates.

(d) The use of simple words, phrases, or colloquialisms to insure readers that the idea or person comes from a background just like that of ordinary, folksy people; for example, the use of dialectical or regional English on the part of politicians, the exhibiting of cloth coats (No expensive furs here, guys!), inexpensive cars, ordinary dress.

(e) The use of famous or prominent people to push an issue, politician, or a product; for example, superstars in various fields.

(f) The use of the argument that everyone is doing it, and so the reader should fall in line; for example, wear your hair in a certain style, vote for a candidate, go to the show with all the gang.

(g) The presenting of only the part of the facts which favors one issue or person; for example, movie ads that use only the positive parts of a critic's comments, or the omission of damaging budget figures that disprove an argument.

(h) The technique of attacking a person instead of debating his or her ideas(s); for example, "If _____ (some politician) is for this, I'm against it!"

26. Teachers: Gather several examples of propaganda. Have children classify them by the various propaganda techniques and find other examples on their own.

27. Teachers: Have students write their own examples of various types of propaganda.

IDENTIFYING STEREOTYPES

Sample Activities for Discussion, Task Cards, Learning Centers, Reading Contracts

1. Suppose you were a Martian who had never read any other thing about earth but this story: What would you think girls were like? What would you think boys were like? Would you rather be a boy or a girl? Why? What would you think men were like? What would you think women were like? Would you rather be a man or woman? Explain. How would you think people looked? What color would Earth people be? How tall would Earth people be? What would you think Earth people would spend most of their time doing?

2. Compare the list of editors and publishers for two or more magazines or newspapers: Which has the highest percentage of women on the total staff? Which department has the most women? The least? For each magazine or newspaper? Compared to each other? Make a graph or write a summary of what you found.

3. Make a list of all the types of activities the author had each of the following do: men, women, boys, girls. Make some guesses about the author's feelings about each of these groups.

4. How many boys are pictured in your book? Girls? Men? Women? What do you think this means? (Alternate: older people.)

5. Make up a checklist to select books that are free from stereotypes. Consult the checklist that your teacher or librarian has to help you. Compare five books using your own or someone else's checklist. (Your librarian can help.)

6. Judging from the pictures (or content) in the book, would you rather be a boy or a girl, a man or woman?

7. Who has power in the story (article, etc.)? What sex, age, race, etc.?

8. Who is shown as more tolerant or understanding? What race? What sex? What age?
9. How does this writer handle religion?
10. How does this author describe occupations?
11. Pantomime an age level, sex, religion, race, or occupation. What did your actions reveal about yourself? About your audience?
12. How many stories in this book have male and female main characters? (Alternate: race of main characters.)
13. Make a chart of the number of times these things happen: Someone solves a problem. Someone is active. Someone is the leader. Someone cries. Someone is strong. Someone earns money. Someone is foolish. Someone is beautiful. Someone works in the kitchen. Someone cleans house. Someone comes from a different family structure.
14. What kinds of families are described in this book? What kinds are left out?
15. Make a representative list of adjectives used to describe different sexes, races, ages, or religions. What conclusions can you draw?
16. Teachers: Cut out five pictures of professional men and five pictures of professional women fron newspapers or magazines. Have the children try to predict their occupations. Discuss reasons, possible sources of errors.
17. Teachers: Cut out ten pictures of men and women representing various occupaions. Give a list of their occupations. See who can correctly match the most. Talk about which attitudes helped and which did not help accuracy in solving this.
18. Teachers: Have children take pictures of men and women workers in the community. See who can guess what they do.
19. Teachers: Play What's My Line? with community resource people; e.g., police officers, shopkeepers, workers, parents. Try to get persons who are not stereotypic.
20. Teachers: Read a paragraph or two aloud from a story, article, poem. Have children guess whether the author was a man or a woman. Why? Have students check their predictions.

DETERMINING THE RELIABILITY
AND VALIDITY OF WRITTEN MATERIAL

Sample Activities for Discussion, Task Cards,
Learning Centers, and Reading Contracts

1. As you read this book (article, pamphlet, etc.), keep asking yourself if it seems reasonable. Possible? Be ready for a discussion on those two points after you finish.
2. Have you ever read or heard something that makes you believe or disbelieve what you read in this book (article, etc.)? Which is the more reliable source? On what do you base your judgment?
3. Does the author include any statements that begin, "All _____," which say that everyone or all people do a certain thing or believe a certain thing, or the like? Are the statements accurate?
4. What should be the background and qualifications of a person who writes this kind of book (article, story, etc.)?

EVALUATING CONTENT AND FORMAT
OF READING MATERIALS

Sample Activities for Discussion, Task Cards,
Learning Centers, and Reading Contracts

1. Is this the book you need for your purpose? In what way?
2. In what ways would other readers find this book useful?
3. For what grade level would you recommend this book?
4. If you were going to interview this author on a television talk show, which questions would you want to ask her/him?
5. When was the material written? Did the date of publication affect the material in any way?
6. Are the facts presented in the story true?
7. Can you find mistakes in any of the pictures illustrating the story?
8. What is your opinion of the way the book is put together?

(a) The cover design and material?
(b) The type of print?
(c) The paper used?
(d) The layout of the pages?
(e) The jacket design?

9. Choose a book that has won an award. In your opinion, what were the reasons for this? (Advanced students: Compare your opinions with those of one (or more) reviewers.)

10. What are the names of references that review children's or young people's literature. Choose a book on the basis of a review that you read in one source. Did you make a good choice? Can you explain why or why not?

11. Would you want your name to be listed as writer of this book? Editor? Layout designer? Printer? Illustrator? Jacket designer? Publisher?

12. Why would another student disagree with your opinion about this book? An adult?

13. Is this book a good source of information for our problem (study, research, needs)?

14. Choose a subject that will run for several days in the newspapers. Collect the articles for a week. Compare what happens to the subject day by day (number of words, page order, position on the page, headlines, etc.). What does this tell you?

15. Compare first, second, and other editions of the same book. What similarities did you find? What differences?

16. Is the quality of a book just a matter of opinion?

17. What are the ways to tell if a book is a good one? Are the criteria the same for all types of books?

18. Pretend you are a critic and write a review of your book or story. Alternate for advanced readers: Write a review of your book in the style that a critic would use for *Ms.* magazine, for *Sports Illustrated*, etc.

19. Teachers: Have children on a panel to review books for classroom or library purchase. Help them draw up a list of criteria for use in judging books.

20. Teachers: Discuss types of books with the class that they would choose for younger children; for older students. Discuss the dangers in choosing books for others.

COMPARING TWO OR MORE SOURCES

Sample Activities for Discussion, Task Cards, Learning Centers, and Reading Contracts

1. Which author is the best known?
2. Which author's style appeals most to you?
3. Compare a list of other books written by each of the authors. What does this say to you?
4. Which materials or books are the most recent? Does this affect their contents? In what way?
5. Look up the copyright date on each book. Locate a news magazine and a newspaper front page from that same time. What was going on in the world at that time? Did the authors differ in what they said?
6. Subscribe to two newspapers for the class.
7. Find at least two newspapers or news magazine stories on a given subject:
   (a) What was included in each story?
   (b) What was different in each?
   (c) What do the differences in the story headlines tell you?
   (d) Are there any other comparisons you can make?
8. Find write-ups about the same news story in at least two different newspapers. On what pages did the story start? How long was each story? How big were the headlines? What guesses (hypotheses) can you make about the policies of each newspaper as a result of your analysis? How can you find out if your hypotheses are factual?
9. In two newspaper or news magazine articles on the same story:
   (a) What facts are included in each?
   (b) Are there any ways in which the articles contradict each other?
10. Substantiate an opinion of yours by using at least two different sources.
11. Interview two people on a subject from the book. Make a chart of the ways they agreed and disagreed with the author. Which of the three do you feel is more correct? Why?
12. Find a film, film strip, or another book on the same subject. Which would you recommend for a seven-year-old? Which for a high school student?

13. Compare five articles or features in your local newspaper with the coverage of the same subjects in a national newspaper for the same date.

14. Compare two books about the same topic (e.g., biographies about one person, stories about an era of history, stories about an event). How were they alike? How did they differ?

15. Compare an autobiography with a biography about the same person. How are they alike? Different?

16. Compare the *who, what, where, when, why* for two selections written by two different writers about the same event, idea, or person.

17. Find two descriptions of the same person, event, happening, etc. Which do you consider the best?

18. Find two books or two newspaper or magazine articles that express opposite opinions on the same topic.

19. Read two books which are written on a similar topic. Choose the one you like best. Make a list of all the things you can think of that cause you to like one book better. Compare your list with lists that other students make. What did you leave out? What did you see that no one else saw? Compare the lists with those drawn up by librarians and teachers' groups. Rank the criteria according to their importance to you. Again, compare to others' rankings.

ANALYZING SELF THROUGH CRITICAL READING

Sample Activities for Discussion, Task Cards, Learning Centers, and Reading Contracts

1. Keep a list of all the books you read for a certain period of time (a month, a week, a year, etc.):
   (a) What does this list tell about you?
   (b) Are you limiting yourself in any way to certain subjects, authors, or type of book?
   (c) What books would you like to read that you haven't as yet read?

2. Look at the new books in the library. Which interest you? Which do not?

3. If you followed some of the behaviors suggested in this book, would you be a better person?

4. What was one thing you learned from the story? Anything else?
5. Did you change your mind about anything as a result of reading this story (article, etc.)?
6. What place does this book have in your life?
7. Out of all the books you have ever read, how does this book compare?
8. Would you list this book among the best five you've ever read? Among the worst five books you've ever read? Anywhere else?
9. Make up a checklist that would help other people select a book for you.
10. Read the story a second time:
    (a) What did you skip the first time?
    (b) Do you see anything new the second time?
11. What new things does this story make you want to know?
12. From where do you and your family get most of your information?
13. Read a book that you have read before. Did you change your opinion? Did you react differently? Did it mean the same thing to you? Do this with both a book you liked and one you disliked at first reading. Any differences?
14. Do the story characters have the type of life you wish you had? Which parts of their lives would you like to experience? Which not?
15. Look through newspapers and magazines and cut out things of interest to you (hobbies, favorite things, weekend trips, family fun, interesting people, menus or recipes, clothing, hair styles).
16. Tape oral reading for self-evaluation.
17. Which of the characters in this book have lives similar to yours?
18. Keep a log of your reading for a month, listing ideas, suggestions, actions, etc., of interest to you.
19. What do you know or what past experiences have you had that can be applied to understanding this selection?
20. How are you and the author similar? Different?

A FINAL WORD ABOUT CRITICAL READING

Young people need to know how to evaluate what they read. An author can have a tremendous influence on young

readers, especially if the writer is skilled in his/her craft. Therefore, young readers need to realize that an author can satisfy
for one purpose or for one period in life and, perhaps, not for
another; that some writing is better suited to recreational reading than to serious research. All authors have biases, points of
view, and values. The more proficient reader learns to recognize this and take these leanings into account in judging written material. In this way, students can begin to see that writers
are people much like themselves; that is, sometimes authors
write for noble, altruistic reasons, and sometimes for personal
advantage, and sometimes (and usually) for both. The ultimate
test of a writer, then, is the possibility for growth that his or her
writings give our students. Judged in this way, reading becomes a mirror in which the student can learn about and better
the self.

3

Creative Reading Skills

* * * * * * * * * * * *

The moment we educators see one of our students recognize (even a little) that reading is one of the most creative processes—that reader input and output is every bit as essential as author input and output, that there is very little difference, really, between being a reader and being an author—is a heady one. We educators drive home after such a day feeling fulfilled, knowing that our creativity sparked that of another. We may even feel a little smug; it's a good feeling.

This feeling helps us continue to watch for this spark each day, to accept the fact that none of us or our students can be functioning at our peak of creativity one hundred percent of the time. In fact, plateaus and regressions in ourselves and our students are a part of this very creative process—a time to regenerate, to rethink, to evaluate, to incorporate knowledge into our own systems and lives. This leaves us free, then, to try out other new ideas we get from reading that, in turn, will have, in their time, to be integrated into ourselves in a similar fashion.

DEVELOPING AUTHORS' SKILLS

Sample Activities for Discussion, Task Cards, Learning Centers, and Reading Contracts

1. Write a story about your prediction of something in the future. (Variety of Authors' Tasks)
2. Keep a poetry journal (your own or favorites you have read). (Variety of Authors' Tasks)

3. Keep a feelings journal of how you react day by day. (Variety of Authors' Tasks)

4. Pretend to be an inanimate object in the room. Write up your adventures during the day. (Variety of Authors' Tasks)

5. Keep a diary of your activities. Check famous books that are diaries for clues as to what you want to include. (Variety of Authors' Tasks)

6. Rewrite your book using the same plot line, but in a different setting and time. (Variety of Authors' Tasks)

7. Write your own autobiography and illustrate it. (Variety of Authors' Tasks)

8. Be a historian. Write a history of your community. Find photos if you can. (Variety of Authors' Tasks)

9. Be a research consultant for younger children in your school. Research people, events, etc., of interest to them. (Variety of Authors' Tasks)

10. Interview a story character or a friend of the character. (Interviewing)

11. Interview your parents, teachers, and classmates to find their favorite parts of the newspaper. (Alternates: favorite foods, colors, film stars, songs, etc.) (Interviewing)

12. Prepare a list of questions you would ask someone famous if you were to interview her or him on a TV show. (Interviewing)

13. Interview your teacher about his or her interests, education, hobbies, projects, hopes for your class, pet peeves, or the like. (Alternate: Be a roving reporter. Interview classmates, friends, or parents on the same topics.) (Interviewing)

14. Compare your interviewing skills with those of other students. Form a panel and invite a visitor whom you would enjoy interviewing. Each person on the panel should prepare a set of interview questions beforehand and write up the interview afterwards. Then, compare questions and write-ups. (What questions did others think of that you forgot? What did they include in their write-ups that you overlooked, etc.) (Interviewing)

15. Write an imaginary query that the writer might have written to his publisher selling him the idea for this book or story. (Reference: *Writer's Market*.) (Selling a Story)

16. Write a query letter to a magazine editor or book publisher about some of your own work. (Selling a Story)
17. Make up a list of chapters you would include in a book titled, *What School Is Really Like,* or make up a tentative list of chapters for a book you would like to write. (Selling a Story)
18. Make up three beginnings for other stories which use the same style of opening that this author used, then make up one in your own style. (Developing and Recognizing Individual Writing Styles)
19. Write or tape-record some new dialogue for a character in the story. Make the character sound just the way the writer had him talk. (Alternate: Rewrite the dialogue the way you feel it should have been written.) (Developing and Recognizing Individual Writing Styles)
20. Which authors write in a way that you would like to write: Describe. (Developing and Recognizing Individual Writing Styles)
21. Take any picture from a magazine or elsewhere. Make up an ad for a real or imaginary product using that picture. (Writing Ads)
22. Using a camera, pose classmates or group objects for an ad for a real or imaginary product. (Writing Ads)
23. Select a product that is usually advertised in magazines. Prepare a display of the advertisements of that product over a period of several years. Share your conclusions about the audience to whom the advertisement is directed and the effectiveness of the series of ads. (Writing Ads)
24. Prepare ads for the same product for each of the following magazines: *Town and Country, Jack and Jill, Ms., Esquire, Time,* or similar magazines.
25. Think of something that, if it were invented, would make your life better or more exciting (Example: a portable flat tire repairer). Pretend it has already been invented. Make up an ad to sell it. (Writing Ads)
26. Sometimes a writer is also an artist or photographer. Pretend that you are an artist-writer or an artist-photographer. Illustrate some of your work. (Illustrator-Writer Skills)
27. Using a tagboard sliding frame, decide what part of each photograph should be used to illustrate the story. This is called cropping. (Illustrator-Writer Skills)

28. Crop a photo in several different ways. Observe the effects. Compare your cropping with that of your classmates. (Illustrator-Writer Skills)

29. Look at various uses of photographs to illustrate magazine and newspaper articles. Find examples of different ways to lay out words and photographs—e.g., words over picture, words cut from pictures, picture to edge of page, etc. Collect and display them. (Illustrator-Writer Skills)

30. Look at several magazine covers for the same magazine. Note where the editors customarily place titles and captions. Find or take photographs that would be suitable for the covers of these magazines. (Alternate: Make a sample magazine cover for these magazines.) (Illustrator-Writer Skills)

31. Look at several different magazines. Decide what kinds of pictures or illustrations each editor wants. Take pictures that you feel would be appropriate for that magazine. (Illustrator-Writer Skills)

32. Research and list five potential markets for the kinds of photographs you like best to take. (Use *Writers' Market* or *Photographers' Market*, or similar sources for information.) (Illustrator-Writer Skills)

33. Sell one of your pictures to a publisher using the steps listed in various writers' or photographers' market sources. (Illustrator-Writer Skills)

34. List five headlines you'd like to see in the newspapers. (Caption Writing)

35. List the headlines in the newspaper for the day you were born. (Look them up in the library or at a newspaper office.) (Caption Writing)

36. Make up captions for a series of pictures of your best friend. (Alternates: one of your parents, your teachers, your classmates.) (Caption Writing)

37. Collect several examples of a cartoonist's work; describe her or his style. What do the cartoons tell you about her or his beliefs? Make up captions for his or her work; compare them with the original. (Cartooning)

38. Make up a cartoon or cartoon strip about the happenings in our class today. (Alternates: About your day, your best friend's day, etc.) (Cartooning)

39. Using only three pencil or brush strokes, make a sketch of

your teacher. (Alternates: A classmate, yourself, your parents, etc.) Do the same with five strokes. (Cartooning)

40. Make a collection of ideas various cartoonists use to express movement, action, ideas, danger, etc. (Cartooning)

41. Draw three ways in which you could express grief, surprise, and hunger in a cartoon. (Cartooning)

42. In journalism classes, students are often taught that the lead paragraph should contain *who, what, where, when, how,* and sometimes *why.* Look at a page in the newspaper. Check three beginning paragraphs. List the *who, what, where, when, how* and *why* for each. Think of a class event. Write a lead paragraph including all these elements. Write a lead paragraph for a newspaper article following this pattern for an event in your book. (Reporter-Journalist Skills)

43. Newspapers often have men whose job it is to write headlines and story titles. Count the number of letters in small and large headlines. Write headlines for stories about incidents in your book. Write headlines for these paragraphs. (Teachers: Cut lead paragraphs from newspapers for students to use.) (Reporter-Journalist Skills)

44. Proofread an article of your own, of a classmate, or from already published work. (Reporter-Journalist Skills)

45. Make a daily newspaper of class happenings. Have an early edition and/or a late edition. Put out an occasional extra. (Reporter-Journalist Skills)

46. Which happenings in our class would make a good article for the local newspaper? Write the story, send it to the editor, and share his/her response with us. (Reporter-Journalist Skills)

47. Write a gossip column about class happenings. (Reporter-Journalist Skills)

48. If you were the reporter assigned to this class, which events that happened today would you write up? (Reporter-Journalist Skills)

49. Be a film critic. Review a recent film you have seen. Send a copy of your review to the producer of the film. (Alternates: television series, new books.) (Reporter-Journalist Skills)

50. Be a photo-journalist for your school. Snap action pictures of school activities. Offer the articles you write to parents' groups, teachers, classmates, reporters, yearbooks, or pub-

lish your own book about your school. (Reporter-Journalist Skills)

51. First grade texts are written with a limited vocabulary. Check a standard word list (e.g., Dolch) or a basic book. Write a story for first graders using only those words and proper nouns. (Writing to Specifications)

52. Write a poem of three verses, each verse of which has four lines, with the same line ending each of the three verses. (Alternate: Ending with the same word) (Writing to Specifications)

53. Compose the melody and lyrics for a song that uses the ABAB or AABA melodic line. (Writing to Specifications)

54. Write a riddle, verse, or sentence where all, or almost all, of the words begin with the same letter of the alphabet. (Alliteration) Example: Peter Piper. (Writing to Specifications)

55. Look up the definitions for *rhyming couplets, triplets,* and *quatrains.* Find or write a sample of each. (Writing to Specifications)

56. Write a poem using only one word per line, each word of which is one letter longer than the one above it. (Writing to Specifications)

57. Make up a story where the principal character repeats the same line of poetry all the time. (Example: "Fee, fie, foe, fum," from *Jack and the Beanstalk.*)

58. Write a haiku poem of three lines. The first line contains five syllables, the second, seven, and the last five. Compare yours to haiku in poetry books. (Alternate: Cinquain poetry uses a 2-4-6-8-2 syllable pattern.) (Writing to Specifications)

59. Write a limerick about someone or some event in the classroom (or yourself). (Writing to Specifications)

60. Pretend you are a gag writer. Make up a joke in your favorite comedian's style. (Writing to Specifications)

61. Write a story (sentence) using every letter in the alphabet. (Writing to Specifications)

62. Design a screenplay that would make a good Disney movie. (Writing to Specifications)

63. Write a story for a kindergartener, including pictures. (Writing to Specifications)

64. Write an outline for an original story in less than seventy-five words. (Writing to Specifications)

65. Write a story, poem, or article. Put it aside for a few days. Then look at it with fresh eyes. Which parts run smoothly? Which parts are unclear? Which parts are redundant? Which parts should be left out? Rewrite it as necessary. Look at it again a month later. What would you change now? (Editing, Proofreading, and Publishing Skills)

66. Read the writings of a classmate. Make suggestions as he or she asks for them. (Editing, Proofreading, and Publishing Skills)

67. Be a magazine editor. (a) Select the cover story from stories cut from magazines or written by classmates. (b) Choose a balance of articles for the magazine. (c) Pretend that you receive an article that does not fit the format of your magazine. Write a rejection letter. (Editing, Proofreading, and Publishing Skills)

68. Take a newspaper or magazine article. Pretend that you have to fit it into 200 words. Rewrite the article to fit. (Editing, Proofreading, and Publishing Skills)

69. Proofread a page of a newspaper or magazine to see if you can find errors in it. (Teachers: Keep a file of pages containing errors for this exercise.) (Editing, Proofreading, and Publishing Skills)

70. Be a publisher for a book of stories for your class to give to parents, to donate to a class at younger grade level, etc. Read, edit, and select the poems, stories, plays, etc., to be included. (Editing, Proofreading, and Publishing Skills) Think up a good name for your publishing company.

71. Teacher: Have a Typewriting Club. Use an aide, a programmed text, or an experienced student to teach typewriting skills. Later, have students compose some of their writing directly on the typewriter. (Using Authors' Tools)

72. Teacher: Have a dictation corner where students practice dictating stories and dialogue directly on a dictation machine or tape recorder or to a "rewrite" person. (Using Authors' Tools)

73. Teacher: Set up a photography club for students to learn basic photography skills. (Using Authors' Tools)

74. Teacher: Invite a photographer to talk to the class about camera equipment he or she uses to cover a football game, a party, a fire, an accident, an important visitor, and the like. (Using Authors' Tools)

75. Teachers: Set up a center for a unit on letter writing for the students. (a) Have a list of interesting people to write to. Examples: Yourself, your teacher, congressmen, pen pals, the editor of a magazine or newspaper, consuls, travel agents, sick classmates, parents, grandparents. (b) Display the kinds of notes students can write: thank you, holiday, hello, trips, etc. (c) Display or have students make a display of post cards. (d) Display or make a collage of the kinds of letters they could write: business, telegrams, postcards, etc. (e) Have a variety of stationery and envelopes available, or have students design their own. Include a variety of pencils and pens. (Letter Writing)

76. Teachers: Have a list of interesting ideas for letters. Examples: (a) Write a diary letter to someone special. Make her feel as if she had been with you for the week (month, or day) of the letter. (b) Describe your home and your life to a pen pal. (c) Write and decorate a letter to someone who has been good to you this week. (d) Write a post card about a trip you took—even a field trip! (e) Write a telegram as if you were one of the characters in the story. (f) Write a letter as if you were some animal in danger of dying of pollution. (g) Pretend to be an inanimate object in the classroom. Write letters to various people in the class about your reactions to them. (Letter Writing)

77. Teachers: Form a Writers' Club, where a story, poem, or other evidence of writing must be submitted in order to be a member. (Variety of Writer Tasks)

78. Teachers: Provide a series of story beginnings, middles, and endings that students can draw from envelopes or from a flip book for creative writing. (Variety of Writing Tasks)

79. Teachers: Write group compositions where students alternate lines. (Variety of Writer Tasks)

80. Teachers: Set up a letter writing system within the classroom for classmates and outsiders. (Letter Writing)

81. Teachers: Provide a box of flannel board story characters for children to use to make up their own stories and shows. (Alternate: puppets of various kinds.) (Variety of Writer Tasks)

82. Teachers: Show the illustrations from a book with which the students aren't familiar. Have them write a story to go with the illustrations. Share, stressing the varieties of ideas, then compare with the original—not to match it, but to understand the possibilities. (Variety of Writer Tasks)

83. Teachers: Make books in the shape of the main characters, objects, or geometrical forms for students to write about. (Variety of Writer Tasks)

84. Teachers: Have students use one of these topics in a story: My Dreams, Things I Like to Do, If I Were . . . , If You Were I, Best Friends, My Favorite . . . , My Mother, Invisible, The Strangest Thing I Ever Saw, What Would I Be Doing If I Were At . . . ?, I Wish, My Own Special Monster, A Letter To An Imaginary Friend, What Will I Be, My Life In Twenty Years, etc. (Variety of Writer Tasks)

85. Teachers: Have an "I Was Once A Baby" day when students can set up a center or a display of whatever they wish to share. (Variety of Writer Tasks)

86. Teachers: Publish or display student writing. (Variety of Writer Tasks)

87. Teachers: Have students list ten sentences that show the author's sequence: (a) Have them rearrange the sentences in as many ways as they can to vary the sequence and still come out with the same story. (b) Have them rearrange the sentences to change the story. (Sequence)

88. Teachers: Read the middle of an unfamiliar story aloud to the students. Have students write or draw individual beginnings and/or endings. Read some of them aloud. Then read the author's beginning and/or ending. Discuss differences and similarities. Concentrate on the excitement of looking at diverse opinions. (Sequence)

89. Teachers: Have students write, draw, record, videotape, or act, etc., a sequel to the story. (Sequence)

90. Teachers: Introduce a sequence of books by reading aloud a beginning, ending, or middle book in terms of publication dates. (Oz, Pooh, etc.) Feature the other books of the author in a special display for free reading. Discuss, chart, and/or draw sequence. (Sequence)

91. Teachers: Take the series of photographs from an article.

Cut off all captions. Have the students read the article and write suitable captions for the story. (Alternate: Have a caption learning center with several articles to be captioned.) (Caption Writing)

92. Teachers: Take or have a student take a series of photographs about a school event (e.g., assemblies, visitors, awards, newcomers). Have students choose and caption those photographs that they feel best illustrate the story. Discuss differences and perceptions of the event. (Caption Writing)

93. Teachers: Have students make up their own captions for comic strips. (Caption Writing)

94. Teachers: Cut out a series of picture captions. Have the students draw what they think the caption describes. Compare and contrast their results with the actual picture, discussing various perceptions. (Alternate: Use headlines.) (Caption Writing)

95. Teachers: Read the first few lines of a newspaper story or cut out these lines for students to read. Have them write the rest and compare what they did with what the reporter wrote. (Reporter-Journalist Skills)

CREATION OF ORIGINAL MATERIAL

Sample Activities for Discussion, Task Cards, Learning Centers, and Reading Contracts

1. Tell a younger person (or friend) a story you made up about additional adventures of a favorite story character.

2. Create a speech that one of the story characters would make.

3. Make up a song about the story, a story event, the author, or a story character. (Alternate: Make up a poem, a costume for one of the story characters, a puppet show, or a dance based on the story.)

4. Write a story about what would have happened if you were one of the story characters.

5. Teachers: Give the class an oral or written inventory similar to this sample: Things Done On Your Own. These are some activities that boys and girls sometimes do on their own.

Check those you have done. Don't check any that you were assigned or made to do.

_____ 1. Wrote a poem.
_____ 2. Wrote a story.
_____ 3. Wrote a play.
_____ 4. Made a collection of your own writings.
_____ 5. Wrote a song.
_____ 6. Gave a puppet play.
_____ 7. Kept a diary.
_____ 8. Played word games.
_____ 9. Used a thesaurus.
_____10. Used a dictionary.
_____11. Recorded an oral reading, story, or the like.
_____12. Found errors in printed material.
_____13. Made up a new game.
_____14. Wrote a letter.
_____15. Read a science book or magazine.
_____16. Made a written record of an experiment.
_____17. Kept a notebook on some subject.
_____18. Made a scrapbook.
_____19. Counted the yearly rings in a tree section.
_____20. Made a collection of some sort.
_____21. Figured out a way of improving something.
_____22. Followed a map.
_____23. Made a map.
_____24. Made out a budget.
_____25. Illustrated a story.
_____26. Took photographs.
_____27. Other _____.

6. Teachers: Activities for students' creations: sound stories, finger plays, murals, games, dioramas, displays, exhibits, recordings, film strips, slide shows, booklets, choral speaking, radio and television programs, songs, films, roll movies, clay, impersonations, dramatics, dance mobiles, shadow plays, peep boxes, book fairs, allover designs, potato prints, greeting cards, design notepaper, design monograms for self or story characters, cattle brands, book jackets, calligraphy, book cover designs, comic book stories, cartoons, stationery or letterheads for self or story characters.

DESIGNING GAMES PUZZLES, ANAGRAMS, AND THE LIKE

Sample Activities for Discussion, Task Cards, Learning Centers, and Reading Contracts

1. Design a reading learning center for our class. Include at least one of the following: (a) new words to learn; (b) something to draw, paint, listen to, read, answer, write, evaluate, feel, see, taste, smell; or (c) a new book no one in the class has read.
2. Create a different world, including geography, intelligent beings, society, language, etc. Write a story about that world.
3. Find five words, each of which you can use to make another word by scrambling the letters. (Use all the letters.)
4. Make up a crossword puzzle, word scramble, or word search game using new vocabulary words, story characters, or chapter headings from the story.
5. Make a flip book for other students to use to write stories. Have at least ten examples in each of the following flip sections: Characters, Settings, Incidents. Add two other flip categories of your own.
6. Design an identikit for making different faces. Include eyebrows, eyes, noses, etc. Use the kit with your classmates to identify how various story characters look. Or ask a police officer to demonstrate an official kit.
7. Design an all-purpose game board which can be used for at least five separate games.

DEVELOPING CREATIVE THINKING SKILLS: CONVERGENT, DIVERGENT, AND EVALUATIVE THINKING

1. Draw a picture of the meaning of a new word in the story. (Convergent Thinking)
2. Draw a picture of the meaning of a familiar word. See who can guess the word. (Convergent Thinking)
3. Write a rebus story where pictures are substituted for words. If you are good enough, write a rebus story substituting pictures for sounds. (Convergent Thinking)

4. Play Concentration and see if you can solve the rebus. (Convergent Thinking)
5. Choose a rebus book. Write down in words what one of the pages means. (Convergent Thinking)
6. How are you and the main character of your story alike? (Convergent Thinking)
7. Place five objects on the floor. Think of all the ways they are alike. (Convergent Thinking)
8. Make a chart of the categories of types of stories read by the class this month. (Convergent Thinking)
9. Make up a follow-the-numbers picture based on your story. (Convergent Thinking)
10. Invent a story character and a name to go with these initials: R.W.C. (Divergent Thinking)
11. Play a game where you have to think of various objects that could fit a given description. Examples: (a) Name something that is the color of Santa's suit and makes a noise. (b) Name something that swims in water. (c) Name a toy that bounces. (d) Name something you eat that is sweet and cold. (e) Name games you can play in a car on a long trip. (Divergent Thinking)
12. Put the scrambled lines of a poem in sequence without ever having heard or seen the poem. Compare to the original. (Divergent Thinking)
13. What is reading? Write (or discuss) your definition and compare it with that of other students. (Alternate: Make an illustration of what reading is to you. Compare with other definitions.) (Divergent Thinking)
14. Different stories or other selections for writing mean different things to different people. Interview some classmates who have read the same selection to see what it means to each. (Divergent Thinking)
15. List as many occupations as you can where reading is unimportant. Support your choices. If possible, interview someone in that occupation to see if they agree. (Divergent Thinking)
16. Choose some object. Tell all the ways that it could fit into the plot of your book or story. (Divergent Thinking)
17. Give at least ten definitions of the following: school, reading, thinking, learning, creativity. (Divergent Thinking)

18. Make up five sentences whose words begin with the letters ABCD, FOTHT, etc. (Divergent Thinking)
19. Judging by current films, make up a list of five titles of movies that should be huge successes with today's audiences. (Divergent Thinking)
20. If a learning center, an exhibit, or a bulletin board were entitled, "Write On," what could be included in it in the way of games, activities, ideas, assignments, audio-visual materials, etc. (Divergent Thinking)
21. Make up at least ten titles for "If" stories. Example: If You Were As Tiny As An Ant, What Would You Do? (Divergent Thinking)
22. Write a report or prepare a talk on how we could improve something at school. In reading class? (Evaluative Thinking)
23. If all reading materials (books, newspapers, etc.) disappeared, how would it affect your life? (Evaluative Thinking)
24. Prepare yourself for a debate on the following: Reading is Less Important Nowadays. Be ready to take either the pro or con side. (Teachers: Assign by the drawing of cards labeled *pro* and *con*.) (Evaluative Thinking)
25. Evaluate your book on a ten-point scale using antonyms at opposite ends of the scale. Examples:

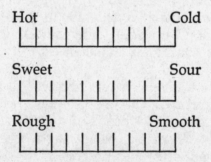

Hot   Cold

Sweet   Sour

Rough   Smooth

Make up other pairs. (Alternates: Rate authors or story characters.) (Evaluative Thinking)
26. When and under what conditions do you do your best reading? (Evaluative Thinking)

27. Design a "Tell It Like It Is" box where students can write out their ideas, thoughts, complaints. (Alternate ideas: Label the box: The Doctor Is In, Suggestion Box, Dear Abby.) (Evaluative Thinking)

28. Watch a TV story. Who was the most interesting person? What did you like/dislike about the presentation? What feelings did you have throughout the story? (Evaluative Thinking)

29. Be a movie critic. Evaluate a recent film. (Evaluative Thinking)

30. Personal opinion plays a part in any writer's work. Some examples of opinion writing are newspaper editorials, essays, book and film reviews, etc. Make a book entitled, *In My Opinion*, and include stories that you write about your views of life. Some suggestions: For Me, Luxury Is _____; The Best Care Is _____; The Ten Best Films Are _____; etc. You can think of even more exciting ideas to write about in your book. (Evaluative Thinking)

31. If you had $25 to spend today, what would you buy? (Evaluative Thinking)

32. If someone offered the main character in your story a horse, what would be his or her reaction? If it happened to you, would you take it? What would be your reaction? Your parents'? Your friends'? (Evaluative Thinking)

33. Choose a series of poems for special days and events, weather changes, classroom happenings, etc. Make a collection to be displayed at these or other appropriate times, such as Sad Days, Success Days, etc. (Evaluative Thinking)

34. Be a student teacher. Select a book you feel would be good for younger children. Evaluate your selection after reading it to them. (Evaluative Thinking)

35. Serve on a committee to take an inventory of classmates' opinions on the magazines they most want ordered for the classroom. Research other magazines that are available that your classmates don't yet know. Make a presentation to the class of the strengths and weaknesses in these other magazines. (Evaluative Thinking)

36. Make a collage entitled, *Me*. Include everything you have enjoyed in magazines this month. (Evaluative Thinking)

DEVELOPING PROBLEM-SOLVING SKILLS

Sample Activities for Discussion, Task Cards, Learning Centers, or Reading Contracts

1. Did this reading selection give you ideas about how to solve any problems you're working on?
2. What books would help you solve some of your current problems?
3. Make up an experimental design to test the theory that plants grow better when they are talked to. (Alternate: When they hear soft music.)
4. What would you do if: (a) Your boat sprang a leak? (b) You fell off your horse? (c) You saw a shark when you were scuba diving? (d) Your father was seriously injured on a hiking trip and you were the only person around? Make up some problems of your own similar to these and tell how you could solve them.
5. Make up a list of at least seven things you could suggest to a teenager who says he or she is bored. (Alternate: To a seven-year-old)
6. Make up a list of ten things you could do on a stormy day.
7. If the school principal asked our class to set up a plan to solve a school problem, what do you think the problem would be? List the steps the class would have to take to solve the problem. (Collect information, set up groups, etc.)

DEVELOPING PLANNING SKILLS

Sample Activities for Discussion, Task Cards, Learning Centers, or Reading Contracts

1. Plan and carry out a dramatization of a favorite story. Be prepared to describe what a play producer has to do. (Alternates: A film, a parade.)
2. Design a custom paint job for the main character. (Primary grades: "What color car do you think ____ would have?")
3. Design a puppet stage that second graders could use to put on plays.
4. Plan some machine that would have made a great deal of difference in the plot of your book or story.

5. Plan to have an author visit school to discuss his or her writing.
6. Plan your ideal school where everyone would be a good reader.
7. Plan a weekly schedule for yourself which will help you become a better reader.
8. What do you need to do today to help you become a better reader?
9. Plan a list of things to do if you finish your assignment early.
10. Plan a trip for the class that will include visits to some of the things or places we have been reading about.
11. Plan a campaign to help students want to be better readers. Design posters, bulletin boards, and displays. Make up slogans. Rearrange the room, etc.
12. Draw up the plans for a workable post office for your classroom for students to write letters to each other or to outsiders.
13. Plan a field trip for your class—first, an imaginary one; then a possible one.

FORMULATING QUESTIONS

Sample Activities for Discussion, Task Cards, Learning Centers, and Reading Contracts

1. Find out what a multiple-choice question is, then write five for your story. Be ready to discuss what happened as you tried to write the questions. (Alternates: Write five multiple-choice questions that are funny, ridiculous, or exaggerated, etc.)
2. Make up questions that you think a first grader could answer about your story. A third grader? A high schooler? How did you decide which questions should be asked at each grade level?
3. Play *Twenty Questions* about book titles, characters and/or authors.
4. Think up three clues about the story. Give the class one clue at a time, the hardest clue first. See if they can guess the story. (Alternates: five or ten clues; authors, story characters.)

5. Design a series of questions for a public opinion poll for your class (school, parents, etc.) Conduct the poll and present the findings. Evaluate your questions. Were they good ones? Explain.
6. Research the various, possible types of questions. Make up one of each kind about your story.

UNDERSTANDING THE RELATION OF READING TO OTHER MEDIA

Sample Activities for Discussion, Task Cards, Learning Centers, and Reading Contracts

1. Listen to the evening news. Write a prediction of an editorial opinion that your morning newspaper will have on the subjects mentioned. Check your predictions the next morning. (Alternate: Predict tomorrow's headlines.)
2. Tape-record everything a television commentator says about a news story. Transcribe his/her comments onto paper. Compare with a newspaper story on the same event. How many words does each contain? What differences do you see in the way sentences are composed? Are there differences in vocabulary or kinds of words used? What do all these comparisons tell you about television and newspapers? Reverse the procedure by reading aloud a newspaper article on a subject or event. Compare this tape to a tape of a television report on the same story. What did you find out?
3. How long do you estimate it would take you to read this story out loud? Do it and see how close your guess was.
4. Listen to a story that the teacher or someone else reads aloud to you, then read the story yourself. Compare how you felt about the two ways of learning a story. Reverse: read a story first, then listen to it aloud and compare.
5. Read a selection aloud to half the group and have half the group read the selection for themselves. Give the same test. Which group scored higher?
6. What is the difference between the words, *compare* and *contrast*? Give examples from two books that you have read.
7. Watch a television or film presentation of a story, then check out the book and read it (or reverse the procedure).

Was the story changed for television or the movies? Which story did you enjoy more? Why do you think the changes were made?

8. Select television or film stars to star in a TV or movie production of a book you have read. If the book has been made into a film, compare your choices with the producer's.
9. Make a film, filmstrip, or slide show of the story.
10. Hold an authors pageant. Come dressed appropriately. (Alternates: Story characters, book titles.)
11. Translate a fairy tale into a foreign language you know or are studying.
12. Make a woodburning picture of the story, a story event, or a story character. (Alternates: frieze, panel, sculpture, all-over design, mural, stained glass window, collage, line design, torn paper design.)
13. Write a brief description of a new TV show that you think would be successful. (Alternates: Base it on a book you have read; do a similar presentation for a proposed new film.)
14. Write and produce a play for the class to give for other classes, parent groups, and/or other schools. (Alternate: Design and produce a comic book.)

EVALUATING ONE'S OWN WRITTEN WORK

Sample Activities for Discussion, Task Cards, Learning Centers, and Reading Contracts

1. Make a bulletin board, a scrapbook, or a collection of stories or poems you feel good about writing.
2. Put aside one of your written efforts for a week or more. Read it as if it were someone else's. Is it well done? What does it say well? What does it leave out? Where does the word rhythm flow? Where does the rhythm falter? Where would you rank it in terms of all the writing you have ever done? First? Last? Bottom tenth? Top two percent? Etc.
3. After finishing a written assignment for your teacher, on a separate sheet, write your predictions of your teacher's reactions and comments on your work. See if you were correct.
4. What do you consider the best creative writing or composi-

tion work you have ever done? Share with us why you feel so good about it and why you consider it so successful.

IMPROVING SELF-CONCEPT AND SELF-DEVELOPMENT THROUGH READING

Sample Activities for Discussion, Task Cards, Learning Centers, and Reading Contracts

1. What can you do better than each of the story characters?
2. Did any books influence you to study or learn about anything?
3. How did this story make you feel better about yourself?
4. What did you learn from this story (book. etc.)?
5. Prepare a "This Is Your Life" learning center for a classmate, a story character, an author, or for yourself.
6. Record or write childhood tales of your father (mother, yourself, etc.) Present him (her) with a copy as a present.
7. Make a family tree charting your family as far back as you can.
8. Write a description of a holiday that you invent especially for yourself.
9. Write a list of the things you like about yourself.

DEVELOPING READER PURPOSE SKILLS

Sample Activities for Discussion, Task Cards, Learning Centers, and Reading Contracts

1. Make a list of books about which you wish the teacher would not have you answer questions. Do you know why you'd rather not?
2. How can this book (article, etc.) help you have a better life?
3. Would you read this book if it were not assigned? Share your reasons with us.
4. Who in the room do you think could benefit most from reading this book (article, etc.)?
5. Which parts of this book are helpful to you and which are not?
6. What did you learn from this book? Facts? Things about people? New thoughts? New ideas? New ways to solve problems?

7. Reading serves many purposes. For what purpose would you suggest someone read this book? Why are you reading it?

8. Write down why you think you want to read a new book before you start it. Is it for enjoyment? To learn? Read the book. Did you fulfill your purpose? Did you get any unexpected results?

9. You have only $100 to spend on books for yourself for a trip you are taking to a desert island for five years. You will not be able to get any other reading material. Which books would you buy? Show prices and give reasons. Compare your list with others. What magazines or other reading materials would you include?

10. If you had $25 to purchase books, which books would you buy? Why?

11. Make a list of all the reasons why a person should read.

12. Teachers: Sample questionnaire to determine reading selections: What are your hobbies ? What is reading? What kinds of books do you like to read? Which books did you read last? Which books did you read this month? Which books did you read that weren't assigned? Which books do you own? Which books do you wish you owned? What kinds of books do we need in this classroom to satisfy your reading purposes?

DEVELOPING RECREATIONAL READING SKILLS

Sample Activities for Discussion, Task Cards, Learning Centers, and Reading Contracts

1. Teachers: Select a group of children to help you plan a recreational reading center, including materials, furniture, books, arrangements, and rules.

2. Teachers: Assign a committee or an individual to make bulletin boards about recreational reading. Examples: (a) A display of all the books one student has read in a month; (b) A display of book jackets from new books; (c) An open book on display, selected for its reading quality, changed daily.

3. Teachers: Have frequent discussions with students about books they are reading at home, other home reading materials, and their use of the public library.

4. Teachers: Check to see if any students are in the midst of a "reading enthusiasm"; that is, reading all the books on one subject (baseball, for example) or all the books written by one author.

5. Teachers: Discuss who is reading the dictionary or the encyclopedia in his recreational reading or who is reading unusual material. (All these, by the way, are fine diagnostic questions that you can use to discover your highly creative students.)

6. Teachers: Schedule a time during the day when everyone (including you) reads for pleasure.

7. Teachers: Set up a newspaper learning center where children can browse without having to answer questions.

8. Teachers: Have a group of children plan and set up a display of books on a common interest.

9. Teachers: Display some of the children's own writing in the recreational reading center. Some of the books can be attractively bound, as can collections of poetry.

10. Teachers: Assign topics similar to these: Write all the things you like about reading. If you were to receive a subscription to a magazine as a gift, which one would you like to get? Why? Which book? Which magazine would you give to your best friend? Your relatives? Your teacher? What are the most exciting things you do? What do you want to learn more about? What books do you plan to read soon? Who is your favorite author? What are your favorite activities outside of school? What kinds of books do you like to read best? (Examples: Mystery, fiction, biography, science fiction, fairy tales, plays, how-to, other _____.) How has reading helped your leisure time?

DEVELOPING READER EMOTIONAL RESPONSE

Sample Activities for Discussion, Task Cards, Learning Centers, and Reading Contracts

1. How did you feel after reading this story?
2. Make a chart of your different emotions as you read the story. Tell us each of your feelings and where in the story you experienced them.
3. Have you ever felt the way the characters in the story felt? Share with us what happened.

4. Complete the following for one of the characters in the story: (a) _____ feels happy when _____. (b) _____ feels sad when _____. (c) _____ feels angry when _____ . (d) _____ likes to _____. (e) For _____, school is _____. (f) For _____, family means _____. Make up and complete other feeling sentences for your character.

5. Do you feel better or worse about yourself than the story characters feel about themselves?

6. What color does this story remind you of? What taste? Smell? Feel? Sound?

7. What would you have done if you were one of the story characters? How do you feel about what the character actually did?

8. What do you think _____ (story character) daydreams about?

9. Have you ever read a story or book that made you feel as if you were actually there or experiencing it for yourself? Tell us about it.

10. What was your first impression of your book? Did you change your impression as you continued to read?

11. In the setting and time of which book would you prefer to live? Share your reasons with us.

12. How did this writer cause you to feel about _____ (story character, event, book, etc.)?

13. What problems do you see the characters in your story as having? Do you have any similar ones?

14. For which story character do you feel empathy? For which do you feel sympathy? What is the difference between the two terms, *empathy* and *sympathy*?

A FINAL WORD ABOUT CREATIVE READING

Including creative reading in the reading program is one of the primary ways to develop positive student self-image because it produces students who are better prepared in academic reading skills, as well as better able to understand the meaning, importance, and stimulation reading offers to them. There is a certain playfulness, a certain humorous quality to creative reading. Help students understand that playing or organizing is a good way to learn, that fun is a legitimate part of learning.

Creative reading, as well, gives us the opportunity to help

students develop a more rounded, more practical approach to thinking; one which recognizes the importance and the uses of linear and nonlinear thinking alike; one which teaches students to think beyond the obvious and the easily apparent; one which encourages them to think of the possibilities and potentialities in what they read; one which helps them use reading in every-day problem-solving situations; and one which opens a whole new world of ideas to them.

4

Literature Appreciation Skills

* * * * * * * * * * * *

A student's appreciation of literature develops over time, and changes as he or she changes. It is not a one-time thing a student "gets" and has forever, nor is it a learning that appears in final form at any time. Students change, grow, expand, as does their taste in literature. Indeed, student growth and taste in literature are mutually enhancing; as one expands, so does the other.

Possibilities are endless in literature. There is no need to limit the teaching of literature appreciation to a curriculum of standard, accepted classics. Use these classics, yes, but include also well written books that facilitate personal growth and self understanding; that stretch the imagination, senses, emotions; that expand views and viewpoints; that offer escape, fantasy, pleasure, enjoyment; and that give opportunities for new learnings.

VALUE OF READING

Sample Activities for Discussion, Task Cards, Learning Centers, and Reading Contracts

1. Make a list of books for a person who "hates to read." Defend your choices.
2. If some natural or man-made catastrophe threatened to destroy all books and you could only save one book, which

would it be? Which math book? Which recipe book? Others?

3. Make up a real or imaginary list of books that would be valuable for a child in the following cultures: Pre-Columbian Mexican, Australian aboriginal, New York City ghetto, New Mexico ranch, Beverly Hills, your culture.

4. Why would a mathematician want to read well? A scientist? Other occupations? A consumer?

5. What kinds of books would a second grader need to help him/her choose a bicycle? A camera?

6. What "how-to" books have you found to be especially valuable? Why?

7. What do you know that would make you a better driver or cyclist that you might not know if you couldn't read?

8. What books would you require a bad driver to read?

9. Give reasons why reading would be important in three different career choices.

10. Make a list of books that you think would be important in planning a new home? Why?

11. Make a list of the ways in which reading makes your life better. Compare with lists of other class members.

12. How many ways did you use reading this week? Today? (Examples: solving problems, locating information, etc.)

13. Share names of books that really made a difference in your life.

14. Share books that you have read or that you asked someone to read to you more than one time.

15. Interview three adults, three high school students, and three classmates about the value to them of reading good literature. Chart or record their answers in an interesting form. (Graphs, pictures, tape recordings, collage, and the like)

16. Why would people in the following situations need to read well? (a) A third grader who had saved enough money to buy a softball bat? (b) A family planning a summer vacation to Argentina, Hawaii, India, or Alaska? (c) A photographer who wants to sell pictures for a living? (d) An artist who wants to illustrate children's books.

17. Think about how reading has been of value to people you know. Be prepared for a discussion on the topic.

18. Why would the following want to read good literature:

(a) A pop music star? (b) A famous athlete? (c) A national television commentator? (d) A politician?

19. What effect does the book business have on our economy? How big a business is it? Primary grades: Visit a local bookstore or interview a book dealer or book salesman.
20. If you were collecting first editions of books for investments, which would you choose from the past? From current best sellers?
21. Research the names of books you think would be helpful for someone who wants to make more money next year.
22. List career possibilities in the book marketing, editing, or selling fields.
23. How many children's books were published last year?
24. People in which occupations would be the most interested in your book? Justify your choice.
25. Which books have made a difference in their societies; e.g., Stowe's *Uncle Tom's Cabin*?
26. Make a list of books about which you wish the teacher would not have you answer questions. Do you know why you'd rather not?
27. Which books have been important in changing stereotypes; e.g., sex, age, race, etc. Example: Friedan, *Feminine Mystique*.
28. Which magazines do you wish the school would subscribe to for shop students. For other classes?
29. How has reading been of value for your family?

STORY ELEMENTS: MOOD, STYLE, PLOT, THEME, CHARACTERIZATION

Sample Activities for Discussion, Task Cards, Learning Centers, and Reading Contracts

1. Make a family tree showing the family history of one story character. Compare it to your own family. Make up a predicted family tree of the future for one character. Did family patterns change?
2. What could you see of yourself in the main character?
3. If you were to choose classmates or friends who reminded you most of the main characters in the story, whom would you choose?

4. What kind of mood do you prefer in the books you read—serious, comic, tragic, mysterious, etc?

5. Design a custom paint job for the car of the main character. Primary grades: What color car do you think _____ would have?

6. Design a puppet stage that we could use to put on plays. Use color to help set the mood.

7. Choose a book that you think is particularly well illustrated. Describe how the illustrations fit the mood, style, plot, theme, characters.

8. Make a series of cartoons or pictures that show the plot of your book.

9. What song lyrics can you find that tell a good story? A good joke? Describe a person well?

10. Many writers invent a new setting, culture, and/or language for their stories; e.g., *Lord of the Rings, Dune, Alice in Wonderland.* Can you find other examples?

11. Who is your favorite character in literature?

12. Find examples of the use of flashback techniques in stories.

13. What words, phrases, or formats tell the reader the setting of this story? The mood?

14. In what setting for what book would you most like to live?

15. What effect does the economic setting have on the story? The climate? The geography? The characters' health? Transportation methods?

16. Categorize the story: real and make-believe parts, character likenesses and differences, etc.

17. Make up a table of contents for a magazine for readers 500 years from now. Make up an imaginary list of best sellers.

18. How much do you estimate the story characters knew about math? In what sciences do you think the characters in this story would be interested?

19. How do you suppose the leading character thinks government should be run? What causes you to think so?

20. Find phrases or sentences that add to the book's realism.

21. Does any character in this book remind you of a character in another? Why?

22. Who would be the ideal hero or heroine of a book for this culture?

23. Share descriptions of the geographic settings of stories that you thought were well written. What geographic knowl-

edge would the author have to have to write this book?

24. How did the main character feel about his/her economic status?
25. Design three changes of scenery that you could use if this story were a play.
26. Design a wardrobe for one of the characters in the story.
27. What kinds of drivers do you think the main characters would make? Why?
28. How would the story change if the characters didn't have careers or had different ones?
29. Write a critique of your book as if you were a book reviewer for *Ms.* (Alternates: *Rolling Stone, Time, Family Circle.*)
30. As you reread the story a second time, what do you see that you didn't see the first time?
31. What is the theme of this book? Do others agree with you?
32. Write a story by using envelopes, flip charts, spin-a-wheel, etc., to get: (1) main character, (2) plot, (3) setting, (4) theme, and (5) outcome. Examples: Main character: tiger, circus performer, rock, writer, etc.; Plot: takes a journey, grows up, loses something, etc.; Setting: below the sea, on another planet, etc.; Theme: right makes might, friends, try, try again, etc.; Outcome: makes a friend, changes life, new clothing, new ways, etc.
33. What do you think are the elements that make a good mystery? Science book? Historical novel? Other type of book?

DIFFERENT LITERARY FORMS

Sample Activities for Discussion, Task Cards, Learning Centers, and Reading Contracts

1. Haiku is based on a mathematical ratio of number of syllables (5-7-5). Write or find some examples.
2. Find examples of science fiction where the author's knowledge of math makes the story more interesting. (Example: Asimov, *Mirror Image*)
3. Write a prediction of what literature will be 100 years from now (or 1000). What kinds of writing? What forms of books, etc.?
4. Rewrite the story in a different format and era.
5. The theme of three wishes or Aladdin's lamp is common.

What would you wish for if it would come true for you by magic or by rubbing a lamp?

6. Which famous speeches (oral literature) are your favorites?
7. What was the most prevalent form of literature for this culture?
8. Make up a list of ten best sellers (fiction and nonfiction and real or imaginary) for the ancient Hawaiians or for Nubians.
9. Write a poem or a prose selection in the shape of a favorite geological formation (for instance, a mountain, a river, etc.)
10. Rewrite this story to fit the title, *The Journey*.
11. Which historical character do you wish had written a book? What kind of book?
12. Rewrite a Greek myth in a modern-day setting.
13. Note the use of flashback techniques in stories.
14. How close to the reality of life in this setting do you feel the author came?
15. Write a proposal for an imaginary new political system. Which format did you choose? Why?
16. Paradox, especially economic paradox, is a form used in novels. Complete: First, the good news/then the bad news. Fortunately/unfortunately, etc.
17. Which forms of literature sell best at Christmas? At Mother's Day? Other holidays?
18. Who are some of the best current translators of books from one language to another?
19. How did some passages in the *Bible* change in format as a result of translation from one language to another?
20. How did the literary form that the author chose contribute to the effectiveness of what he/she wrote?
21. Compare an old and a new form for the same fairy tale. How did it change?
22. Take the story and convert it into a different writing format (poetry, prose, lead front page story for a newspaper, etc.)
23. Which film version of a book do you feel remains closest to the author's interest? Which is least close?
24. What kind of theatre production do you think your book would best make? TV production? Film production?
25. What forms of writing have people's desires for goods influenced?

26. What are the characteristics of science fiction, mysteries, and other literary forms?
27. Write a fairy tale that could take place today.
28. Write a modern story in biblical phrases.
29. Make a display of myths from various countries; e.g., Greek, Roman, Norse, African, etc. Find and display books on the story of creation from various cultures (Armenian, Indian, Hawaiian, South American, Egyptian, etc.)
30. Make a chart of the different kinds of literature you have read this year. Keep it up-to-date. Include: Nature stories, science fiction, fiction, science, animal, family, myths, legends, fairy tales, historical fiction, biography, autobiography, sports, hobbies, travel, adventure, classics, poetry, mystery, and any other types you read.
31. What do you think are the elements that make for good writing in various literary forms; e.g., science fiction?
32. Rewrite the story from the viewpoint of a story character.
33. What kinds of books do first graders like? How do you know? If you were a librarian, how would you organize a library for first graders? (Alternate: For our grade level?)
34. What kinds of literature do students your age like? How do you know? Is this true for all pupils your age?
35. Decide on your favorite type of literature. What would you want a student your age, who had never read this type of literature, to know about it? What would you tell them about why you read it?

CULTURAL ANALYSIS THROUGH LITERATURE

Sample Activities for Discussion, Task Cards, Learning Centers, and Reading Contracts

1. Choose and read a book about a mathematician or someone with another occupation who influenced society.
2. Make a time line of story events.
3. What one scientific invention do you think would have the most impact if it were introduced into the story?
4. Can you make a comparison of a country's climate and its literature?
5. Does the author present a stereotype of any group, race, age, sex?

6. In books like *Little House on the Prairie*, what part do economic conditions play in story development?

7. If you had to pick five books explaining our culture for a time capsule, which would you pick?

8. What do you think the author would consider to be an ideal society? Chart it.

9. Make a map of a make-believe place you have read about. (Examples: Little Red Riding Hood's route. The Hobbit's home country.)

10. Make a journal for a character in the story comparable to the journals of Lewis and Clark. Make five entries.

11. What kinds of books would a student your age have read 50 years ago? 100 years ago?

12. Make a list of best sellers in the country you are studying. (Consulates and embassies can help you.)

13. Which speech patterns in the book tell the cultural background of the characters?

14. In which cultures was speech an important part of oral literature? (Example: American Indian, etc.)

15. Choose five books that you think give the fairest representations of current affairs.

16. What was literature like in the era you are most interested in?

17. How did the cultural biases of the writers affect the book?

18. What do you think the author feels about men, women, and/or children?

19. Design a set as if this story took place in ancient Rome, old China, or in Viking days.

20. Create appropriate makeup for a story character. What if he or she had lived in China? Someplace in the eighth centry B.C.? Other times or places?

21. What kinds of goods would you consume if you lived in the time and setting of the story?

22. What careers would be open to you in the time era of the story?

23. Compare how businessmen, artists, and/or athletes are treated in three different stories. What does this tell you about our culture?

24. List advantages and disadvantages of being a writer in our society.

25. What do you think a weekly grocery shopping list would include for families in your favorite novels?
26. Make a floor plan for the house in this story or design an appropriate one for the culture.
27. How did the family life of the book's characters affect the plot?
28. From your story, tell about the following: food, music, handicrafts, literature, transportation, family, schooling, etc. Was this true for all families in this setting?
29. Make a display of books about an American subculture; e.g., Spanish-speaking, teenage, Hawaiian, etc. (Alternate: Make a display of books about the subcultures in your local community.)
30. Sometimes authors are persecuted by their societies for what they write; sometimes they are acclaimed as heroes or heroines. How do you think this society reacts to this author?
31. Which social class or caste would you prefer to belong to in the culture of this story?
32. Would you rather be a boy or a girl in the society described in the story?
33. What would you have to do before you would know the geographic setting well enough to write this selection?

BIBLIOTHERAPY

Sample Activities for Discussion, Task Cards, Learning Centers, and Reading Contracts

1. How did you feel about one of the characters in the story? Find sentences or phrases in the story that affected your opinion of this character.
2. What books would you recommend for a girl who isn't sure it is feminine to study math?
3. Which story characters do you think would be better at math than you? Which worse? What about science? Other content areas?
4. How do scientific inventions affect the time you have available to read?
5. Which historical character in literature do you admire most? (Alternate: Which story character?)

6. If you wrote a book, to whom would you dedicate it? Make up a sample dedication page.

7. Look at some of the dedications in books. Why do you suppose the authors dedicated the book to the people they did?

8. What satisfactions do you think the author got from writing the story? What satisfactions did you get from the way the literature was written?

9. Based on what you have read of economic conditions, where or when do you wish you had lived?

10. How does your allowance (or salary) compare with that of the main character?

11. Which character do you think would most sound like you?

FAMOUS WRITINGS AND AUTHORS

Sample Activities for Discussion, Task Cards, Learning Centers, and Reading Contracts

1. Which authors would you like to invite to speak at Book Week?

2. There are many yearly awards given for best children's and adult's books. Who received awards last year?

3. Make a display of books that were written by famous writers of a certain culture; e.g., Black, American Indian, Appalachian White, Asian-American, and the like.

4. Play *Author Rummy* using a deck of cards featuring four different titles by the same author for 13 authors (52 cards).

5. Play *Twenty Questions* using famous authors. (Alternates: Story characters, objects, titles)

6. Play flash card games where the author's name is given and the player must respond with a book he/she has written, or vice-versa.

7. Put the names of authors (books, story characters) on the back of the student (or team) who is *It*. See who can ask questions and identify themselves first.

8. Play "Who Am I?" by writing five progressively easier clues about authors with which the class is familiar. Give a decreasing amount of points as the clues become easier.

9. What facts about the author's life help you understand his/her writing?

10. What are the following and how do they relate to litera-

ture? *The Children's Catalog; The New York Herald Tribune* Awards; The Laura Ingalls Wilder Award; The Regina Medal; Book of the Year for Children; Hans Christian Andersen Award; Carnegie Medal; Kate Greenaway Medal; Newbery Medal; Caldecott Medal; The Children's Book Council.

11. Teachers: Play games designed to acquaint students with authors, famous literature, and/or literary quotations; e.g., literary baseball, football, and the like. (Alternate: Have students design the questions for the games.)

SELECTING APPROPRIATE MATERIALS FOR SELF AND OTHERS

Activities for Discussion, Task Cards, Learning Centers, and Reading Contracts

1. Write or hold a debate on censorship and books.
2. What kinds of books do you feel seven-year-olds should not be allowed to read? (Alternates: Ten-year-olds? Seventeen-year-olds?)
3. What books would you recommend to a mathematician? Why?
4. How are best seller charts computed?
5. List your selections for a science library for yourself. Which geography books would you include? Other kinds of books?
6. Which current best sellers deal with science?
7. How do you think feminist leaders would feel about this book? Older people? Different racial groups? Different religious groups?
8. If Earth were being destroyed and you only had room in your spaceship to save ten books, which would they be? Interview others on this subject and chart their answers. Arrive at a group consensus on the ten books.
9. What landscape books would your best friend enjoy? Other kinds of books?
10. What books would you select for a new millionaire? A pauper?
11. What books would you suggest for our classroom library? Magazines? Reference materials?

12. Look at a best seller list for children's or adult's books. How many have you read? Which would you like to read?
13. Make a best sellers book list for students in your classroom.
14. If you were a newspaper book critic, what would be your selections for the ten best books for this year?
15. Which book critics give you the most help in your choice of reading matter?
16. What book would you recommend to the average family to help them with their purchases?
17. If you were going to open a bookstore, what kinds of books would you sell? Explain.
18. Make a list of literature that gives some insight into career choices.
19. Where would you find suggestions for good books for children? (Answer: *Children's Catalogue*, *The Horn Book*, *Saturday Review*, *Ms.*, *Childhood Education*, *Elementary English*, *The New York Times*, *The Christian Science Monitor*, etc.)

A FINAL WORD ABOUT LITERATURE APPRECIATION

As we seek, in all good will, to add creativity to the reading process, let us not make the mistake of believing that creativity and analysis are mutually exclusive. Analysis of literature can, if handled with caring and perception by a teacher who feels literature appreciation to be important, add insight, sparkle, diversity, and intense pleasure to the enjoyment of reading throughout a student's life. The creative mind is not necessarily the uninitiated one.

One of the bonuses of a good literature appreciation program is the opportunity for unexpected learning. Literature provides chances to learn of and to evaluate other ideas, attitudes, and cultures, as well as chances for our students to respond in a personal way to the writer's mind and thought patterns. Thus, reading becomes, for our students, an important means for making life richer, deeper, more exciting, more satisfying, more creative.

5

Vocabulary Development Skills

* * * * * * * * * * * *

We educators are fortunate in that our work on one reading skill doesn't remain in isolation, but spreads to reinforce and strengthen other reading skills, as well, Then, this same energy rebounds doubly to reinforce the first skill with which we started. This seemingly magical increase from a minor expenditure of our energy is a gratifying and humbling experience with which we are blessed and which reminds us again and again how much we receive personally from being teachers. Such is the case with our efforts put forth in developing vocabulary skills. As we work to increase vocabulary development in our students, we see them sometimes making quantum leaps in their general reading ability; this, in turn, cycles back to improve their vocabulary skills, the original starting point. Thus, reading reinforces vocabulary development; better vocabulary increases reading ability.

VOCABULARY PATTERNING

Sample Activities for Discussion, Task Cards, Learning Centers, and Reading Contracts

1. Write a script which you could use to teach non-English speaking people to be able to converse in English: (a) When meeting someone for the first time; (b) When getting gasoline for their car; and (c) When asking directions. Make up other situations and write scripts for them.
2. Make up scripts for yourself in a language that you want to learn for similar situations to those in activity number one.

3. Make up a poem in which every line begins with the same two words. (Examples: Blue is _____; Anger is _____.)
4. Describe a special friend or story character in a poem, each line of which begins with the same two words. (Example: Diana is _____.)
5. Make up a yell or a cheer about some event that happened today, about a person in our class, or about something we learned.
6. *Alphabetical You*. List words that describe you for each letter of the alphabet. (Alternates: A relative, your teacher, a friend.)
7. Write a "Fortunately-Unfortunately" story.
8. How many words can you think of that would fit alphabetically between the words *same* and *seen*?
9. Choose a pattern from a story, poem, or song and repeat it as many ways as you can: Some examples: Good news _____, bad news _____; Because I _____, I _____; If it weren't for _____, I would _____.
10. Find words that contain two parts that rhyme (Example: backpack).
11. Find words composed of two identical parts (Example: tutu).
12. Find words that can be read forwards and backwards. (Examples: was–saw; rat–tar).
13. How many words can you think of that begin with *B*? Every word must contain at least four letters. (Alternates: How many words can you think of that begin with *bo*? How many words can you think of that begin with *reg*? Use the same procedures, but have words end with these letter (s) or have the letter (s) in the middle of the word.
14. How many words can you think of that have little words in them?
15. Make a list of five words that contain the same three letters in sequence. (For example: bean, reanalyze, peanut, meant, protean (ean).)
16. How many words can you list that end with *all*? *ish*?
17. How many different ways can you think of to say hello? To say goodbye?
18. Teachers: Put macaroni or written letters into piles of consonants and vowels. Students can draw letters using the word patterning you are studying (CVC, CVCV, etc.) They

get two points if they can make a word from their draw in the order in which it was drawn, one if they can arrange all the letters of the draw into a word in any order.

19. Teachers: Music is one of the easiest patterns to remember. Set to music new words, facts, etc., that you want the children to remember. (Example: an alphabet song.) Or have the students make up a tune or a song about reading.

20. Teachers: Read much poetry or other rhythmic writing to the class. These words are easy to remember. Have the students write down all the rhyming words they can hear.

21. Teachers: Study the various patterns used in different types of poetry with the children; e.g., haiku, tanka, sijo, etc. (*Tanka* is a heartfelt poem, the first three lines of which follow the haiku pattern of five syllables, seven syllables, five syllables, increased by two more lines of seven syllables each. *Sijo* is a poetic form of six lines, each line of which contains six to eight syllables, for a total of forty-two to forty-eight syllables.)

22. Teachers: Have the students practice matching the rhythmic pattern of limericks.

NEW VOCABULARY

Sample Activities for Discussion, Task Cards, Learning Centers, or Reading Contracts

1. Many authors make up a new language for their story. Give examples. (Examples: *Dune, Ring Trilogy, Alice in Wonderland.*)

2. Invent some new words for a book you might write. Or invent a new pattern for sentences.

3. Make up a packet of new words you want to learn. Check with the teacher as you master each one.

4. Learn a new word a day for the next two weeks. Be ready to discuss with me why you chose those words, what they mean to you, and how you learned them.

5. Teachers: Put all the new words that you are introducing on cards or pieces of paper in the shape of leaves, feathers, or the like. As a student learns the word, he or she can add it to his/her pile, tree, headdress, etc. (Alternate: Use the new vocabulary in phrases written on cards, trees, feathers, etc.)

6. Teachers: Ask questions such as, "What words do you almost always mix up?"
7. Teachers: Schedule a weekly, "Talk Walk," for the class—a visit in the neighborhood or a field trip—where the object is to identify words with experiences; e.g., baker, asparagus, shocks.
8. Teachers: Read aloud to the class from books by authors who use a rich variety of language.
9. Teachers: Have a new word for the students to learn each day. Choose words pertaining to current interests or words that are interesting all by themselves.
10. Teachers: Have students describe unfamiliar objects only by their feel. (Alternates: Shape, size, dimensions, smell, taste, etc.)
11. Teachers: List all new vocabulary from a reading selection on the board or on word strips. Discuss the new words before the students read the story. Check how many they can recall afterwards.
12. Teachers: Make individual dictionaries for students to use in their written work. Include a basic word list (Dolch, for instance), then list individual words as students ask for them, making appropriate comments to help students remember their location. (Example: The word *know* sounds as if it should be listed under *N*. How are you going to remember it's listed under *K*?)
13. Teachers: Have students play *Vocabulary Checkers*. Print new words in each square, then play checkers in the usual way. Students must know how to read the word before moving into the square.
14. Teachers: Have students play *Bingo* with new vocabulary words.
15. Teachers: Have students play regular and three dimensional *Scrabble*.

TECHNICAL AND SPECIALIZED VOCABULARY

Sample Activities for Discussion, Task Cards, Learning Centers, and Reading Contracts

1. Teachers: Schedule speakers from various trades and businesses to talk about ten words important in their work

or to talk about and demonstrate the ideas, tools, machines, etc., that they use in their work.

2. Teachers: Ask your students to write down (or, if they're too young, tell you), words you use that they find to be new, used in a new way, or difficult to understand.

3. Teachers: Hold a hobby day when students exhibit their hobbies, including lists of words that are unique to that hobby.

4. Teachers: Have the students make dictionaries of words used by police officers, truck drivers, post office workers, etc.

5. Teachers: Choose books containing technical or specialized language to read aloud to the class.

6. Teachers: Have students make a collection of specialized or technical language that they encounter in their reading.

7. Teachers: Give students a chance to listen to police channels and tell about what they hear. (Alternate: C.B. channels.)

SPECIAL RELATIONSHIPS AMONG WORDS: SYNONYMS, ANTONYMS, HOMONYMS, AND HOMOGRAPHS

Sample Activities for Discussion, Task Cards, Learning Centers, and Reading Contracts

1. Which way would you rather be described: "He is skinny," or "He is slender"? Look up other pairs of synonyms and see which one you would rather have used in describing you. Do these synonyms mean exactly the same thing?

2. Why would a writer need a thesaurus?

3. One of the difficult tasks of being a writer is dealing with the word, *said*. Make a list of words you can use in the place of *said*. (Alternate: find a book by a good author and list his or her ways of dealing with *said*.)

4. Draw a line under the words that mean the same or almost the same as _____.

5. What is a word you could use in the place of tale? Ran? Fled? Hurried? Bull?

6. Rewrite a paragraph or a short story using words that mean

the same thing as the words in the story but are different words. (Synonyms)

7. What prefixes can you think of that completely change the meaning of a word?

8. Write the opposite of top, hot, etc.

9. Take three words that have almost the same meaning and point out exactly how they are different. Use your dictionary. (Examples: Said, stated, declared, and glance, glimpse, look.)

10. Write synonyms and antonyms for all new words in the story.

11. Make synonym paper chains, where every link has one synonym printed on it for the word with which you are working. (Alternate: Paper fans)

12. Rewrite a fairy tale into modern language.

13. Rewrite a modern tale into Biblical language.

14. List all the words and expressions, including slang, that could be used in place of the word, *strange*.

15. List a word that sounds like *bare* but is spelled differently. *Hear*? *See*? *Too*? Can you find other examples in your reading of words that are pronounced alike but are spelled differently? What are they called?

16. How many sentences can you think of that use the word, *run*, in different ways? (Alternate: *Spot, figure, blue*?)

17. Make a collection of words that have the same sound but different spellings and different meanings. (Example: Two, to, too; blew, blue, etc.) What are these words called?

18. Teachers: Play *Synonyms* with the class. Divide the group into two teams. Give a word. The player tries to give a synonym for that word. If he or she cannot, the next player for the other team gets a chance. One point is given for each correct answer. (Alternate: Use antonyms, singulars and plurals, etc.)

19. Teachers: Give the first of a pair of homonyms and see if students can give the second with its correct spelling.

20. Teachers: Have a contest to see who can list the most homonyms, antonyms, and homographs to be displayed on a bulletin board or made into class books.

21. Teachers: Play *Concentration*, *Old Maid*, or *Bingo* games using synonyms, antonyms, homographs, or homonyms.

VARIATIONS OF VOCABULARY DUE TO REGIONAL DIFFERENCES, AGE, AREA AND THE LIKE

Sample Activities for Discussion, Task Cards, Learning Centers, and Reading Contracts

1. Make a dictionary of current teen-age slang in your area. (Variation: Make the dictionary at the beginning of the year. Check to see how current it is at the end of the year.)
2. Interview teachers, parents, other adults. Ask them for slang phrases that were used when they were teenagers. Date the phrases and put them into a chronology or time line.
3. Interview new students in your school: Are there any slang expressions used at your school that were new to them? Are there slang expressions that they used in their old school that no one uses here? Are there differences in words or phrases used in either place? List the results by state.
4. What phrases in your story could be used to show the geographic area in which the story took place?
5. There are many words in our language that originated from the name of a person or an inventor. Can you find any? (Example: Lynch.)
6. Families have a way of inventing words or phrases that only people in that family understand. For example, in one family, one son was unable to say "scissors" correctly when he was young; he said "sorsees," so everyone in the family still says that. Does your family or your group of friends use special words or phrases no one else could understand?
7. Words are added to our English vocabulary every year; for example, in the 1950, *Sputnik:* in the late 1960s, space jargon. What words have been added to the language in the last five years? In the last year?
8. Make a linguistic map of regional words; e.g., sucker–lollypop, carry–take, dinner–supper.
9. Find and share books that are written in nonstandard English.

10. What words, phrases, or formats tell the reader the setting of the story?
11. Find two books that include various regional or other dialects and be prepared to read a sample of each.
12. In Hawaii, residents often speak of Aloha time. What does this mean? Do you know any other ways people in other places refer to the same concept?
13. Make a list of words or phrases that only people in your classroom would recognize and use.
14. Make up a test on words that only people from the barrio (the quarter, the ghetto, etc.) would be likely to answer correctly.

DEVELOPING APPROPRIATENESS OF VOCABULARY

Sample Discussion, Task Cards, Learning Centers, and Reading Contracts Activities

1. If you were making this book into a film or a TV movie, which passages of dialogue would you want to be sure to include?
2. Find five sentences in the book where you might have substituted another word for one in the story.
3. Rewrite some written instructions so they are easier to follow.
4. Teachers: Have students tape-record a talk or the sharing of an event in their lives. As they listen to the recording, have them remember or jot down notes of words, phrases, expressions, and the like, that they used that they feel are inappropriate or not suitable, and those words, phrases, expressions, etc., that add to the effectiveness of their talk.
5. Teachers: Have students interview five classmates on the following topics: What word do you hear me (the interviewer) using most often? What phrase? Then have students discuss their findings and whether they should change their speech patterns.
6. Teachers: Give students an anonymous questionnaire on words that they feel you overuse, words you use well, or words you don't use enough.
7. Teachers: Share some of Edwin Newman's examples from

his books on inappropriate language. See if students can find comparable examples.

8. Teachers: Have students evaluate the language of bulletins to be sent home to parents.
9. Teachers: Discuss the suitability of the language in a book for a particular grade level. Could first graders read it? Why or why not? Etc.

VOCABULARY DEVELOPMENT THROUGH THE STUDY OF ETYMOLOGY

Sample Activities for Discussion, Task Cards, Learning Centers and Reading Contracts

1. Which current best sellers are based on translations from another language?
2. Which current books would you suggest could be successfully translated into another language? Explain.
3. Invent new sounds or words for things you see every day. Have a club where members must use those words instead of the real ones or set aside a certain period during the day when everyone uses those words.
4. List ten new words that have been added to our vocabulary in the past ten years (or the past year).
5. Make a book giving the meaning of every student's name in the class.
6. Read a place name book for the cities and geographical features of your state. (Example: *California Place Names*.)
7. Make a history of the street names of your city.
8. Do research on the history of our alphabet.
9. Interview your parents and grandparents about expressions that were popular when they were in high school. (Examples: *hubba hubba, peachy keen, I dig*.)
10. What common words in our language have we borrowed from French? Spanish? Italian? Arabic? Russian? Japanese? Etc.
11. What does your name mean? What do your family members' names mean? What do your best friends' names mean?
12. Where did the days of the week get their names? The months of the year?
13. Make a book of words of interest to you and their histories.

14. What do these combinations of letters mean in a word and from where do they come? *Aqua, bene, dic, man, sect.* Make up a card for each for our word history file.
15. What kinds of people settled in your area? How did they influence the language of the region?

FIGURATIVE OR IDIOMATIC LANGUAGE: HYPERBOLE, METAPHOR, SIMILE, PERSONIFICATION, ANALOGY, MALAPROPISM, PALINDROMES, ONOMATOPOETIC WORDS OR PHRASES, ALLITERATION, AND PUNS

Sample Activities for Discussion, Task Cards, Learning Centers, and Reading Contracts

1. List all the phrases, proverbs, sayings, adjectives, etc., that you feel describe you. (Figurative Language)
2. List all the phrases or words you can find in the story which convey images or a sensory feeling. (Figurative Language)
3. Make a list of figurative speech from your story and then write what the selection really means. (Figurative Language)
4. What figure of speech do you use the most? Your best friend? Your teacher? Other family members? Your sister? Your brother? (Figurative Language)
5. Make a list of figurative expressions from your reading that especially appeal to you. (Figurative Language)
6. Which expressions from your reading have you added to your speech? (Figurative Language)
7. How does each car manufacturer name the cars that the company produces? How are washing machines named by various manufacturers? Housing tracts? Dress styles? Consult magazines and newspapers for the answers. (Figurative Language)
8. Have a classmate listen carefully to your speech for a day, then tell you the figures of speech you often use. (Or, choose a group of friends to write down those expressions they remember that you often say. See if you want to continue using them so often.) (Figurative Language)
9. Play "More of It." Think up phrases similar to, "A desert is like a sandpile, only there is more of it." (Simile)

10. Play "First the . . ." Example: First the raindrop and then the flower. (Analogy)

11. Play a proverbs game. Write a series of proverbs on slips of paper. Students draw a slip of paper and act out the proverb written on it (or pantomime the proverb). The audience tries to guess the proverb. (Figurative Language)

12. Play one of your favorite music selections. Keep track of figurative and idiomatic language in the words of the song, especially phrases that appeal to you. Be ready to talk about the effectiveness of the lyricist. (Figurative Language)

13. Does a skyscraper really scrape the sky? Give examples of other names of things that exaggerate what the thing is or what it does. Hint: Centipede. (Hyperbole)

14. Does this author really want you to believe everything he or she writes or is he/she exaggerating? (Hyperbole)

15. Can you remember a time when a speaker you were listening to exaggerated to make a point? (Hyperbole)

16. What is the difference between hyperbole and propaganda? Between hyperbole and lying? (Hyperbole)

17. Tell about a time you exaggerated to make sure the point you were making went over. (Hyperbole)

18. Finish each of the following in at least five ways: as quiet as _____, as big as _____, trees are like _____, water is like _____. (Simile)

19. When do you feel strong as an ox? Flat as a tire? Think up similar clichés or well-used expressions that fit you on occasion. (Simile)

20. Advertisements frequently use similes. Make a collage of similes from ads in newspapers and magazines. (Simile)

21. The most famous example of personification is Smokey the Bear. Research his background. Make an exhibit of the ways Smokey has appeared through the years. (Personification)

22. Make a scrapbook or collage showing the use of personification in ads. (Personification)

23. Make a list of characters in storybooks that are personified by the author. (Example: The wolf in *Little Red Riding Hood*.) (Personification)

24. Write a story from the point of view of one of your boots or of one of your pets. (Personification)

25. What would a rock say if it could talk? (Personification)

26. What, in your opinion, makes personification work well in a story that you have recently read? (Personification)
27. Make a list of all the phrases that compare something to a rock. To a duck. (Analogy)
28. Put a word for person, place, or thing together with words not normally used to describe them. (Hint: ferocious stone.) See if the combinations make sense. (Analogy)
29. Work five word comparisons using this model. _____ is to _____ as _____ is to _____. (Hint: *Knew* is to *new* as *real* is to _____. *Came* is to *come* as *ran* is to _____. Etc.) (Analogy)
30. Choose an object in the classroom. Pretend to be that object for a day. Write a story of your experiences. (Analogy)
31. Complete the following sentence. If I were _____ (story character), I would be happy because _____, sad because _____, thankful because _____, anxious because _____, eager because _____. (Choose other emotions to describe in a similar fashion.) (Analogy)
32. Pretend that you are your reading book. What would you say? How would you feel? Etc. (Analogy)
33. How are clouds similar to television? Make up other examples of how two different things are alike. (Analogy)
34. Complete the analogy: A poem is to a novel as a _____ is to a _____. (Fill the blanks with car terminology.) (Analogy)
35. If your main story character were an animal, what kind would he/she/it be? (Alternates: color, weather, song, drink, food, etc.) (Analogy)
36. Use math symbols to design a book cover. Try to design the cover in such a way that the math symbols really point up what the book is about. (Analogy)
37. Make a collection of malapropisms or puns (where one word is used in such an evidently incorrect way, perhaps unintentionally, that the use is funny or where someone plays with words). Collect either those you hear someone say, those you read, or those from a book on malapropisms or puns. (Malapropism and Puns)
38. Give an example of a malapropism or pun, then give the word that should have been used. (Malapropism and Puns)
39. Invent some malapropisms or puns about people or happenings in our class, about politicans, or for TV. (Malapropism and Puns)

40. What names can you think of that are read the same way backward and forward? (Examples: Nan, Bob) (Palindromes)

41. Find words in your reading that are read the same way forward and backward. (Examples: Rotor, dad, madam) (Palindromes)

42. Find a book in the library that gives examples of palindromes. Share some of the ones you appreciated most. (Palindromes)

43. List any film or TV show names that are palindromes. (Palindromes)

44. Make up a word that sounds exactly like a rooster crowing. Find out how various foreign languages represent the same sound. (Onomatopoetic Language)

45. Make up a word that sounds exactly like these sounds: a car door closing, opening a zipper, a creaky chair, a brush going through your hair. What other sounds can you make words from? (Onomatopoetic Language)

46. Vachel Lindsay and other poets wrote some poetry in which they tried to use words which sounded exactly like the subjects they were describing. Find some examples of his and others of poetry where this was done. (Onomatopoetic Language)

47. Listen to sounds outside the classroom or on a record. Write actual words that fit the sound as closely as possible. (Onomatopoetic Language)

48. There are some musicians (Peter Frampton or Alvino Rey, for example) who play music with an attachment that causes the guitar (or other instrument) to sound as if it were a human voice. Find examples of such music and share these with us. (Onomatopoetic Language)

49. Write a song using words that sound as if they were the thing sung about ("Old McDonald Had a Farm," for example). (Onomatopoetic Language)

50. Find and share onomatopoeic song lyrics. (Look up *onomatopoetic* if it's a new word for you.) (Onomatopoetic Language)

51. Play an alliteration sentence game with friends. The object is to build sentences in which every word begins with the same letter. The beginning player says a word. The next player must say a word beginning with the same sound

which makes a part of the sentence. (Example: sand, sand seems, sand seems silky, etc.) If a player misses or can't think of a word, he or she must drop out. The last one left wins. (Alliteration)

52. Find examples of sentences in your reading in which every word or almost every word begins with the same letter of the alphabet, or where that letter is used constantly in any position in the words—beginning, medial or ending sound. (Alliteration)

53. Find examples of single words that contain the same sound at least three times within the word. (Examples: Mississippi, Popocatepetl) (Alliteration)

54. Teachers: Have the children put together words not normally associated with each other to create interesting images. Examples: Demon trees, limitless fences, cold warmth. (Metaphor)

55. Teachers: Keep a class notebook of metaphors that the students have found in their reading, in popular music, or in sayings and proverbs. (Metaphor)

56. Teachers: Make a metaphor flip book consisting of nouns and verbs. Discuss the possibilities and plausibilities of each combination. (Example: The bridge dived _____.) (Metaphor)

RELATING WORD STRESS, PITCH, AND INTONATION TO WORD MEANING

Sample Activities for Discussion, Task Cards, Learning Centers, and Reading Contracts

1. Teachers: Have students make up a series of sentences; substitute an *m* sound for every syllable; then say the sentence, using the *m* sound and the same stress, pitch, and inflection as if they were saying the actual words. See if someone can guess what kind of sentence was said.

2. Teachers: Read a brief selection out loud. Have students move their hands up and down to follow your voice pitch. (Alternates: Have students read aloud and move their hands up and down at the same time or tape-record the selection and follow their own pitch with the appropriate hand movements.)

3. Teachers: Have students read the same sentence aloud

several times, each time stressing a different word. Discuss how the difference in stress affects the meaning of the sentence or what the speaker feels.

4. Teachers: Have students read a sentence aloud in a normal tone, then use intonation that completely reverses the meaning of the same sentence.

5. Teachers: Hold auditions for parts in a play by having the potential actors try out behind a screen (or with listeners covering their eyes) so that only their voices are heard. Select the person who uses the most appropriate stress, pitch, and tone for the role. (Alternates: Audition for roles in radio dramas, tape-recording stories, etc.)

WORD MEANINGS

Sample Activities for Discussion, Task Cards, Learning Centers, and Reading Contracts

1. Make up funny definitions for familiar words and phrases.
2. Make a meaning collage for a new word. Paste pictures and words associated with the word into a pleasing design.
3. Suppose there were an accident outside our classroom. Write up the accident from the point of view of the participants, a teacher, a principal, a caretaker, a parent, or a police officer.
4. Write up an event in the story from the point of view of three story characters.
5. Select three words from the story and write them in such a way that their meaning is clearly shown. Example: drip.
6. When there is a word in a sentence that could mean more than one thing, how can you tell which meaning to use?
7. Teachers: Have students describe a word and see if other students can guess it.
8. Teachers: Have students make picture dictionaries illustrated by their drawings or by pictures from magazines. These dictionaries can be as simple as one on circus animals for younger children or on more complex idea words for older students. Add new words often.
9. Teachers: Make multi-meaning illustrated dictionaries, where students illustrate the multiple meanings of various words such as run, hit, etc.
10. Teachers: Make a list with students of feeling words and of

what the words mean. Use for a bulletin board labeled, "Feelings," "Warm Words," "What Are Feelings?," etc.

11. Teachers: Give students sets of words to complete; for example, "Ready, set, _____."

12. Teachers: Give exercises similar to, "The word _____ always makes me think of _____."

13. Teachers: Play a game using phrase cards. Students draw a phrase card and use the phrase in a sentence. One point is given for each word in the sentence.

NONVERBAL VOCABULARY DEVELOPMENT

Sample Activities for Discussion, Task Cards, Learning Centers, and Reading Contracts

1. Pretend you are a cave man or woman. Use only gestures to speak. Act out a scene. See if the class can follow the action.

2. Pantomime a word. See who can guess the word. (Alternate: Use facial expressions only.)

3. Pantomime an event in your story. See who can guess what is happening.

4. Pantomime one of the characters in the story. See who can guess what the character was like.

5. Learn and demonstrate some of the hand signs animal trainers use.

6. List all the times when gestures and facial expressions are not present to help people communicate. (Example: telephone conversations)

7. Lip-read with a friend. Read a list of words to him or her and have him or her read a list to you. See if you can understand each other. Note which sounds are easiest to lip-read. See if your friend agrees.

8. Act out, without words, the usual gestures of someone in the classroom. See who can guess who it is.

9. Look up how to play the American Indian guessing game where an object is hidden in the hand and the opposing player tries to guess which hand it is in.

10. Research and be ready to share with us how acting in a TV show would be different from acting in a play.

11. Teachers: Have the class play, "Black Magic." (One child is "It" and goes outside the room. All agree on one object.

The leader calls "It" back, then asks questions beginning, "Is it _____?" The leader asks if it is any of several objects, then if it is a black object. (The correct answer is always the object following the black object. When the one who is "It" catches on, send someone else out. Only the teacher and the first leader know the secret. The person who is "It" does not tell others when he/she catches on.)

12. Teachers: Cut pictures of people's faces apart horizontally. Give the portions that include the eyes to half the group and the portions with the mouths to the other half. Have the students write down the emotion(s) they see in the expression on their half of the picture, then see if the person who has the other half agrees or disagrees. Discuss differences in perceptions.

13. Teachers: Have the class practice lip reading for a day, where all instructions, discussions, and the like are given silently, or work with learning to lip-read a few words or sentences.

14. Teachers: Teach the class American Indian sign language.

15. Teachers: For older students, include popular books on nonverbal language as part of the classroom library.

16. Teachers: Work with pantomime or shadow picture activities. (Examples: Pantomiming the meaning of a word, acting out an episode from the story.)

17. Teachers: Videotape each student at work in the classroom. Give the students a chance to watch themselves without sound. Have them write comments about how they feel about the way they use nonverbal language when they talk.

WORD ENRICHMENT

Sample Activities for Discussion, Task Cards, Learning Centers, or Reading Contracts

1. Make a list of ten words that describe the main character in your story.

2. What things could each of these color words describe: Red? Pink? Blue? Violet?

3. What interesting words did the author use that helped you see pictures in your mind; that made you be aware of your

senses; or made you feel the way the people in the story did.

4. What words do you consider especially beautiful, either to hear, to see, or to think about?
5. List all the words you can think of to describe reading.
6. Write a description of the most beautiful thing you ever saw. Describe it so well that we can see it, too. (Alternates: The most exciting event, the most frightening moment, your proudest time, etc.)
7. Interview people of various ages and from various parts of the United States and the world about how they celebrated Halloween (or other holidays) in their part of the world. Give an oral presentation with displays, pictures, etc., of what you learned to the whole group.
8. Describe your ideal school. (Alternate: Your ideal bedroom or home.)
9. Make a list of words that you enjoy that your favorite grownups use. (Alternate: That you do not enjoy.)
10. Play categories, using this board or design your own.

	A	B	C	D
Games				
States				
Foods				
Books				
Authors				

11. Play, "Guess Who" or "Guess What" with a group of friends. Cut out pictures of film stars; pin one picture on the back of each person playing. Players have to guess who is pinned on their backs. They can ask questions of anyone, but all questions have to be answered *yes* or *no*. (Alternate: use baseball stars, new vocabulary words, foreign language words, etc.)
12. Design and produce a play for your age level or for younger children using stick puppets. (Alternates: Marionettes, paper bag puppets, finger puppets.)
13. Make up your own words for four activities that you do every day.

14. Write a story around an imaginary word.
15. What are clichés? Can you find five examples from your reading?
16. Hold a telephone conversation between two characters in your story.
17. Teachers: Real aloud frequently to the class, especially books that use words in innovative ways.
18. Teachers: Show your own enthusiasm for words—creative uses of words, unusual uses of words, etc. Comment on your own reaction to words that authors use. And don't forget to comment on effective word use by students in the classroom.
19. Teachers: Have students choose a word to use for a day and see how many times they can use it.
20. Teachers: Have a vocabulary club where a student introduces a new word at each meeting.
21. Teachers: Write a category on the board. Have each child write as many words that fit that category as possible. The one who writes the largest number of correct words gets to choose the next category. (Examples; School, cars, etc.)
22. Teachers: Play, "Who said that?" Have students read paragraphs they have drawn from a pile of excerpts from books most of them have read. See who can identify the author. (Alternate: Use dialogue passages and see who can identify the story character.)
23. Teachers: Read a story aloud, then have the students list as many of the words that moved the story along as they can remember. The one with the longest list wins. (Alternates: Words that evoke imagery, feeling words, etc.)
24. Teachers: Encourage students to read widely. Occasionally, mark progress in fifty-page increments rather than by number of books.
25. Teachers: Have students keep a record of words that give difficulty or that the student doesn't understand. Be sure to use the lists often for practice. Students may mark out the words as they add them to their vocabulary.
26. Teachers: Encourage students to bring in any unusual, interesting, or arresting words or word usage they run into in their reading or as they listen to the language of others.
27. Teachers: Compile a slang dictionary of local phrases and words with the students.

28. Teachers: Play *Password* with the class.
29. Teachers: Divide the class into groups (or choose individuals) to share the daily paper—editorials, sports, front page, comics, etc. Each group (or person) should summarize in an interesting fashion any items worth sharing with the class.

A FINAL WORD ABOUT VOCABULARY DEVELOPMENT

Reading brings to our students the excitement of words well used; of words arranged in splendid and unusual beauty; of words written by persons far away and long ago; of words used reverently and expertly by men and women who can describe a better us, a better life. These words serve to delight, instruct, and broaden our students. They bring richness to their speech and to their reading, helping students understand the immense, exciting possibilities within the English language. To be able to offer students this gift of love and enjoyment of language takes a special kind of teacher.

6

Word Perception Skills

* * * * * * * * * * * *

More attention has probably been paid to word perception (or word attack or word analysis skills—the more common synonyms for word perception) than to any other phase of the reading program. Much of this attention has been deservedly directed at three special types of word perception skills— phonic cues, sight cues, and, to a lesser extent, structural analysis cues. These three, important though they may be, represent only a small part of the totality of skills involved in word perception. Although their emphasis in most reading programs has accelerated the growth of many, many students, these three skills, used alone as a word perception curriculum, would handicap all students in their growth by limiting their range of potential word attack behavior, especially those more advanced students who tend not to use these word attack procedures as much as they do other word identification processes. These three word perception skills tend to be limited, also, to one type of learning style based on a slower, more linear thinking pattern. None of this, however, negates their importance, especially considering their effectiveness in helping young readers read unfamiliar words and the emotional hold that phonics, in particular, has on the general public.

This chapter can serve as a checklist for us educators to remind us to look occasionally at our reading instruction to see if we are limiting our curriculum to these most popular word attack techniques and are leaving out such processes as etymological, configurational, linguistic, meaning or semantic, kinesthetic, contextual, syntactical, and encoding and decoding cues.

ETYMOLOGICAL CUES

Sample Activities for Discussion, Task Cards
Learning Centers, and Reading Contracts

1. Investigate the origins of your first, middle, and last names.
2. Research the history of the words for ten common objects in our classroom.
3. Look up the origin for the words for the titles of people who work in our school (teacher, principal, nurse, caretaker or janitor, etc.).
4. If you wanted to look up the history or the origin of a particular word, where would you look? List at least three sources. Consult a librarian for your answer.
5. Make up new words to use for the school activities we work on each day (reading, etc.). Try to make your original words fit their subject.
6. Is there a word of Greek origin in your story? Italian? Latin? American Indian? Spanish? French? German? Scandinavian? Arabic? Any other source?

CONFIGURATIONAL CUES

Sample Activities for Discussion, Task Cards,
Learning Centers, or Reading Contracts

1. If you had to remember how this new word looks, how would you do it?
2. Draw or write a word in such a way that it looks like what it means. (Examples: *tall*, *rain*, etc.)
3. Many words fit into the same shape of configurational pattern. Show some shapes and several words that can fit into each.
4. In order to use configuration (or word shape) to learn new words, you have to be able to see words rapidly. Choose ten words you are sure you can read. Use a tachistoscope or a slide projector with a timing mechanism. See how fast you can set the machine and still read the words. Next, practice with words of which you're not so sure. (Use

highway signs to practice your configurational skills while traveling.)

5. Teachers: Cut a word or a sentence in half diagonally. See if the students can complete the word(s).
6. Teachers: Play *Hangman* with the children. (Blanks represent a letter in a sentence.) Each child guesses one letter at a time until the sentence is clear. The first player to read the sentence aloud correctly wins.
7. Teachers: Have students write a new word, trace around it, and cut it out. Have them look at the shape from several angles to see what it looks like (animal, person, plant) and draw a picture using the shape of the word.
8. Teachers: Play, "All Aboard" with the class. Have students arrange their chairs as though they were on a train. Give each person a flash card with the name of a local street on it (or nearby towns). The teacher or game leader has an identical set of flash cards and flashes them one by one. Each student recognizes his "stop" by matching the station to the "ticket" in his hand.
9. Teachers: Play, "Turn Around." The students line up facing the teacher or game leader, who shows a card with a word on it. When a student recognizes the word, he turns and faces the opposite way. The teacher calls on the first one to give the word orally.
10. Teachers: Hold up cards, each of which has a different outline of shapes that several words could fit. Ask students to list as many words as they can that would fit into each shape.
11. Teachers: Describe the outline of a word orally to the children. See how many words they can recall that fit this oral description.
12. Teachers: Use word dominoes, on which are written new words to be taught, as a learning or an interest center.
13. Teachers: Put up a rack of magazines. See who can find a given magazine the quickest. (Alternate: Use a paperback rack to have students look for a specific paperback book.)
14. Teachers: Use a U.S. map puzzle, where states are identified by outline (alternate: shapes of countries) as a class activity.

SIGHT CUES

Sample Activities for Discussion, Task Cards, Learning Centers, or Reading Contracts

1. How are *come* and *came* alike? How are they different?
2. If you had to remember how these new words looked, how would you do it?
3. There are some words with which we just have trouble. Perhaps we learn them once or even twice, and then simply forget them. What are some of these words for you?
4. Make a series of flash cards for words you would like to study.
5. Teachers: Play *Bingo* or *Concentration* with new words.
6. Teachers: Play "Magician" with new words. Make a magician's hat from black construction paper and make several paper bunnies. Write new words on each bunny. Fold the bunnies horizontally, so the words are hidden inside, and place the bunnies in the hat. Give each student a turn at waving the magic wand and pulling a bunny from the hat. If the student knows the word, he or she can read it or ask someone in the audience to read it.
7. Teachers: Have each student make a set of word cards from a list of new words on the board. The teacher or leader calls out a word and each student should show the card that matches the word.
8. Teachers: Have students learn sight words based on traffic words and signals, names of children in the class, objects in the classroom, names of streets near the school, names of TV shows, etc.
9. Teachers: Have students make a list, a personal dictionary, or a set of cards of the basic sight words they know.
10. Teachers: Sometimes use a tachistoscope for teaching new words.
11. Teachers: Play *Name Bingo* with the names of students in the class.
12. Teachers: Take your class to view the driver training equipment if this equipment features a film as part of the mock auto setup used in some courses.
13. Teachers: Speed up a film as rapidly as it can go. Have

students try to read any words they see in the film on buildings, signs, title credits, and the like.

CUES FROM WORD SIMILARITIES AND DIFFERENCES

Sample Activities for Discussion, Task Cards, Learning Centers, and Reading Contracts

1. Make a list of ten words new to you. Categorize the list into as many similarities and differences as you can think of. (Alternate: Choose two new words. Explain all the ways they look alike and the ways they look different from each other.)
2. Play "How Are We Alike." Choose three classmates to stand in front of the class. List the many ways they are alike.
3. Explain the difference between a flower and a weed.
4. How does a new word remind you of a familiar word?
5. Write the opposite of: Kindness, white, rainy, steamy.
6. Write as many words as you can think of that begin with *ch* on the chalkboard.
7. How many pupils' first names begin with *B*?
8. Make up a crossword puzzle based on your story.

KINESTHETIC CUES

Sample Activities for Discussing, Task Cards, Learning Centers, and Reading Contracts

1. Teachers: Cut out a large cardboard letter shape. Have students write as many words on the letter as they know that begin with that letter.
2. Teachers: Have students trace new words in the air and say them at the same time. (Alternates: Trace on sandpaper, clay, sandboxes; paint the word; water paint the word; sprinkle sand to make a painting; make paper mosaics; etc.)
3. Teachers: Shape cookie dough into words or letters (or have students make cookies into these shapes). The student eats them when he or she knows them.
4. Teachers: Form words on the playground with students just like a band does at half time at football games.

5. Teachers: Provide letter stencils of all kinds for making posters, book covers, name cards, etc.

6. Teachers: Have students act out the meaning of a word. See who can guess the word.

7. Teachers: Have students make a word chain for a new word. One letter of the word is printed on each link.

8. Teachers: Other ways for students to learn words and letters kinesthetically: Shape clay into long snakes and form letters and words. Use a sand or salt tray or box. Trace sandpaper letters. Cut out construction paper letters. Use alphabet macaroni or cereals. Paste small stars in the shape of words. Squeeze cake topping into words. Decorate crackers with cheese squeezed from a tube in the form of words or letters. Make standup, cutout names for each student's desk. Cut letters from magazine pictures or from printing. Use string or yarn to form words. Write on the chalkboard. Use Magic Slate plastic (that peels off or wipes off cleanly) for tracing words. Use a wood burning set to shape words. Use a jumprope to shape words, then walk around it.

LINGUISTIC CUES

Sample Activities for Discussion, Task Cards, Learning Centers, and Reading Contracts

1. Linguistic methods of teaching reading start with words in which each letter has only one sound, usually three-letter words with a consonant–vowel–consonant pattern with short vowels. Sample exercises: List as many words as you can that fit this pattern. Use this list of words to write a story. Illustrate that story.

2. Put the following words together to make a sentence; put them together in as many ways as you can: I, the, at, like, walk, barefoot, seashore, to.

3. Pretend you are a linguist (a person who studies words, word patterns, and the way people use words). Take ten creative writing stories that classmates have written. Classify the ten most common words in the stories and the ten least common words. (Alternates: Classify the words from ten of your own stories. Do the same with student discussions that you have tape-recorded.)

4. Ask your teacher to let you look at a teachers' manual for a

reading book the class is using. Find the sentences or paragraphs that tell how the particular words the author uses in the book were chosen. Compare this to the way words were chosen for other reading books.

5. Hide three letters in a word (yet keep them together in the same sequence) so other people would have trouble finding them; example, eno-enough, or keno, and the like. (Alternate: Make up a list of five words that have the same three letters kept together in sequence and see who can guess the letters the fastest; e.g., made, adequate, laden, invader, lemonade (ade).)

6. Pretend you are a linguist researching the words in a book. Make a list of the number of words and the times each is used in one hundred lines of print.

7. Count the number of *E*'s used in one hundred words; the number of *Q*'s. What does this tell you about our alphabet?

8. What is the most frequently used word in the first 100 words in your story?

9. Critique your speller and the sequence in which it has you learn to spell. Does it put words on the same page that are confusing to spell when you have to learn them together? Are there words that should not (or should) be learned at the same time, etc?

10. Interview people who were born in different parts of the United States to find out words that are used in different regions. Put these words on a map.

11. What is a linguistic map?

12. List the words you had trouble with in the story. What is your thinking as to the best way to study these words? What skills should you use to identify each?

13. How many times did you find the word, *is*, in your story?

MEANING OR SEMANTIC CUES

Sample Activities for Discussion, Task Cards, Learning Centers, and Reading Contracts

1. Teachers: Give the students a definition of a word and have them give you the word.

2. Teachers: Discuss with the students what each new word makes them think of or remember.

3. Teachers: Have students draw a picture of what one new word in the story means.

4. Teachers: Ask students these questions: What types of words would make sense here where this new word is in the sentence? What other words in the sentence or sentences surrounding the new word give us hints of what the word could be? Do you recognize any familiar parts of the new word? What does this word do in the sentence? Does this word describe one thing or several? Etc.

CONTEXT CUES

Sample Activities for Discussion, Task Cards, Learning Centers, and Reading Contracts

1. Teachers: Choose an unfamiliar word from the story. Have the students guess the meaning from a sentence containing the word, then look up the word to see the dictionary definition.

2. Teachers: Make a cloze passage by blacking out every fifth word of a reading passage. Number the blanks. Have students write the words that they think belong in each blank. (Alternates: Blank out every eighth word, every second word, etc., depending on students' skill.)

3. Teachers: Have students write a paragraph about a certain word, but omit the word every time it is used in the sentence. See if the class can guess the word.

4. Teachers: Have students work on: (a) Finding the word that doesn't belong. (Example: Green, red, run, pink.)
(b) Supplying the missing word. (Example: See _____ bird.)
(c) Completing sentences. (Example: Susan _____. (hurried)(helped)

5. Teachers: Cover one word in a sentence written on the chalkboard or on a strip of paper. Have the students guess what word is covered.

6. Teachers: Have students read aloud only the nouns in a sentence. Discuss the clues in the sentence that helped them locate the nouns.

7. Teachers: Read a short selection, pause at various places, and omit a word. The student who can supply the correct missing word reads the next excerpt and leaves out a word.

STRUCTURAL ANALYSIS

Sample Activities for Discussion, Task Cards, Learning Centers, and Reading Contracts

1. Look at these new words. What is there about the words or in the words that will help you remember them? Later we'll discuss this to see what others in the class found.
2. Here are some unusual ways to begin words. Think of five words that begin with each of these combinations of letters: ad, ang, arc, em, im, ob, ot, us, ute.
3. How many words can you think of that end with *end*?
4. Make at least five new words from each of the following roots: cause, calm, rich.
5. Draw a line under the root word: changed, enabling, etc.
6. What is the root for these three words: labor, belabor, labored?
7. Why do you suppose a scarecrow was named that? Can you make a list of five compound words (words that put two or more words (roots) together)? Hint: skyscraper.
8. Make up a compound word crossword puzzle.
9. Teachers: Make up a series of cards on which are written singular and plural nouns. Have students separate them into plural and singular piles.
10. Teachers: Use a wheel of root words and affixes (prefixes and suffixes) chosen from new words in books students are reading. Ask students to make up as many pretend and as many actual words from the wheel as they can. (Alternate: Have students make their own wheels entirely of actual words. Slip boards, flip books, etc., can also be used.)
11. Teachers: Have students make a root tree where the trunk has the root written on it and where every leaf is a different word containing that root.
12. Teachers: Have a card pile of affixes (prefixes and suffixes) and a pile of root words turned upside down. Have students in turn draw a card from each pile and decide if they make a word. They get to keep those that make a word. The other cards go to the bottom of the piles. The student with the most words at the end of a certain number of draws or minutes wins.
13. Teachers: Create new words with students. Decide what

certain prefixes and suffixes will be and mean (example, *pil* for *un*), then make up a few root words. Put the creations together and talk your new language for a week. (Alternate: Use foreign languages.)

14. Teachers: Have students make a file or a book in which they list all affixes and their meanings encountered in reading.

15. Teachers: Have students draw a ring around the suffix (prefix) in lists of new words.

16. Teachers: Have students try to write a paragraph without using a prefix. (For more advanced learners, without using any affixes.)

17. Teachers: Have students listen to a tape recording of conversation, sound tracks of films, etc., and list all the contractions they hear.

SYLLABLE ANALYSIS

Sample Activities for Discussion, Task Cards, Learning Centers, and Reading Contracts

1. Teachers: Play "The Most Syllables Game." Examples: What name has the most syllables of any name you ever heard? What TV or film star has the most syllables in his/ her name? What book title? What country? What word that you have ever read? What word in your book? Make up a "most syllables" question of your own.

2. Teachers: Divide the names of all the students in class into number of syllables. (Alternates: Space words, car terms, etc.)

3. Teachers: Have students draw from a stack of cards containing numerals from one to seven (or make up your own top limit according to class proficiency). Students must give a word containing the number of syllables listed on the card they draw. Give one point for each correct answer. The winner is the student with the highest number of points at the end of a set time limit.

4. Teachers: Have students write haiku, sijo, and tanka poetry, three poetic forms based on syllables.

5. Teachers: Play "Syllable Whirl." Have students spin a dial or roll dice marked with the numbers 1 to 10. The first one

of two players representing two teams to come up with a word of that number of syllables wins a point for his or her team.

6. Teachers: Play "Syllable Math" with the number of syllables in words. (Example: Add the number of syllables in Pennsylvania to the number in Kentucky. Multiply the total by the number of syllables in California.)
7. Teachers: From a list of words already divided into syllables and accented, ask the students to pick the word you are pronouncing.

ACCENT ANALYSIS

Sample Activities for Discussion, Task Cards, Learning Centers, and Reading Contracts

1. Teachers: Make up a set of sentences with the class, each of which contain two words which are spelled the same but which are accented in different places. (Example: con/tént, cón/tent.)
2. Teachers: Choose sentences from a current reading assignment. Have students read the sentences as if they were surprised, angry, hostile, aggressive, etc. (Alternate: Have students read sentences as if they were having certain feelings, then see if the class can guess the emotions they are expressing.)
3. Teachers: Listen with the class to popular songs that are in nonstandard English. List words that are accented differently; e.g., Black English, Southern, etc.
4. Teachers: Listen with the class to records or tapes of people who speak English with an accent. In what ways do they differ in pronunciation and accent?
5. Teachers: Make a chart with students which shows the rules for accent; e.g., if a word ends in a suffix, the root word is usually accented, etc.
6. Teachers: Read sentences aloud in such a way that the listener can tell whether you are reading a question, a declarative sentence, or an exclamation.
7. Teachers: Read sentences aloud, stressing the important words. See if your listeners can tell which words you stressed.

SYNTACTICAL CUES

Sample Activities for Discussion, Task Cards, Learning Centers, and Reading Contracts

1. Teachers: Write each word from a sentence on a separate card. Give each card to a student. Have the students group themselves in line in as many ways as they can get the sentence to make sense.
2. Teachers: Choose twenty words randomly from the new words list at the back of the reader. See how many sentences the students can make from the list of words.
3. Teachers: Have students write cinquains. Cinquains use types of words in a special pattern to form a poem: First line—one word for a title; second line—two words describing the word above; third line—three words about an action for the title word; fourth line—four words expressing feelings by or about the title; fifth line—another word for the title.
4. Teachers: Diamantes are also poems based on word class. The pattern:

noun

adjective   adjective

participle   participle   participle

noun   noun   noun   noun

participle   participle   participle

adjective   adjective

noun

The two nouns for the first and last lines of the diamante are usually antonyms; the words on the top part of the diamond refer to the first noun, and the words on the bottom part of the diamond refer to the second noun.

5. Teachers: Have students supply antecedents for pronouns. (Example: Who is the sentence about? She ran all the way home. *Mary*. He can play. _____.
6. Teachers: Have children make sentences by drawing from a pile of subject phrases, verb phrases, and any additional phrases you wish.

7. Teachers: Play word games based on word class; for example, something that is big, noisy, flighty, etc.
8. Teachers: Play popular records or tapes. Have students keep track of word classes—nouns, verbs, etc.
9. Teachers: Have students write poems, each line of which is based on the same sentence pattern; e.g., Red is _____; Go _____; Ah, _____; etc.
10. Teachers: Have half the class think of nouns and half think of verbs. Read a short story aloud. Call on the noun group to supply a noun from their list each time there is a noun in the story and the verb group to supply verbs. Advanced groups can supply other parts of speech.

ENCODING—DECODING: PHONIC CUES, WHOLE WORD PHONICS, GRAPHOPHONIC CUES, GRAPHEMES, AND SECRET CODES

Sample Activities for Discussion, Task Cards, Learning Centers and Reading Contracts

1. Practice writing your initials until you have a pattern you would be proud to sign on an oil painting or other art work.
2. Write your initials in the center of a large piece of paper. Outline your initials with one color of crayon. Continue outlining, using a different color each time, until you have filled in the whole sheet.
3. Find a book in the library that uses illuminated capital letters.
4. Make a display of different types of print used in books in our library.
5. Make a display of various types of alphabets other than the one we use.
6. Make up a series of letters for our alphabet that look like the sound the letter makes. Sometimes you'll have to make up more than one sound for a letter. Check your inventions with some of the phonetic alphabets (ITA, etc.).
7. Make up a series of pictures to represent specific words. Translate a paragraph from a book into your new language.
8. Make a chart of how you felt today. For every hour draw a face. Put on the expression for each face that describes your feelings at the time.
9. Make up a secret code for messages.

10. Read about the use of code during wartime.
11. Write down at least ten ways you can think of to improve our alphabet.
12. Teachers: Teach the international highway sign codes.
13. Teachers: Have students collect airline baggage destination strips. Examples: ABQ = Alburquerque, LAX = Los Angeles International.
14. Teachers: Teach newspaper or magazine proofreaders' symbols.
15. Teachers: Have students plan and perform a card section stunt just like the ones college students do at football games.
16. Teachers: Give students a readability level formula. See if they can estimate the reading level of stories, books, newspaper or magazine articles, directions, and government or political publications.
17. Teachers: Have half the students make up a code and write a message of at least 24 words. Then give the other half of the class time to try to decode what was written. Every so many minutes, have the encoders give the decoders a hint.
18. Teachers: Bring braille books and typewriters for students to see.
19. Teachers: Set up a small hand-operated printing press in the classroom.
20. Teachers: Set up a mini-library featuring books on the alphabet, pictographs, sign language, and other alphabet systems.
21. Teachers: Write down a paragraph in which all the letters of each word are reversed. See who can decode the message first.
22. Teachers: Use the pronunciation guides in dictionaries as if they were a secret code.
23. Teachers: Teach and use Morse code for special "surprise" messages.
24. Teachers: Have students research the Hoboes' Code for leaving signs for others.
25. Teachers: Make up nonsense or calypso songs with the students that use as lyrics the rules for phonetic analysis; e.g., if a word ends in e . . .
26. Teachers: Make up or have students make up riddles to fit phonic rules. A vowel in a three letter word is usually

_____. (Alternate: Make up or have children make up riddles to fit phonic irregularities; e.g., the *gh* is usually silent when preceded by a vowel as _____. (might, right, through).)

27. Teachers: Play *Jeopardy* using phonics rules: An example of the rule is given; or the answer is given and the phonics rule is to be given by the contestant.
28. Teachers: Have students make individual picture dictionaries of special words; e.g., "Words That Intrigue Me," "Words That I Find Hard," "Words That Would Be Interesting to Me."
29. Teachers: Have students cut or draw pictures to make a collage for a letter. See who can guess the letter.
30. Teachers: Have students cut out letters to form a word. Make each letter a collage representing the meaning of the whole word or the beginning, middle, or ending sound of that particular word.
31. Teachers: Play "What's Left Out?" Write the alphabet, leaving out five to fifteen letters. Have students complete the puzzle.
32. Teachers: Have students design a game that they think would help others learn some phonics rule.
33. Teachers: Play "Connect the Alphabet." Students make pictures by drawing a line from letter to letter in sequence.
34. Teachers: Have students make up "Connect the Alphabet" picture puzzles for others.
35. Teachers: Have the class sing alphabet jingles and songs.
36. Teachers: Have a rhyming box full of small objects. Have students find those that rhyme.
37. Teachers: Write a sentence. See how many ways the students can rhyme another sentence with it.
38. Teachers: Make "Dial-a-Word" wheels where one letter changes; e.g., initial letter, middle letters, endings.
39. Teachers: Play a variation of *Categories*. Going alphabetically; list a food that starts with *A*, etc. Each player goes as far in the alphabet as he or she can, then the next player continues. (Alternates: sports, football players, etc.)
40. Teachers: Have students make collages for the sounds the class is studying; e.g., initial consonants, consonant digraphs, etc. (Alternate: Make an alphabet collage from letters cut from magazines.)

41. Teachers: Have students list all the words on a page or in a paragraph that contain silent letters.
42. Teachers: Have students make a collage or list of words that begin (end, have the same middle letter) as their name.
43. Teachers: Teach and use pig Latin for a day to help students hear sounds in a new context.
44. Teachers: Have students interview people who spoke another language originally on the difficulties they had with English sounds.
45. Teachers: Play records and tapes for the students where regional or foreign accents are prominent. Have them list the sounds that make up an Irish accent, a Boston accent, etc. Play the record several times so most of the sound differences can be spotted.
46. Teachers: Teach students poems and songs that have interesting rhyming patterns.
47. Teachers: Play "Poet." One student is the poet. He or she says a word and points to another student while the poet counts to ten. If the other student comes up with a rhyming word before the count of ten, he or she becomes the poet.
48. Teachers: Give topics similar to these: What words do you nearly always confuse? Why do you think this happens? Make up a rhyming riddle about a common classroom object. Make up a sentence that uses as many words containing *st* as you can.
49. Teachers: Have students name as many words as they can that rhyme with *same*.
50. Teachers: Have younger children put into piles pictures of words that rhyme.
51. Teachers: Decide at the beginning of the day a word that will become the "Magic Word." During the day, each time the teacher uses that word, the first student to raise his/her hand gets a point. Use common words at first.
52. Teachers: Play card games such as *Fish* or *Old Maid*, using whole words on the cards.
53. Teachers: Have students think silently for a time about steps for sounding out an unfamiliar word. What should they do first, second, etc? Then have each student discuss his or her list. Make a combination list for students to use for later reference. (Sample items: (1) Figure out the first sound. (2) Think what word with that beginning sound

would make sense in the sentence, etc. Take these items as examples, not as final solutions.) (Alternate: Play a similar game with letter cubes used as dice.)

54. Teachers: Give students exercises where part of a word is already written for them. Examples: It is a s____ day. We took a drive in our new c__r. ___hat is a good idea.

55. Teachers: Write sentences, including only the consonants, and substituting dashes for the vowels. See who can interpret. (Alternate: Use vowels only.)

56. Teachers: Write each letter from a word on a separate card. Give each card to a student. See how many ways the students can line up to form a word using all of the letters.

57. Teachers: Scramble letters from various words. See who can unscramble them.

58. Teachers: Make up word searches for students (or have students make them up). Subjects can be animals, film stars, and the like.

59. Teachers: Have students make a collage of different ways a single alphabet letter can be written (upper case, lower case, gothic, etc.).

60. Teachers: Have students use various media to letter posters, signs, book covers, etc.: (a) Two different colored pencils held and used as one; (b) shapes consisting of a circle, half circle, and straight line; (c) an inch piece of chalk or crayon used sideways for printing; (d) letters cut from potatoes; (e) hand-printing type; and so on.

61. Teachers: Write a series of sentences from which you have deleted one alphabetic letter. See if the class can figure out which is missing. Alliteration is hardest to do. (Example: ___lue ___onnets ___loomed ___eside the ___rook.)

62. Teachers: Have the class make a book of abbreviations.

63. Teachers: Have students choose describing words that begin with the same letter as each letter in their names. (Alternates: For their friends, relatives or—if you're brave enough—for you.)

64. Teachers: Give students crossword puzzles about the story to work or have them make up a crossword about the book.

65. Teachers: Have a crossword puzzle center where students can solve puzzles from newspapers and magazines or from crossword puzzle books. One of the activities could be designing crossword puzzles. (Alternate: Acrostics.)

66. Teachers: Have students write and act out a play about Gutenberg and the printing press.
67. Teachers: Have students roll alphabet dice and see how many words they can make from each toss.
68. Teachers: Have cardboard letters of the alphabet available and have students make up new games using them.
69. Teachers: Use a *Scrabble* game (or a three-dimensional *Scrabble* game) at a learning or an interest center.
70. Teachers: Play a word scramble game using names of students, states, foreign countries, presidents, and the like.
71. Teachers: Have students make alphabet posters.
72. Teachers: Have students see how many words they can make from the letters in their names. If this exercise is a game, students may draw extra alphabetic letters so that all have as many letters to work with as in the longest name in the group.
73. Teachers: Run all the words from a paragraph or a short page together, omitting capitals and punctuation marks. Have the students find the words and separate them by circling them or by using diagonal slashes.
74. Teachers: Have students cross out all the silent letters in a short reading selection.
75. Teachers: Give students the beginning and ending letters, and have them think of words that begin and end with those letters. They get a point for every letter they add. (Example: B etwee N = 5 points.)
76. Teachers: Play *Phonics Bingo* with individual letters, consonants, blends, digraphs, etc.
77. Teachers: Have a typewriter available as a learning center activity.
78. Teachers: Design word search games tailored to specific kinds of words; for example, things that are red, animal names, days of the week, months of the year, etc.
79. Teachers: Play word puzzles where students have to find common alphabet letters in a list of words.
80. Teachers: Have students build words by adding one letter at a time to either the word beginning or ending.
81. Teachers: Have students make designs by cutting out students' names along a doubled, folded sheet of paper.
82. Teachers: Have students make words by having letters keyed to numbers on a telephone dial.

83. Teachers: Give students words that contain *dr*. Then have them make up a question to which one of the *dr* words is the answer.

84. Teachers: Have students change one word into another in the fewest possible steps one letter at a time, each step a new word: Example: Feat, fest, fast.

85. Teachers: Play *Anagrams* with the students, the object being to rearrange the letters of one word to form another. Example: silent-listen.

86. Teachers: Play "Chain Gang." Divide the class into teams. The first player gives any word; the next player on the other team must give a word that begins with the last sound of the first word, and so on. Example: run – near – rather, etc.

87. Teachers: Play "Alphabet Hunt." Have students find objects around the room or in books that begin with each of the letters in the alphabet. The first one correctly finished wins. (Alternates: Flowers, animals, cities, countries.)

88. Teachers: Play "Spin-a-Word." Students spin a numbered dial for the number of letters in a word. The first one to think of a word with that many letters wins a point.

89. Teachers: Make up sheets of letters of the alphabet. Be sure to include plenty of vowels. Students use a crayon or a pencil to make a word in a certain number of strokes (three, etc.). Moves are only one space at a time, either horizontally, vertically, or diagonally.

90. Teachers: Give each student a pile of alphabet cereal or macaroni. Give a familiar word aloud. The first student to form the word from the letters wins a point.

91. Teachers: Have students make words from two medial letters. Examples: __ap__, __ix__.

92. Teachers: Have students make up their own word circles or wheels from a beginning sound. See how many endings they can add.

A FINAL WORD ABOUT WORD PERCEPTION

Of all the precautions we teachers need to observe in teaching word perception skills, the most important is that we teach reading so that students will read. Because of the relative ease of designing word perception exercises and activities, many reading programs concentrate on this area rather than on the act of reading. The thoughtful educator will provide students with interesting, exciting activities that stress meaning as well as analysis, that ground students as thoroughly in the esthetics as in the basics of reading. Otherwise, our students' scores on the meaning section of standardized reading tests will continue to fall.

7

Auditory Perception Skills

* * * * * * * * * * * *

For a long time, most educators delegated the teaching of auditory perception skills to beginning reading instruction in the primary grades. More recent thinking has recognized the importance of auditory perception skills to all grade levels, elementary and high school alike, and there are even some pilot programs in auditory perception skill development at the university levels.

Remember that most students who grew up in a television world may need extremely elementary instruction in auditory perception simply because they have had no opportunity to develop those skills. They may need step-by-step guidance, for example, in learning to use auditory ways of inducing mental images of actions in a story. Don't give up. Their world has been the matter-of-fact one of television, where much of the stimuli were presented to them in a passive mode.

AUDITORY FIGURE-GROUND SKILLS

Sample Activities for Discussion, Task Cards, Learning Centers, and Reading Contracts

1. Teachers: Play a song in a foreign language. Have students try to write down the lyrics in phonetic fashion.
2. Teachers: Have students listen to foreign languages to answer: What sounds does the language have that English doesn't? What sounds does English have that the foreign language doesn't? What words from that language have become a part of English?

3. Teachers: If students are learning a new language or if the class is using bilingual teaching methods, have a learning center with listening posts or with a radio turned low. Keep the radio tuned to a foreign language station. Have students listen for five minutes. See if anyone heard a word, a phrase, or a sentence he or she understood.

4. Teachers: Play a recording or listen to a police broadcast. Have students try to pick out calls for a particular car.

5. Teachers: Play a recording or listen to a control tower operator talking to planes. Have students try to understand the instructions.

6. Teachers: Have students think of as many occupations as they can that require the ability to hear one group of sounds out of many sounds. (Examples: Police officer—radio calls; airplane pilot—radio calls; restaurant cook—orders; speech therapist—sounds; singer—cues, music, tone; orchestra conductor—every instrument; control tower operator—poor radio reception; court reporter—testimony; dispatcher—radio calls; teacher—students' responses; sports participants—play calls, etc.; ornithologist—bird sounds; safecracker—sounds of the tumbler; mechanic—automobile sounds.)

7. Teachers: Set up a C.B. center in the classroom where students can learn to hear what is said. Later, they may begin to broadcast.

8. Teachers: Have an autoharp tuning center where students may sign up to be responsible for tuning the autoharps. Give careful instructions or ask a music teacher for help. (Alternate: guitar tuning center.)

AUDITORY MEMORY SKILLS

Sample Activities for Discussion, Task Cards, Learning Centers, and Reading Contracts

1. Student instructions: You are a telephone operator. Operators have to be expert at hearing a number and remembering it. Practice with a friend to see if you can hear and write down ten numerals in a row (three area code, three prefix, four ending numerals).

2. Teachers: Ask students to be the secretary at a dictation center for classmates or for younger children, to write or type stories as other students dictate.

3. Teachers: Tell a story once only. Ask the students to recall the main events or main characters or retell the story.

4. Teachers: Ring a bell a certain number of times or in a certain order. See who can duplicate it. Add more rings, more complicated patterns, and longer sequences as the students improve.

5. Teachers: Play memory games: (1) In Grandmother's Trunk . . . (2) My ship has come from China. What was it loaded with? It was loaded with . . . Each player adds an item: Player 1, an item beginning with *A*; Player 2, an item beginning with *B*, etc.

6. Teachers: Play *Bingo* using number of hand claps for numbers. (Alternate: rings from tone bells.)

7. Teachers: Have students list occupations where auditory memory is essential. (Examples: Actor—remembering lines/remembering cues; secretary—remembering directions; doctor—remembering patients' symptoms; nurse—remembering doctor's instructions; traffic controller—remembering what pilots said; singer—remembering song lyrics; psychologist—remembering patient's problems; short order cook—remembering orders; waiters—remembering orders; cocktail waitress—remembering orders; reporter—remembering facts; speech therapist—remembering sounds; telephone operator—remembering telephone numbers.)

8. Teachers: Make class poems from lists of students' favorite sounds and from sounds they don't like.

9. Teachers: Play "Waiter" or "Short Order Cook." See who can remember the most orders for the most number of people.

10. Teachers: Give oral directions for students to do things (move around the room, get something, etc.). Start with one direction; increase to three or as many as they can handle.

11. Teachers: Each day ask a student to be responsible for remembering instructions to tell absent students.

12. Teachers: Ask students to make a list of words they simply have trouble remembering how to pronounce. (Examples: *statistics, problem*.) Have a class discussion where the group gives suggestions or the person thinks of ways to remember the pronunciation. Keep the lists current. Add new words and delete the ones that no longer cause difficulties.

AUDITORY CLOSURE SKILLS

Sample Activities for Discussion, Task Cards, Learning Centers, and Reading Contracts

1. Complete this jingle. Winston tastes good, _____.
2. This is the last broadcast from a ship. The ship is overdue. What could the message mean? ____ ____ ____ waves are ____ ____ ____ ____ high ____ ____ ____ Captain ____ ____ ____ all ____ ____ ____ ____.
3. How many words can you think of that begin with *ch*?
4. Teachers: Have a student use a toy (or pretend) telephone to carry on a one-sided conversation. The other students try to guess who is on the other end and what he said.
5. Teachers: Teach students new song lyrics by handing them a sheet that contains a few words interspersed among blanks. Ask them to listen and fill in the blanks. (Example: Lou, ____. ____ to my ____, etc.)
6. Teachers: Play *Name That Tune* with the class.
7. Teachers: Ask students to list occupations where incomplete messages are common. (Examples: Auctioneer; secretary—when the boss says, "Etc., etc., etc." while dictating; information operator; spy; detective; team of song writers; teachers; doctor; psychiatrist; announcer.)
8. Teachers: Give students opportunities to experiment with a voice-activated microphone similar to those used in space exploration.
9. Teachers: Commercials often make use of the principle of auditory closure. Have the students make a collection of examples.

AUDITORY PITCH, TIMBRE, STRESS, AND INTONATION SKILLS

Sample Activities for Discussion, Task Cards, Learning Centers, and Reading Contracts

1. Listen to regional speech patterns. How are words pronounced differently in other parts of the country?
2. Tape-record new students in your school who have a different accent. See if you can make a regional summary of pronunciation differences. Remember, they may be shy.
3. How do you think the voice of the main character in the story would sound?
4. Try to imitate the voices of famous people or of classmates. Tape-record your try. Listen, then tape-record again. Continue until you have a good imitation. It may help if you can listen to a recording of the person whose voice you are trying to imitate.
5. Why would voice pitch, timbre, stress, and intonation be important in these occupations: Musician? Speech Therapist? Translator? Psychiatrist?
6. Teachers: Play "Echo." The teacher says a sentence using a certain pitch, stress, or tone; the students imitate him or her.

AUDITORY SEQUENCING SKILLS

Sample Activities for Discussion, Task Cards, Learning Centers, and Reading Contracts

1. Teachers: Record a sequence of sounds. Have students tell or write a story using the sound effects in exact sequence.
2. Teachers: Play a game using a series of auditory directions. Examples: (a) Walk to the door, turn around three times, and clap your hands. (b) Count all the buttons on your clothes, hop on your right foot to the nearest person, and tell him or her the number. (c) Find a book with a yellow cover and tell us the author's name. Begin slowly and, as the class improves, increase the speed and number of directions.

3. Teachers: Tap the rhythm of a familiar poem. See who can remember it.
4. Teachers: Use resonator bells and a die to write the music for a song. Assign numbers to tones from lowest to highest. Roll the die to get the sequence of the tune.

AUDITORY BLENDING SKILLS

Sample Activities for Discussion, Task Cards, Learning Centers, and Reading Contracts

1. Teachers: Set up a rebus learning center where students can solve rebus puzzles, read rebus books, and work with rebus puzzle books. Ask students to make up rebus puzzles of their own.
2. Teachers: Play *Concentration* with the group, including the rebus component.
3. Teachers: Play *Name That Tune*, where song melodies are played a note at a time.
4. Teachers: Spell out unfamiliar words in a sort of chant or school yell mode.
5. Teachers: Give each student a sign with one letter of a word. Have them line up in correct order, left to right, and give the sounds they represent in order, faster and faster, until the word is said correctly.
6. Teachers: Play whisper or lip reading games where students try to figure out the mystery word.

AUDITORY DISCRIMINATION SKILLS

Sample Activities for Discussion, Task Cards, Learning Centers, and Reading Contracts

1. Be an impersonator. Listen to famous people (singers, actors, politicians) or to your classmates. See who can sound the most like the person imitated.
2. Teachers: Play the "Sound-Riddle" game. Have the students put their heads down, and see if they can identify common sounds such as cutting paper, pouring water, jingling coins, and the like. (Alternate: Tape the sounds.)
3. Teachers: Give a consonant. Have the students raise their hands each time they hear it in a group of words. (Alternate: Count the number of times silently.)

4. Teachers: Have students draw from a stack a card with a picture on it that can be identified with a certain sound. Then make the noise while the other students try to guess the picture (a train, an animal, etc.).

5. Teachers: Experiment with students with sound effects to try to produce the sound of a fire, a horse, etc. Whoever is able to duplicate the sound most closely records the instructions in a class sound book.

6. Teachers: Experiment with an echo chamber attachment on a tape recorder or other microphone.

7. Teachers: Let students experience the difference in time between speaking and hearing the sound when using a public address system.

8. Teachers: Use a set of tone bells for a learning center. (Alternate: an autoharp.)

9. Teachers: Play bird call records to see which students can learn to identify the sounds.

10. Teachers: Play "Who Am I?" One student is *It* and hides his or her head. Another student disguises his or her voice and asks, "Who Am I?" The student who is *It* has three guesses. If *It* guesses correctly, he or she gets to be *It* again. If not, the student who disguised his or her voice becomes *It*. (Alternates: Ask students to put their heads down or close their eyes. One student reads a short selection aloud. The others try to guess who read it. Or tape-record beforehand so the students won't be able to tell who it is by speaker movements or location.)

11. Teachers: Drop a number of pennies in a pie pan. See who can give you the exact number dropped.

12. Teachers: Tape two pie tins together with a certain number of dried beans inside. Have students tape two others together with enough beans to match the sound. (Alternate: use jars.)

AUDITORY COMPREHENSION SKILLS

Sample Activities for Discussion, Task Cards, Learning Centers, and Reading Contracts

1. Teachers: Read a story aloud to students. Ask questions to check their understanding.

2. Teachers: Have students share puns that depend on auditory similarities.
3. Teachers: Work with students on *Sound Groupings*. Assign individuals or groups sounds to record; e.g., winter sounds, school sounds, home sounds, highway sounds, etc. Have them share with the rest of the class.
4. Teachers: Using a tape of animal sounds, have the class guess what each sound is.
5. Teachers: Have students tell a story using only sounds.
6. Teachers: While the teacher (or a student) reads a story, have students dramatize it with their hands (or pantomime it).
7. Teachers: Give the students scrambled oral sentences to try to put into correct order after hearing them once.
8. Teachers: Ask someone you know who speaks a foreign language to talk to the class in that language for twenty minutes or so. How did the class members feel? What did they learn about how it feels not to understand a speaker?
9. Teachers: Tell students that you will draw exactly what they tell you on the chalkboard, one part at a time. See who can guess first what the student or side who is *It* is trying to have you draw.
10. Teachers: Divide students into teams that will direct a student from another team to do something. That student can do only what is said (for example, walk across a room) in the sequence given. The student's team tries to spot mistakes the other team makes in giving directions.
11. Teachers: Have students close their eyes. Write a letter on the chalkboard. See who can identify the letter only by the sounds of writing. (Alternates: drop an object on the floor.)
12. Teachers: Dial a telephone number. See who can tell you what you dialed. Students should have their eyes closed in this exercise.
13. Teachers: Discuss with the students occupations where workers' ears have to be protected. (Airline maintenance crews, etc.)
14. Teachers: Blindfold a student. Have other students give him or her directions for finding an object. See what happens.
15. Teachers: Play *What's My Line* featuring parents of students

from other classes, school district personnel, or local business people.

16. Teachers: Divide students into groups. Supply each group with a tape recorder. Have them record as many different sounds as possible around the school. Share each group's tape, seeing if the members of the other groups can identify the sounds.

17. Teachers: Ask students questions about sound, such as: What are pleasing sounds? Unpleasant? Softest? Loudest? Most unfortunate? Etc.

18. Teachers: Ask students to identify each story character with a particular sound. See if classmates can identify the character from that sound. (Alternate: Have individuals or groups compose a short musical theme for each story character, similar to the themes for characters played in the musical score of a movie or TV show whenever a certain character appears.)

AUDITORY TRACKING SKILLS

Sample Activities for Discussion, Task Cards, Learning Centers, and Reading Contracts

1. Teachers: Hide a buzzer or tape recorder someplace in the room. Leave it on. See if students can locate it by sound.

2. Teachers: Play "Where Is It?" with the students. Have one person be *It* and close his or her eyes. Ring a bell. The student who is *It* has to point to the direction the sound is coming from. (Alternate: Play "Find The Cow." Blindfold one player. Another has a bell and runs around inside a circle formed by the rest of the class. The blindfolded player has to "catch the cow." An easier version is for the "cow" to remain stationary.)

3. Teachers: Have students hide their eyes and point to where you are as you move about the room.

4. Teachers: Have students close their eyes. Choose students to read the character parts of a story or a play. Station each actor in a different area in the classroom.

5. Teachers: Move about as you give instructions for assignments.

6. Teachers: Have students experiment with recording sounds, music, or oral reading on stereo tape recorders.
7. Teachers: Play stereo records and discuss with the students where the various instruments seem to be located. Leave off first one track and then another. Discuss differences in sound.

LISTENING SKILLS

Sample Activities for Discussion, Task Cards, Learning Centers, and Reading Contracts

1. Some people enjoy listening to a story being read aloud as they drive on long distance trips. What story would you enjoy hearing in this way?
2. Listen for a moment with your eyes closed, to all the sounds in the classroom. What did you hear?
3. Later today we will play a listening game. Be alert all day for sounds you can make that will fool the others when they try to guess what the sounds are with their eyes closed.
4. Make rattles or other sound devices to use as rhythm instruments.
5. Look up directions for string and tin can telephones. Make some for us to use in the classroom. Choose people to help you if you need them.
6. Keep a listening diary of interesting sounds or of your progress as a listener.
7. Make a report on noise pollution in our school.
8. Listen to a classmate's problem. Tell him or her what you think was said. Check to see if you heard correctly.
9. Teachers: Play "Where Am I?" One student describes a setting verbally, and the other students try to guess where he/she is.
10. Teachers: Have students listen to tape recordings or record a favorite book. Note inflections to establish characterization.
11. Teachers: Audition students for the voice that sounds most like each story character. Have a panel of students rate all tryouts.

ORAL LANGUAGE SKILLS

Sample Activities for Discussion, Task Cards, Learning Centers, and Reading Contracts

1. Teachers: Make a tape for parents to hear for Open House by having each student discuss some classroom work that he or she is interested in, or record some classroom work project. Retape if some students want to correct their mistakes.

2. Teachers: Experiment with the students on different methods for giving a speech; e.g., with a podium, with illustrations, with a chalkboard, with slides, with listener participation. Discuss personal preferences.

3. Teachers: Have students write anonymous questions on topics that they want the class to discuss. Schedule a discussion time for each question.

4. Teachers: Make up a collection of pictures to illustrate consonants, consonant blends, and digraphs to check sounds that students cannot perceive and/or articulate.

5. Teachers: Ask students to decide what famous speeches they wish they had made.

6. Teachers: Have students write a speech for a story character to deliver. Where would the speech be made and to whom?

7. Teachers: Have a student lecture bureau, using students in the classroom to talk to other grade levels about their interests, their studies, travel, etc.

8. Teachers: Set up a cassette center where students can record stories, conversations, poems, songs, etc.

9. Teachers: Have a telephone dramatization lesson. Students draw situation cards and make a telephone call based on the description.

10. Teachers: Ask one student to describe an object, while the rest of the students try to draw what the object is.

11. Teachers: Ask one student to be ready to tell absent students what they missed and give them the directions they need to catch up.

12. Teachers: When scheduling guest speakers, have a discussion beforehand to decide on pertinent questions.

13. Teachers: Tape a class discussion and critique it later with the students involved.

A FINAL WORD ABOUT AUDITORY PERCEPTION

There are many ways that good auditory perception skills help students read better. Auditory perception helps students read new words more easily through phonological (or sound) cues; adds life to dialogue passages through pitch, stress, and intonation sound patterns; and provides an auditory flow to the reading of good writing that is pleasurable to experience. This flow is not simply subvocal speech, but a ring, a feel, a stream of elegant word usage that partially (perhaps wholly) stems from good auditory awareness. Most of all, however, good auditory perception skills enhance students' visualizations or imageries of story characters, actions, and backgrounds when auditory imagery of speech patterns, background noise, and sound effects are a part of the imagined scene.

8

Visual Perception Skills

* * * * * * * * * * * *

Reading is essentially a visual experience in that in reading we take in a visual pattern and make it meaningful to us. At the base of this process is visual perception—not mere seeing, as such, but the perceiving of the symbol, adding our own individual meaning components, and sifting our thoughts through those of the author's to complete a creative act called reading. These visual symbols have the power, through this combining of author-reader thoughts and experiences, of literally changing our lives, the way we believe, think, act, cook, relate, feel. Each page we read may contain information that will turn our world around. Consequently, good perception of these visual symbols is of vast importance to us.

These acts of visual perception can range from the simplest recognition of small differences in written symbols (*m* and *n*, for example) through an experienced reader's taking in of whole words or phrases and, for the most capable readers, of whole pages at a time as they read.

VISUAL COMPREHENSION SKILLS

Sample Activities for Discussion, Task Cards, Learning Centers, and Reading Contracts

1. Teachers: Use highway signs to teach younger students that they can already read. Teach older students in a driver's test format. (Alternate: Use labels from familiar products.)

2. Teachers: Have the students work for a few moments either with their eyes closed or blindfolded. Talk about the experience.

3. Teachers: Hold discussions of how different people see different things in the environment. Share a picture or a photograph. Discuss what a diver would see in it. A mother? A three-year-old? A teacher? A student? Etc. Do the same with views from the classroom windows, scenes on the playground, etc.

4. Teachers: Hold up a picture. Have everyone write down what he or she sees in the picture. Compare similarities and differences in perception, what was seen first by whom, what some saw that others didn't, etc.

5. Teachers: Play an eyeglasses game. Have students cut out and decorate frames for eyeglasses for various ways people can look at the world. (Examples: Eyeglasses for rose-colored viewing, for put-down, for nervous sight, for blinded-by-love sight, for can't-see-the-forest-for-the-trees viewing, for jumping-to-conclusions, etc.)

6. Teachers: Real aloud to your students while they have their eyes closed. Discuss the experience.

7. Teachers: Ask your students to think of different ways a cartoonist might show motion, anger, surprise, winter, excitement, happiness, hunger, etc.

VISUAL FIGURE-GROUND SKILLS

Sample Activities for Discussion, Task Cards, Learning Centers, and Reading Contracts

1. Teachers: Ask students to see how many ways they can hide triangles in their drawings. Can anyone else find them? (Alternate figures: circle, square, rectangle, heads, animals.)

2. Teachers: Have students write the alphabet using only circles, straight lines, and parts of circles.

3. Teachers: Have students hide printed words or letters of the alphabet in a picture they draw.

4. Teachers: Have students make words look like what they mean; e.g., rain:

```
r a i n
, , , ,
, , , ,
, , , ,
, , , ,
```

5. Teachers: Play *Word Dominoes*: With a partner, students write a word horizontally. Each person can add two letters at a time, but must complete another word; e.g.,

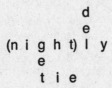

```
          d
          e
(n i g h t) l  y
          e
       t i e
```

6. Teachers: Play "Add A Letter." Start with a vowel. Each player can add one letter and it must make another complete word; e.g., a at hat that that's . . . (Variation: Add a letter, but rearrange the letters if desired.)
7. Teachers: Have a learning center for commercial doodle books or posters. Most of them come with a variety of colored pencils or pens.
8. Teachers: Form a Birdwatcher's Association. Keep records of individual and class finds. Provide bird identification books. (Alternates: Wildflowers Club, Archaeological Society.)
9. Teachers: Have children look at a picture to see how many times they see a specific color.
10. Teachers: Take walks to look for specific colors; e.g., red; or specific shapes.
11. Teachers: Have students write a paragraph that includes the names of five books hidden in it. See who can find them. Do not capitalize the words.
12. Teachers: Use word hunt exercises and books as a learning center.
13. Teachers: Have students roll a piece of paper into a tube or telescope and use it to find something interesting to draw.

14. Teachers: Have students look through a camera lens using various sizes of lenses and describe or draw the differences they see.
15. Teachers: Set up a maze center featuring maze books.
16. Teachers: Play "Alphabet Creatures." Have students make some kind of creature from a letter of the alphabet.
17. Teachers: Have a police officer talk to the class about what officers look for on foot or car patrol.
18. Teachers: Get several versions of what happened at any event at school—assemblies, visitors, accidents, etc. Discuss how all versions could be true.
19. Teachers: Have word hunts on a page of a book. See who can count all the *the's*, for instance, in the quickest time.
20. Teachers: Have a tachistoscope or film strip projector with a timing mechanism set up as a learning center for students to use for experimentation.
21. Teachers: Invite representatives from various speed reading firms to talk to the class.
22. Teachers: Give students two paragraphs on different topics set together so every other line continues one of the paragraphs. Set each paragraph in a different style type. Example:

> "Come into the house," he
> *It was cold that day, and*
> said in a friendly tone." I
> *she planned to make popcorn.*

23. Teachers: Ask students to write down how many times they find a certain word on a page.
24. Teachers: Stock a learning center with books similar to Joan Loss' *What Is It?*, a book of photographic puzzles.

VISUAL MEMORY SKILLS

Sample Activities for Discussion, Task Cards, Learning Centers, and Reading Contracts

1. Teachers: Prepare charts similar to the following. Use a different word and a different picture in each box as indicated. Ask students to look at the chart silently for one minute. Have them recall as many items as possible. How many words did they recall? How many pictures? Is it easier to remember words or pictures? What part of the

chart did they forget? (left hand, right corner?) What part of the chart did they remember? How many items can they recall the next day? Can the students remember the exact location of any words? Any pictures? Make the chart contain more or fewer items according to class or individual memory capacities. Use similar charts for mystery games, detective games, police clue games, etc.

(picture)	(word)	(picture)	(word)
(word)	(picture)	(word)	(picture)
(picture)	(word)	(picture)	(word)
(word)	(picture)	(word)	(picture)

2. Teachers: Stage a dramatized event in the classroom. Videotape the dramatization. Ask each student to write down what happened. Compare perceptions with the videotape.

3. Teachers: Have either a regular or a three dimensional *Scrabble* learning center.

4. Teachers: Give students five letters at random from the alphabet. See how many words they can make. (Alternate: List five random letters at a learning center. Have students individually try to make as many words from the letters as possible. Do not share until all have a chance. Comment on differences, unusual words, likenesses, etc.)

5. Teachers: Play *Concentration* with pairs of objects on cards. All cards are turned face down. A turn permits a student to turn up two cards; the object is to turn up a pair. (Authors, words, pictures, letters, etc.) (Alternate: Play *Concentration* with a deck of cards; the object is to turn up two of a kind. These are removed as they are matched.)

6. Teachers: Place students in pairs. Have part of the class draw the face of their partner from memory after looking at the partner for ten seconds; have the rest of the partners draw as they look at the person. Talk about what they saw when they weren't looking and when they were. (Alternate: Same person does both.)

7. Teachers: Help the class set up a slide show to share a class project with parents or others. Use a timing device on at least one projector. Set up several projectors. Use other audio-visual equipment. Run all the machines simulta-

neously. Check the effects. Revise until the class members are satisfied, then share.

8. Teachers: Use a series of flash cards. Start with one numeral on each card. Increase to as many as possible. Flash each card for a moment, hide it, ask students to tell you what was on it. Students can work in pairs at this. (Alternates: letters of the alphabet in random sequence, shapes, etc.)

9. Teachers: Have students visualize new words by closing their eyes, seeing the word, first letter by letter in left to right sequence, then again as a whole.

10. Teachers: Show a picture. Cover up part of it. Have students recall what you covered up.

11. Teachers: Have students close their eyes and answer questions about the classroom and their classmates. Examples: What color shirt does Richard have on today? What is in the window? Who is wearing a blue dress today? Etc.

12. Teachers: Make silhouettes of prominent local or national landmarks. See who can identify them.

VISUAL CLOSURE SKILLS

Sample Activities for Discussion, Task Cards, Learning Centers, and Reading Contracts

1. Sometimes when we try to do something, we can appreciate what other people do even more. Draw a tree. (Teachers: Give time to draw a tree. Next, share with students prints showing trees drawn by various artists.) How did the artist make his or her tree? Did any of the artists solve his or her problem in the same way someone in our class did? Do you want to add to your drawing?

2. Teachers: Have students find, take, or draw a picture which could serve as an illustration for the cover of the book they are reading. Have them explain their choice.

3. Teachers: Have a typewriter center for student use (combining motor skills and visual closure).

4. Teachers: Have students dictate stories to an aide, an older student, or a teacher to type. Have them watch the typing process.

5. Teachers: Ask students how artists suggest possibilities in their pictures without actually painting them. Show a

painting. Sample questions: How do you know the sun is shining? What is the weather like? What kind of climate is this? How do you know? What is the oldest thing in the picture? What season is it? How do you know people live here? What do you think is on the other side of the hill? How does the person in the painting feel?

6. Teachers: Cut a sentence or word in half horizontally. Given only the top part, can anyone tell what the word(s) say? Given only the bottom half? How many other word(s) could this part be? (Alternate: Cut apart diagonally.)

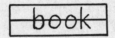

7. Teachers: Provide a box of felt scraps, scraps of construction paper, or cloth remnants. Give directions for making pictures using the scraps. Examples: Make a person. Make a landscape.

8. Teachers: Set up a center featuring books that show a small magnified portion of a picture that lets the reader guess what it is (insect eyes, cross sections of fruit, etc.). The local library can supply current books of this type.

9. Teachers: Play *Hangman* using the names of authors, famous books, and/or literary quotations.

10. Teachers: Make a squiggle on the chalkboard or duplicate it on enough sheets of paper so every class member can have one. See how many ways they can use the squiggle in a drawing.

11. Teachers: Cover up all but a part of a picture. Ask students to tell or write about or draw in the remainder of the picture. Compare differences in perception.

VISUAL SEQUENCE SKILLS

Sample Activities for Discussion, Task Cards, Learning Centers, and Reading Contracts

1. Teachers: Dramatize an event in the classroom or have groups of children stage an improvised event. Videotape the dramatization. Ask children to list the sequence of

events. Compare with the video recording. Compare with each other's reports.

2. Teachers: Have students do exercises similar to this: Unscramble these words: (a) a t i v o c n a; (b) l y p i c o m; (c) s t e b; (d) l n y o.

3. Teachers: Make up lists of scrambled titles, authors, and/or quotations from literary sources and use as individual or team games.

4. Teachers: Have students: (a) choose a macramé project to make, (b) use a crochet pattern to make a gift for someone (maybe themselves?), (c) make an afghan from knitted squares, or (d) design an argyle sock pattern.

5. Teachers: At the jewelry learning center, have students make a beaded necklace or bracelet using one of the patterns.

6. Teachers: Have students work "follow the dots" puzzles in the puzzle center.

7. Teachers: Have students study the front page of a newspaper or a page of a magazine for thirty seconds. At the end of that time, have them tell or make a drawing of exactly where on the page every picture, word, graph, chart, etc., was. Use as a contest if you wish, with one point for every correct item.

8. Teachers: Have students proofread their own writing, stories classmates wrote, newspaper pages, and the like.

FORM CONSTANCY SKILLS

Sample Activities for Discussion, Task Cards, Learning Centers, and Reading Contracts

1. Teachers: Have a jigsaw puzzle center. Use a 500-or more piece puzzle. When students are finished, supply another. (Note: This gives the teacher a good look at working style, especially for those children who are persistent.) Also use jigsaw puzzles of photographs of classroom scenes or children's drawings.

2. Teachers: Have a classroom printing center where the class can set up stories on typesetting kits.

3. Teachers: Set up a paper doll learning center where children can: (a) cut out and place clothes for each doll in separate compartments; or (b) design costumes for each

paper doll. (Alternate: A similar design center for small dolls; e.g., G.I. Joe, Barbie, etc.)

4. Teachers: Set up a typewriting center. Include practice forms, books on how to learn typing. Perhaps a parent or other employed person who uses typing in his/her work could be a guest speaker or instructor.

5. Teachers: Make Shape Books (where cover and pages are the same shape as the title.) Examples: Easter egg books, train books, self portraits for *All About Me* books, etc.

6. Teachers: Have students make birds-eye pictures of their homes, their rooms, or of the classroom.

7. Teachers: See how many different things students can make from a basic shape such as a square, a triangle, etc.

8. Teachers: Set up a copying center where students may copy poems, recipes, etc., in their best handwriting. Supply a variety of papers, pencils, and pens.

9. Teachers: Ask students to circle or copy a word as many times as they can find it on a page.

10. Teachers: Supply books that are written in various types of print for the library table.

11. Teachers: For younger students, have a center with various size jars and lids. The student tries to match lid and jar by sight, then checks by screwing the lids on.

12. Teachers: Set up a learning center featuring books on optical illusions. Have students collect samples of optical illusions or invent some.

13. Teachers: Have students choose two people who are the same height, the same size, or the same weight. Verify their choices by measuring.

FORM PERCEPTION SKILLS

Sample Activities for Discussion, Task Cards, Learning Centers, and Reading Contracts

1. Teachers: Give students pictures of exteriors of houses. Ask them to draw a floor plan that would fit the exterior.

2. Teachers: Give students practice reading an eye chart or with the eye examination equipment at the Department of Motor Vehicles.

3. Teachers: Start a coin or stamp collectors' club where students learn to spot and identify various coins and stamps.

4. Teachers: Have students look up the names of various geometric figures, make each shape, and label them correctly, including the three dimensional shapes.
5. Teachers: Play *Bingo* with numerals, letters of the alphabet, geometric forms, etc.
6. Teachers: Have children identify letters of the alphabet that are upper case, lower case, lying on their side, upside down, and the like. Have children find letters of the alphabet that make different letters upside down or reversed.
7. Teachers: Ask students to make up stories about ink blots.

VISUAL DISCRIMINATION SKILLS

Sample Activities for Discussion, Task Cards, Learning Centers, and Reading Contracts

1. Teachers: Use paint sample cards or chips from hardware stores or house painting suppliers to: (a) Cut apart and see if the students can match pairs of hues of the same color. (b) Cut apart varying hues of the same color. See if students can put them in order, lightest to darkest. (c) Cut apart samples of hues of several colors. See if children can match values (same degree of lightness and darkness.)
2. Teachers: Help children make their kaleidoscope by taking one apart and reproducing it.
3. Teachers: Jewelers have to remember very small differences in color and size of diamonds and other precious stones. Have students try to separate beads by size and tiny differences in color.
4. Teachers: Set up a viewing center. Include a viewmaster, different kaleidoscopes, microscopes, magnifying glasses, telescopes, prisms, light sources, etc., for experimentation.
5. Teachers: Play identification games with silhouettes of all the students in the class. (Alternates: Car, animal, airplane silhouettes.)
6. Teachers: Have younger students match duplicate sets of names of class members, middle grade students be postman to deliver class-written communications, and older students practice calligraphy of various kinds using students' names.
7. Teachers: Have students copy a design or a plan they are

making for a project from a book to give them practice in getting details exact.

8. Teachers: Show students one shade of a color (use construction paper or paint samples). Then show them the same shade along with several shades of the same color. See who can pick out the shade.

9. Teachers: Have students collect examples of minimal pairs (two words which are different phonemically in one sound only) from their reading for a "Minimal Fair" or for a scrapbook. (Examples: initial position, bee–see; medial position, rack–rock; final position, cap–cat.)

VISUALIZATION OR IMAGERY SKILLS

Sample Activities for Discussion, Task Cards, Learning Centers, and Reading Contracts

1. Draw the following from memory. Check to see what details you included and which you forgot: The classroom clock. The front of your home. A car. The front page of a paper. A magazine cover.
2. Play "What Letter Is It?" Describe an alphabet letter or word orally. See who can guess it. (Alternate: The one who guesses it gets to describe another.)
3. Pretend to be a vowel or consonant. Tell: How you would feel if no one knew you? How you would feel if boys and girls recognized you right away?
4. On Halloween, decide what would be appropriate "new" names for each classmate to have to match his or her costume.
5. Prepare a hand shadow play to present to the class.
6. Make a booklet of how to do hand shadow pictures. Invent some new ones yourself.
7. Write a description of how you see the main female and the main male character in your story. Check your description with that of other classmates. (Alternate: Describe the house a story character lives in.)
8. Of all the settings for stories you have ever read, which one would you most like to live in?
9. Of all the characters or people you have ever read about, which one would you rather be? Which ones are most like

you? Which story character had similar problems to your own? Would their solutions work for you?

10. What words in the story helped you to see the happenings in your head?

11. If you were some kind of weather, what kind would you be? Animal? Water?

12. When you daydream, how are you different from what you are in everyday life?

13. Which books have made you a better person? Explain.

14. Teachers: Read an unfamiliar passage aloud. Ask students to visualize what the words make them see. Share differences in perception aloud.

15. Teachers: Have students describe or draw what they picture in their minds when they hear a certain word.

16. Teachers: Ask students to visualize how an object would look if part of it were replaced by part of another.

17. Teachers: Ask students to visualize and describe how the classroom would look to them if they were as small as an ant, as large as an elephant, or as fat as a rhinoceros.

18. Teachers: Ask students to visualize the actions in a particular story. Have them share their images. Comment on differences in perception.

VISUAL TRACKING SKILLS

Sample Activities for Discussion, Task Cards, Learning Centers, and Reading Contracts

1. Teachers: Stand with your back to the class. Draw a letter, a numeral, or a word in the air. See who can guess what you wrote.

2. Teachers: Have a ping pong tournament with side seating for spectators. Ask class members to watch a pendulum swing, a tetherball game, or the like.

3. Teachers: Have students make a list of twenty-five interesting signs they see on a weekend trip.

4. Teachers: Take the class outside to watch birds, butterflies, moths, etc., in season.

5. Teachers: Ask the class to make tubes of paper and look through them at an object. Have them make note of which eye sees the object best.

6. Teachers: Have a target game with moving targets and suction darts or a race car game for a learning center.
7. Teachers: Have students practice following a discussion with their eyes; that is, look at the various speakers as the conversational "ball" shifts from person to person.

EYE MOVEMENT SKILLS

Sample Activities for Discussion, Task Cards, Learning Centers, and Reading Contracts

1. Teachers: Use a tachistoscope, a timer on a slide projector, a slot in a card, or flash cards shown briefly to speed up eye movements. Start with small words, increase to phrases, sentences, and short excerpts. Have students record their weekly increases in the number of words they can read at a specific speed.
2. Teachers: Ask a student to estimate how fast he or she can read a page and still answer correctly five out of seven questions on the material it contains.
3. Teachers: Ask students to hunt for a specific word or item on a newspaper page.

LEFT-TO-RIGHT EYE MOVEMENT SKILLS

Sample Activities for Discussion, Task Cards, Learning Centers, and Reading Contracts

1. Teachers: Make a grid of random alphabet letters. Ask students to cross out all the *e*'s as they come to them in left-to-right sequence. (Alternates: Cross out the alphabet in order, the vowels, the letters in the student's name.)
2. Teachers: Allow certain students, who seem to need it, to use a marker or their finger as they read.
3. Teachers: Hold contests to see how fast students can turn pages (not skipping a page) in left-to-right sequence.
4. Teachers: Ask an optician, opthalmologist, or other eye specialist to bring some of his equipment to school.
5. Teachers: Set up a controlled reader as a learning center for student experimentation.
6. Teachers: Have student observers (perhaps under the direction of a particularly astute school nurse) take notes on the eye movements during reading of student volunteers.

7. Teachers: Videotape a closeup of students' eye movements while reading. Share them in the class.

A FINAL WORD ABOUT VISUAL PERCEPTION

To be able to see a written code is a long way from understanding that code. You can make your students' reading tasks easier, no matter what grade level you teach, by helping them understand the importance of attaching meaning to reading symbols, by giving students plenty of chances to discuss their varying perceptions of what they see, and by helping these students realize that perceptual truths come in a variety of packages. Be sure, also, to allot plenty of time to discussions about students' perceptions and visual images for each new vocabulary word or reading selection they encounter. This creation of a world of images inside their heads, cued by what they read, is one of the most important reasons for stressing visual perception in a reading program. If young readers can become so proficient that this visual cueing of meaning, images, and concepts behind what they read springs to mind spontaneously, their attention can then focus on content, ideas, and feelings on a page—the real reason for reading.

9

Perception Skills

★★★★★★★★★★★★

To perceive is to bring all our senses into focus on a concept, a thing, an object, an idea, a problem, or the like; to interpret or give meaning to what becomes important to our awareness. And forever after, our perceptions of that event, person, or object are colored by our particular perceptive state at the time we first met it. The way we perceive something is the way we learn about, understand, or remember it.

It is, therefore, most important to establish a classroom climate that encourages students to use all their senses in learning so that they will develop rich images and abundant sensory feel for the words they read. To feel the meaning of a word or a concept with our body is about as deep as meaning (and learning) can get.

OLFACTORY PERCEPTION SKILLS

**Sample Activities for Discussion, Task Cards,
Learning Centers, or Reading Contracts**

1. Find a picture of something that smells good to you.
2. Look at a picture in a book. Imagine you could smell everything pictured. Describe the smells.
3. Think of something that would smell sweet, pungent, sharp, calming, happy, etc.
4. In olden days, people used to carry smelling salts and pomanders. What are these? Do we have anything equivalent today?
5. Close your eyes for a few minutes. Open them and make a list of all the smells you smelled.

6. What are the smells you associate with our classroom? The beach? The movies? A car? The dentist's? A bakery? Your favorite story? Etc.

7. Set up a perfume sample shop using bottles that you (and some friends who want to work with you) can get. (Write to perfume manufacturers for samples. Collect leftover bottles from friends, etc.)

8. Hold a toothpaste identifying contest and see who can identify the most toothpastes by smell alone. (Alternates: Foods, perfumes.)

9. Used car dealers have a spray they can use to make old cars smell new. See if you can get a sample. Collect other examples of industrial or sales use of smell.

10. Teachers: Set up a learning center with scratch-and-smell books.

11. Teachers: Hide something that smells good (cookies, perfume, etc.) somewhere in the room. Students must find it by smell alone.

12. Teachers: Have students match by smell two identical groups of fruit extracts. Cover the bottles so coloring doesn't become a factor. Have students compare the smells of fruit extracts with the smells of actual fruits.

13. Teachers: Play "Who Is This?" See if students can identify others by smell alone.

TASTE PERCEPTION SKILLS

Sample Activities for Discussion, Task Cards, Learning Centers, and Reading Contracts

1. Teachers: As a class project, bake cookie alphabets and words. (Students get to eat those they can read. Make sure all get about the same amount.)

2. Teachers: Have students estimate the amount of popped or unpopped popcorn kernels in a glass container. Students get to pop and eat the corn.

3. Teachers: Set up a cooking center: to taste-test different recipes; to invent new recipes; to share family recipes.

4. Teachers: Set up a food center, featuring simple snacks; e.g., peanuts, crackers, fruits. Arrange schedules for serving, hygiene, cleanup, etc. (Especially good in areas where students may come to school hungry.)

5. Teachers: Have a snack tree where children may pick off snacks as rewards for work well done or just for fun.
6. Teachers: Have half the class make peanut butter cookies from one recipe and compare them with the cookies made by the other half of the class using another recipe. (Alternate: Homemade vs. store-bought ice cream.)
7. Teachers: Have a compound tasting day, where students bring foods that are compound words. (Examples: Popcorn, applesauce.)
8. Teachers: Do fingerpainting or creative writing with pudding.
9. Teachers: Teach new words by having students make candy mosaics of them or write them with cheese tubes on crackers, frosting tubes on a cupcake, or out of cookie dough in tubes.
10. Teachers: Make a class A B C book of favorite foods or recipes.
11. Teachers: Have students draw maps of their tongues and locate where they would taste candy, honey, salt, etc.
12. Teachers: Have students investigate and record which foods change form when they are heated or chilled. Make a list and record the changes.
13. Teachers: Have a favorite treat day when each student brings in and shares his or her favorite taste sensations.

TACTILE PERCEPTION SKILLS

Sample Activities for Discussion, Task Cards, Learning Centers, and Reading Contracts

1. Teachers: Have a sandbox center for writing alphabetic letters, words, doodles, longer passages, and the like. (Alternate: Have each child make an individual sand tray.)
2. Teachers: Have a touch-and-feel box of items with special tactile elements; e.g., smooth, rough, soft, wet.
3. Teachers: Play "Who Is This?" A student is asked to close his or her eyes and guess who another child is by touch alone.
4. Teachers: Give a student a yardstick. Blindfold him or her and have two other students walk on either side for safety. Most children can begin to hear the changes in tapping

sounds when near objects and change course to avoid them in 20-40 minutes.

5. Teachers: Play "What Is This?" Put an object behind a student. He or she can only feel it. How soon can he or she identify the object?

6. Teachers: Have a blackboard center where students can write and erase.

7. Teachers: Have students fingerpaint words, letters, and paintings in pudding.

8. Teachers: Have students look carefully at an object, a wall, or a person's face or hand; next, close their eyes and touch it. See if touching makes them aware of something they hadn't known from just looking.

9. Teachers: Have students feel various objects (paper, cardboard, etc.) and match thicknesses with their eyes closed.

10. Teachers: Have students feel various objects and match textures through touch alone.

11. Teachers: Have the room environment full of tactile experiences: depending on age level, include stuffed toys, rugs to lie on as students read, a "barefoot" corner where shoes may be taken off, overstuffed furniture, and the like.

12. Teachers: Use kinesthetic materials for practicing letters, words, longer passages; e.g., clay tablets, sand, sandpaper, twisters (plastic and metal strips used to seal plastic bags), velvet, plastic letters, stencils, button or seed mosaics, glue sprinkled with sand, the palm of a partner's hand, wire screen mesh letters, and fingerpainting.

13. Teachers: Have a "Need a Hug" time. Anyone who wants to can come for a hug from the teacher.

14. Teachers: Have students find pictures of something that is fuzzy, hard, etc.

15. Teachers: Use magnetic boards and letters to teach and practice word perception skills. The slight pull will add a tactile touch.

16. Teachers: Have students make toothpick designs or toothpick words.

17. Teachers: In some cultures, worry beads are used. Share some with the class and discuss other ways people use to relieve tension.

18. Teachers: Have a variety of stuffed animals for younger

children to hold as they work, if they choose. (Examples: Stuffed snake, Snoopy, etc.)

19. Teachers: Have two buckets of water of two different temperatures. See who can guess which is hotter. Check with a thermometer. Gradually bring the two temperatures closer together. (Alternate: Two buckets or other objects, one of which is heavier than the other or filled with more sand.)

20. Teachers: Talk about which members of the class prefer hot and which prefer cold days.

21. Teachers: Have students feel sound vibrations from various sources (records, TV, etc.). Use surfaces, tuning forks, guitar strings, and the like.

22. Teacher: Ask students to discuss or write about pleasant and/or unpleasant things to touch.

23. Teachers: On a push button telephone, have students practice getting a telephone number with their eyes closed.

24. Teachers: Fill the same size cans with sand so they are different weights. Have students sort them according to weight—lightest to heaviest.

25. Teachers: For younger students, have a small scale and various weights with which to experiment.

26. Teachers: Have students do fingerpainting with bare feet on large sheets of butcher paper.

MULTISENSORY PERCEPTION SKILLS

Sample Activities for Discussion, Task Cards, Learning Centers, or Reading Contracts

1. Select a sound, a color, a smell, a view, a taste, a touch, a feel, etc., for a story character. See if your classmates can identify the story character from your multisensory presentation. (Alternate: Select for the entire story or for a holiday.)

2. Find passages in your book that caused you to see something, hear something, feel something, smell something, or taste something. Share them with us.

3. Play "Imaginary Presents." Pretend you are opening an imaginary present you want very much. See who can guess what it is.

4. If you lived in a world where everyone was deaf, how would that world be different? (Alternates: Worlds where people couldn't speak, hear, see color, taste, etc.)

5. Listen to the sounds around you first with your eyes closed and then with your eyes opened. Which way can you listen better?

6. Be prepared to tell of an imaginary walk through your favorite outdoor place. Be ready to tell about the walk in such a manner that your listeners will be able to feel, smell, and experience the walk just as if they were there. (Teachers: Lead the class through a series of imaginary walks before giving this assignment.) (Alternate: Do the same for your favorite holiday.)

7. Make a collection of good "touch" words, or words that describe touch or how things feel. (Alternates: "view," "taste," "hearing," etc., words.)

8. Bring in something you love to taste, to smell, to touch, to hear, to see to share with us tomorrow.

9. Select a poem and a musical background for your part in our poetry recital day.

10. Figure out how to serve a fresh coconut. Compare it with packaged, grated coconut.

HAND-EYE COORDINATION SKILLS

Sample Activities for Discussion, Task Cards, Learning Centers, and Reading Contracts

1. Teachers: Set up a game board with a race track or car race theme. Students try out for the race by seeing how rapidly they can race their pencils (trace) along the track course in individual preliminary races. The two top winners race each other for the championship. (Alternate: Use small racing cars or plastic horses.)

2. Teachers: Use a typewriter, a label maker, dot-to-dot books, and a small print set for a learning center.

3. Teachers: Give exercises in the use of an index or a glossary, where the students need to glance back and forth and match the item in the index with the content on a page. Give students assignments where they have to work with

two or more books at once. (Examples: Compare the actions of Snow White and Cinderella. Make a list of five opening sentences from books that you particularly like, etc.)

4. Teachers: Plan activities that require hand-eye coordination. (Examples: Squeezing clay, pushing in thumb tacks, etc.)

5. Teachers: Have an origami learning center with books, papers, and directions.

GENERAL COORDINATION SKILLS

Sample Activities for Discussion, Task Cards, Learning Centers, and Reading Contracts

1. Teachers: Have students play *Follow the Leader* on playground equipment.

2. Teachers: Have students play *Charades*, the answer to which is a word, a book, an author, etc.

3. Teachers: Have students take labels of names of common classroom objects over to the object. (Primary.)

4. Teachers: Give students cards with *yes* printed on one side and *no* on the other (or two separate cards). Ask questions about the story which may be answered by yes or no. Have each child hold up the correct response.

5. Teachers: Have students practice creative dance movements including walking, jumping, running, swinging the body, stretching, bending, etc. Use this also as a break in the middle of tedious, quiet work. (Alternates: Slide, gallop, polka, slither, etc.)

6. Teachers: Play movement games involving coordination. Examples: Show one way to get from here to there. Show a slow way. A fast way. A funny way. The way a rag doll would walk. A sad way. A floating way. A flying way.

7. Teachers: Play movement games that interpret a story or reading selection. Examples: Move the way Mary did when she learned about the cat. Move the way a mad scientist would as he was creating a monster. Move the way you do when you don't want to do something.

MOTOR COORDINATION SKILLS

Sample Activities for Discussion, Task Cards, Learning Centers, or Reading Contracts

1. Suppose you landed by space ship on a world where language consisted of gestures. How would you express the following: I'm hungry; I come from far away; the name of my planet is Earth. Make up gestures for other phrases you might need to use. Act them out. See who can guess what you said.

2. In a darkened classroom, use a flashlight to write a word you are learning.

3. Prepare a dramatization of your story.

4. Be ready to do a pantomime of any of the following: Walking to school in the rain, buying new shoes, driving a car, helping clean the house, or eating a banana.

5. Teachers: Have a bicycle, scooter or skateboard marathon or rodeo.

6. Teachers: Have a macramé, origami or bead stringing center where students can express their feelings about the stories they read in motor form.

7. Teachers: Have a contest to see who can draw the straightest line or the most perfect circle on the chalkboard.

8. Teachers: Set up a construction center where students may follow directions or work on self-designed projects. Include nails, wood, tools, paints, paper, paste, etc. Have students list rules for the center.

9. Teachers: If a parent or you is a good enough photographer, take a time exposure of students writing words in a darkened classroom with a flashlight.

10. Teachers: Play *Simon Says*.

11. Teachers: Have students do two motor tasks at the same time. Examples; Hop and shake your head, pat your stomach and your head, etc.

12. Teachers: For younger students, set up a water play or water painting center. Include brushes, food coloring, etc. (Alternate: Sand play center.)

13. Teachers: Play *Charades*, using as topics story events, characters, titles, etc.

14. Teachers: Tap or clap syllables, sentences, song titles, and the like. See who can guess the words.
15. Teachers: Ask students to cut out new vocabulary words or letters to spell them from magazines.
16. Teachers: Have stacking contests using cards, dominoes, etc.
17. Teachers: Set up crafts centers such as woodworking, wood burning, leather, bead making, weaving, and the like.
18. Teachers: Have a student pretend to write a word on the chalkboard, keeping his or her fingers about an inch away so nothing appears on the board. See who can guess the word.
19. Teachers: Use rhythm instruments to accompany songs.

POSITION IN SPACE SKILLS

Sample Activities for Discussion, Task Cards, Learning Centers, or Reading Contracts

1. These are the same object. Explain what would cause the change in shape.

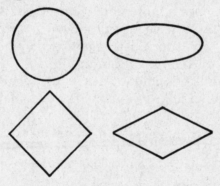

2. Add lines behind, in front of, at the sides, above, below this figure. How many different things could this be?

3. These are the same item. What could have happened to change it?

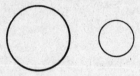

4. Explain how figure A could be the largest, the smallest, the middle sized object.

5. Make up some puzzles that use the same shape in different ways.
6. We need to change the furniture in the classroom. Here are some principles we should follow. Sample principles: No one should face bright light. We need space for our drama work. We need space for our movement activities. We need a new art center for finger painting. How many ways can you think of to arrange the furniture?
7. Pretend you are in interior decorator. What suggestions do you have for a library center? Sketch or make a diagram of your design.
8. Look closely at our classroom: What helps you work better? What interferes with your work? What new things do you suggest to make it a better place to work? What does it lack? What can you do to improve it?
9. Teachers: Play "Where Are You?" Blindfold students, then twirl them around for a few moments. Lead them to some area in the classroom or playground. See if they know where they are. What sensory stimuli gave them clues?
10. Teachers: Have class exercises where students look or respond to things in a different way; for instance, look up at things they ordinarily look down on; describe how an ob-

ject they are feeling looks, even though their eyes are closed; stand on their heads, etc.

11. Teachers: Have students sit on the floor or grass far enough apart so that they cannot touch each other even with hands and legs extended. Ask them to close their eyes and feel everything within reach—grass, floor, etc. Then have them look at the same area with their eyes open. Ask them to share the differences in perception of what's there.

12. Teachers: Sing songs a cappella, where various singers are placed around the room.

13. Teachers: Change classroom displays and bulletin boards often to help students be aware of their visual environment rather than to become too used to it. Remember, two weeks is a long time for a child. Let them help.

BODY AWARENESS SKILLS

Sample Activities for Discussion, Task Cards, Learning Centers, and Reading Contracts

1. Teachers: Have students pantomime feelings or emotions and share various student perceptions of what was pantomimed. (For example: How I Feel About School Today, What I Had for Dinner Last Night, etc.)

2. Teachers: Videotape students at work in the classroom, playing on the playground, walking down the hall, and various other activities involving sitting, standing, walking, running, and the like. Before sharing the videotape with the class members, ask them to write a brief description (or share an oral one) of how they move. Show the videotape. Talk about the realities of their movements versus the fantasies they have of themselves.

3. Teachers: Ask students to create an ideal face by choosing each feature from a separate person in the classroom. (Johnny's nose, Bill's hair, etc.) Share. (Alternate: An ideal body.)

4. Teachers: Have students trace around each other's body. Each colors his or her own life-sized image. Ask them to write stories about the way they feel about their bodies.

5. Teachers: Set up a full-length mirror learning center where

students can write about how they feel about various parts of their bodies, where they can check which colors look good on them, where they can read articles about hair care, etc.

6. Play singing games such as "Hokey Pokey."
7. Teachers: When dramatizing a story, discuss the movements and physical characteristics of each character. Practice the movements for each character as a group.
8. Teachers: Play games related to body awareness. Example: Move the largest part of you; the smallest part; two parts together, etc.

LATERALITY SKILLS

Sample Activities for Discussion, Task Cards, Learning Centers, and Reading Contracts

1. Teachers: Have the students label the left and right hands, feet, or sides of pictures of people or animals cut from magazines.
2. Teachers: Have students cut out pictures facing left and pictures facing right.
3. Teachers: Have throwing contests—left hand, right hand, both hands. Have kicking contests—left foot, right foot, both feet.
4. Teachers: Ask students to write down all the left-handed students in the class without looking.
5. Teachers: Ask students to write or tell about how they came to write, throw, etc., with the hand they do use.
6. Teachers: Have right-handed students try for a few moments to imagine what it would be like to be left-handed and write or tell what they think. Then, have them experiment a few moments with trying to be left-handed and share what happened to them. Have left-handed students do the reverse.
7. Teachers: Have left-handed students make a list of improvements in the classroom that would make their lives easier. Share this with the entire class.

DIRECTIONALITY SKILLS

Sample Activities for Discussion, Task Cards, Learning Centers, and Reading Contracts

1. Teachers: Teach students a chorus line type of dance with balloons, balls, fans, flags, etc., where they have to learn to place the object in a certain position in sequence.
2. Teachers: Have a soap bubble learning center.
3. Teachers: Have students write or tell about their most clumsy moment.
4. Teachers: Ask students to share fears and feelings they have about being able to do a directionality task.

SPATIAL RELATIONSHIP SKILLS

Sample Activities for Discussion, Task Cards, Learning Centers, and Reading Contracts

1. Teachers: Have students work with increasingly complicated jigsaw puzzles, some of which are of one color.
2. Teachers: Have students play three-dimensional *Scrabble*, *Bingo*, or checkers. Have students design three-dimensional games or puzzles.
3. Teachers: Use *Chinese Checkers*, *Scrabble*, *Bingo*, checkers, and/or chess for interest centers.
4. Teachers: Supply many put-together puzzles (tangrams, beebees in the eye, etc.) and similar type games for learning centers.
5. Teachers: Have students work with mazes.
6. Teachers: Have students do rhythms with a partner.

A FINAL WORD ABOUT PERCEPTION

An idea or a word perceived in the full richness of our senses is truly a glorious experience. Such perception gives reading meaning, sensory response, and imagery. It helps students interpret what they read, feel the way story characters feel, and experience the smells, tastes, touches, warmths,

movements, and other sensory parts of their reading. Help
students learn specific reading skills in a sensory way; imprint-
ing these skills, so to speak, into their olfactory, taste, tactile,
kinesthetic, vision, hearing, movement, and other receptor
mechanisms; making reading a part of the total self.

10

Work-Study Skills

* * * * * * * * * * * *

To have to pay equal attention to how we learn at the same time that we are trying to get something out of the content on the pages of print we read is often too heavy a load for young learners—not to mention us adults! Among the most important processes we educators can help our students learn are the work-study skills that will allow them to work on content without being stymied by not knowing how to do that work. In preparing students to work more efficiently and effectively, we are helping them do much more than learn to read better, important as that goal is. We are also helping them to a better organized, more satisfying life style; one in which they can easily secure any information that will make their lives happier, more comfortable, and more secure—whether it's how to look up emergency telephone numbers, research information on the best purchase to make on a car, find the best route to Kansas City, decide what clothing to wear today, or make up their minds whether to go to a movie, stay home and watch television, or go to the opera tonight.

MAP AND GLOBE SKILLS

Sample Activities for Discussion, Task Cards, Learning Centers, and Reading Contracts

1. Give the degrees latitude and longitude to find the locations of some of your favorite stories.
2. Draw a birds-eye view of the setting of the story.
3. Draw a map of the action of the story.

4. Draw the setting of the story from the viewpoint of two of the following: a bird; a worm; someone on the moon; a goldfish; a mosquito; and a driver on the highway.

5. On a map of the school's locality, mark the locations of all class members' homes.

6. Find an aerial view of where you live. Compare it to a map of your area.

7. Make up a game that would teach younger students how to read a map.

8. Make a list of map symbols.

9. Make a map of a story event using standard map symbols.

10. What are some problems a map maker has with a flat map?

11. Show examples of different kinds of map projections: Mercader, polar, etc. Share examples of older maps, too.

12. Show examples of differences in scale on maps for the same area.

13. Make up a series of questions about your neighborhood or city that can only be answered by looking at a map. (Example: If you went two blocks west of the school on Pine Street, at what intersection would you be?)

14. What will this map tell you? What is the scale used for this map?

15. Make a map of the way to your house that you could give to a new friend or use to send out in invitations to a party at your house.

16. Write a definition for the word, *map*. Compare your definitions with those given by two dictionaries. How many different meanings did you find for the word?

17. What things would you want to find on a map of your school? Of your neighborhood? Of your state? Of Iran?

18. Make a map of an ideal classroom, country, city, or neighborhood. Make a globe of an ideal planet. Make a map for a library in the year 2500 A.D.

19. Plan a library for a space ship on a ten-year voyage to outer space.

20. One of the hardest things to do with road maps is to fold them correctly after you use them. Plan a demonstration of how to fold a road map.

21. Make up a list of the maps you think we need in our classroom.

22. Make up a mystery location on a map by listing latitude

and longitude. See who can tell you what your mystery place is.

23. Make a map of the route of the best trip you ever took. Put in the places you visited and the things you did.

24. Show the location of three of your favorite stories on a map, or make up an imaginary map if they didn't take place in a real setting.

25. Find a map of Disneyland, Magic Mountain, or other amusement parks. List the parts you have seen and the parts you would like to see.

26. Teachers: Play "I'm Lost." Give each student a map. Students take turns at being lost by telling where they are on the maps, and where they want to be, and asking someone for directions. If directions are clear and accurate, the direction giver gets a point. (Alternate: Play "Getting to Grandma's.")

27. Teachers: Have students compare two different kinds of maps of the same area; for example, an airline and a road map.

28. Teachers: Have students learn the different kinds of maps; e.g., road maps, topological maps, informational maps, linguistic maps, navigational maps, etc.

29. Teachers: Have students learn to make maps by scale, by compass and tape measure, etc. Have them map the classroom, the school yard, and other close-by locations.

30. Teachers: Have students decide the best way to get from city to city by road.

31. Teachers: Have various travel agents and automobile clubs make presentations of their use of maps.

32. Teachers: Have map puzzle centers where students put together maps of the U.S. by state, and of the world by countries.

33. Teachers: Have students answer such questions as: What direction is New York City from Los Angeles? What is the mountain range near Colorado Springs, Colorado? Near Albuquerque, New Mexico? How would you locate Salt Lake City on this map? Etc.

34. Teachers: Locate the time zones on a map or on a globe. Discuss why time changes from place to place.

35. Teachers: Locate north, east, south, west, and northeast, northwest, southeast, southwest in the classroom.

36. Teachers: Have students fill a time capsule, bury it, and make a map to be left for other students to locate it five years later.
37. Teachers: Share with the students a collection of different maps of the United States over the past three hundred years. (Alternate: Africa.)
38. Teachers: Have a treasure hunt where you hide a treat or a new book or some surprise. Provide a map. Divide the class into small groups and see which group finds the treasure.
39. Teachers: Play a map game by putting names of cities on cards. Have each student select a card when he or she has a turn, tell how far it is, how to get there, the population, etc., all from map information.
40. Teachers: Cut out a small area from a larger map. Use this small map as a mystery. See who can tell you where the smaller area is.
41. Teachers: Study weather maps and talk about the various features and information to be found on them.
42. Teachers: Show the route on a map or globe for every trip a student in the class takes during the school year or vacation time.
43. Teachers: Make a map or have students make a map of the route of a proposed field trip.

SKILLS OF INTERPRETING GRAPHIC MATERIALS (GRAPHS, CHARTS, TABLES, DIAGRAMS)

Sample Activities for Discussion, Task Cards, Learning Centers, and Reading Contracts

1. Take a favorite book that has a historical setting. Make a daily, monthly, or yearly time line. Fill in a time line for two other locations or countries. Example:

Events

	1850	1860	1870	
Book				
China				
California				

Discuss whether these events affected the story or not.
2. Do similar charting for people or dates. (Example: Book setting is 1865.)

1865

	1 Major Event	1 Major Person	1 Major Book
Book			
California			
Georgia			
England			
Russia			

3. Make a circle graph of how a student who lived at the time of your story should have spent his allowance.
4. Make a picture graph of the favorite books of students in this room.
5. Make a block graph of the heights of students in this room.
6. Make a line graph of changes in heights of students in this room for the period of one month.
7. What kinds of graphs would make life in our classroom better?
8. Make a graph for a week or two of the number of people who eat in the cafeteria. What does this tell you about the food served? Anything else?
9. Find a graph in a book. Why was the graph put there?
10. Make a graph about your favorite film stars, the hobbies of students in our class, the favorite books of teachers in this school, your progress in reading this year, or of the five most frequently used words on a page in your book.
11. Find a graph in a book or a magazine that you felt was especially well done and/or helpful.
12. Make a graph predicting the future population of your area. Look at population graphs and figures of past population growth for ideas.
13. Fill in the chart with words from the story:

5 Sound Words	5 Feel Words	5 See Words
1.	1.	1.
2.	2.	2.
3.	3.	3.
4.	4.	4.
5.	5.	5.

14. Compare and contrast the main characters from two stories on this chart. Which would you most like to be?

	Character 1	Character 2
Voice		
Favorite Expressions		
Description		
Height		
Weight		
Color Hair		
Typical Movements		
Clothing		
Other Traits		

15. Take your favorite character from a book. Compare him or her to you.

	Character	You
Ideals		
Voice		
Movement		
Best Friend		
Other Traits		

16. Make a chart of choices of classroom activities that lists student choices, gives students room to sign for their

choices and that will assign students also to an area in which they need to work.

17. Make a time line chart for one year comparing a country's literature and political units. (Reference: Grun, *Timetables of History*.)

18. List four things. Make a chart of how they are alike and how they are different.

19. Make a chart of seven different kinds of books (novels, etc.). List five examples of books that fit each category.

20. Make a chart of directions for some classroom activity, of words that have more than one meaning, or of what happened on our field trip.

21. Make a comparable size chart of five main characters in five different stories.

22. Make a schedule for who gets to keep old issues of magazines or discarded books or have students sign for the ones they want.

23. Make a truly interesting chart for parent visitors to our classroom—something you think they should know.

24. Make a maze for your story.

25. Make a diagram of an ideal community you'd like to live in.

26. Make a diagram showing how to do or make something that you can do or make.

27. Make a diagram of parts of a book.

28. Make a diagram of some collection you have.

29. Make a diagram of a bulletin board you'd like to make about reading.

30. Look at an airline schedule. What times do planes leave Los Angeles for Honolulu? What times do planes arrive in Los Angeles from Salt Lake City? If you took Flight 48 to Dallas from Los Angeles, where else would you land? (Vary cities by location.)

31. Look at a table of mileages on a road map of your state. How far away are three major cities? What is the nearest city of over 1,000,000 in population?

32. Make a table of what activities students in your class were doing at 7:00 last night.

33. Mark a TV schedule for your favorite programs for the week.

34. Make a table of your plans for the week.

35. Make a table of how well you worked in reading during the past week.
36. Look at the tide tables or sunrise and sunset tables in your newspaper. What will happen tomorrow?
37. Make a time table and route map for a school bus.
38. Collect various time tables for buses, trains, planes, etc. Share what kind of information can be found on each one.
39. Make a comparison table showing prices for certain items at two local stores.
40. Make a time line table for four stories you have read.
41. Make a time line table and schedule for a field trip for our class. Make a checklist of items to be done beforehand.
42. On the instructions that come inside a box of film, what information does the table of guide numbers for flash bulbs give you?
43. Make a table of stopping times for various mileages for cars, trains, planes, and/or bicycles.

PICTURE AND ILLUSTRATION INTERPRETIVE SKILLS

Sample Activities for Discussion, Task Cards, Learning Centers, and Reading Contracts

1. Teachers: Show a picture. Have students write or draw what happened before, next, later, off to one side of, in front of, or behind the picture.
2. Teachers: Have students look over the illustrations in a story, then write what they think the story is about. Compare their predictions with the story in the book.
3. Teachers: Select three students. Send them out of the room. Have them come in one at a time and tell you what they see in a picture they have never seen before. Have the class discuss similarities and differences in perceptions the three had of the picture. Talk about what other students see differently in the picture.
4. Teachers: Ask students how well they feel the illustrations fitted the story, story mood, author's style of writing, and, in general, added to the book? Or did they take away from the book?
5. Teachers: Ask students to discuss or write about whether they would rather read a book that was illustrated or not.

Both views are right. Try to help both sides see the point of view of the other side.

6. Teachers: Ask students to look for inaccuracies in any illustrations or pictures they find in a book. Share the examples they find with the entire class.
7. Teachers: Ask students to think about and draw how they would have illustrated the book differently.

READING TECHNIQUE SKILLS: SURVEYING, SCANNING, AND SKIMMING

Sample Activities for Discussion, Task Cards, Learning Centers, and Reading Contracts

1. Teachers: Have students locate five books that indicate from the titles that they would be of help in their project. Have them look at the table of contents, index, chapter headings, etc., and make a list of the different kinds of information on their project each book gives. (Surveying)
2. Teachers: Ask students to look through a newspaper article to see who can find out the *who, where, when, what,* and *how* parts the fastest. (Skimming)
3. Teachers: Have students read only the first paragraph of a newspaper story, then predict what the remainder will be. Have them check the accuracy of their predictions. (Skimming)
4. Teachers: Have students skim content book chapters before silent reading: to see if they have questions; to see if they can read graphic materials; and to see if there are words that they need help reading. (Skimming and surveying)
5. Teachers: Have students skim a paragraph and then try to summarize it in one sentence. (Skimming)
6. Teachers: Ask students to skim a short story and then ask them if they would want to read it in more depth. (Skimming)
7. Teachers: Ask students to look for the number of times the word *said* is used on a page. (Or use any word or punctuation mark.) (Scanning)
8. Teachers: Have a menu center, where menus from various restaurants are available for scanning.
9. Teachers: Set up a newspaper center for quiet, relaxed scanning.

10. Teachers: Have each student scan a magazine or a page from a newspaper for about a minute. Then ask him or her what they saw that they would enjoy reading in greater depth. (Scanning and skimming)

11. Teachers: Ask students to look as quickly as they can for answers to specific questions about the reading material; e.g., Who went to town? How many eggs were there? Where was the goat? Etc. (Scanning)

12. Teachers: Have students make a tally of how many times a favorite film or TV star appears in a newspaper or magazine. (Scanning)

13. Teachers: Ask students to find how many times a pronoun is used on a page. (Scanning)

14. Teachers: Have students look for a word on a page by looking for the first letter in the word. (Scanning)

15. Teachers: Have students scan a telephone directory to locate a particular name or business.

16. Teachers: Have students scan a dictionary to look up a particular word.

17. Teachers: Have students scan to see if the story they are going to read took place in the past, present, or future.

18. Teachers: Have students scan the story to find out who the main character is.

19. Teachers: Have students scan a volume of an encyclopedia to find something they want to read or to find certain information.

SKILLS OF FOLLOWING DIRECTIONS

Sample Activities for Discussion, Task Cards, Learning Centers, and Reading Contracts

1. Teachers: Put all directions for classroom equipment in a central place. Students can refer to directions as they use: cameras, videotape recorders, projectors, ovens, films, etc.

2. Teachers: Ask students to write directions for others to use: in using a mail order catalogue; in cooking something; in serving something; or in going somewhere.

3. Teachers: Have a collection of repair booklets for bicycle repair, home repair, auto repair, and the like, in a how-to learning center.

4. Teachers: Show students how to fill out various forms such as library card applications; checks; bank applications (such as savings accounts); income tax forms; bicycle license applications; motor bike license applications; automobile license applications; catalogue mail order forms; and the like.

5. Teachers: Have directions and papers for folding origami figures or for Eskimo string figures at a learning center. (Alternate: Have students invent an origami figure and write directions for it.)

6. Teachers: Have a pattern file for doll's clothes and scraps of material available. (Alternate: Clothing patterns for students.)

7. Teachers: Have handwork patterns and materials available for quilts, crocheting, knitting, needlepoint, beadwork, weaving, jewelry, etc.

8. Teachers: Set up a learning center for making crystal radios from directions.

9. Teachers: Set up a sewing center with a sewing machine, patterns, scissors, etc.

10. Teachers: Set up a living center where students follow directions for caring for plants, pets, gardens, etc.

11. Teachers: Have students collect examples of clear and of unclear directions—both oral and written (maybe some of yours or mine). Also, have examples of easy-and difficult-to-follow directions.

12. Teachers: Write directions and set up supplies for a holiday card or other art project at a learning center.

13. Teachers: Have students write directions on how to do something related to their hobbies.

14. Teachers: Write directions (or have students write directions) for a treasure hunt in which they have to follow one set of directions to find the place where the next set of directions is hidden until they reach the treasure.

15. Teachers: Have students write directions for what they think would develop the ideal reader.

16. Teachers: Choose a student to pretend that he or she is a tourist telephoning from an airport, bus depot, or train station. He or she wants to visit the school. Have another student give directions.

17. Teachers: Have students take turns giving directions on

how to reach other rooms in the school or how to get to
their homes.

18. Teachers: Read aloud or have a student read aloud some
recipe and see if the class can guess what it is.

19. Teachers: Have students write or give oral directions on
how to use simple tools.

20. Teachers: Make up directions tapes or cassettes for small
groups of students. Individualize the tapes by referring to
specific students by name. Examples: "How's it going,
Greg?" "Linda, you can skip this part, since you did so
well on it last week." Etc.

NOTE-TAKING SKILLS

Sample Activities for Discussion, Task Cards, Learning Centers, or Reading Contracts

1. Interview classmates to determine their favorite recipes.
Take notes. Make up a folder or book of these recipes.

2. Make up a list of things you would want to take for a trip to
the place described in this story. Graph or head the list
appropriately.

3. Make up a menu in the appropriate style for restaurants in
the setting of this story.

4. Make a card file of facts or ideas that interest you.

5. Survey your classmates about an opinion expressed in your
book.

6. Make up a system for keeping track of the information you
get as you work on a project of your own.

7. Pretend you are a sailor with Columbus. Write down notes
you might have taken. Take notes that a Taina Indian
might have made as he or she saw Columbus land.

8. Make up a set of notes that the author of your book could
have written to himself or herself before writing the book.

9. Take notes on parts of the story you would like to share with
us.

10. Take notes on parts of your reading that you need help on
or about which you need more explanation.

11. Look up material in three books on some subject of interest
to you. Organize your notes so you can remember what
you read.

12. When would it be better to take notes and when would it

be better to use a tape recorder? Jot down some notes for an answer, then compare your thoughts to those of others.

13. Invite a speaker to your class. Have him or her speak on some interest of yours. Have three people take notes. Compare what they write down.

14. Act as secretary to take notes during the next class meeting.

15. Listen to a story that the teacher reads aloud or one on a record or tape. Jot down notes of things you would like to share, question, or comment on later.

16. Take a walking tour of our classroom, the school, and the playground and make notes of suggestions you have for improving each area.

OUTLINING SKILLS

Sample Activities for Discussion, Task Cards, Learning Centers, and Reading Contracts

1. Pretend you are an astronaut chosen to take a five-year trip to Saturn. Write an outline of what you have to do before blastoff in two weeks.

2. Give a speech about reading, using only an outline.

3. Make an outline for a film or group of photographs you plan to make about your study.

4. Make an outline for each of the following: (a) The major causes for accidents to children are _____; (b) The different states where students in our class were born are 1. _____, 2. _____, 3. _____, etc.

5. Tell the main thought in each paragraph on the page (or in the story) in one sentence.

6. List the events in the story in chronological order.

7. List the characters of the story in order of importance, with the most important character number one. Tell why you placed each character where you did on the list.

8. What are five things you would like to know about _____?

9. In what order should numerals, alphabetic letters, and Roman numerals be used in an outline?

10. Make an outline for a proposed book on your favorite subject or interest.

11. Outline the main points in the story. Compare your outline with that of other students.

12. Make up an ideal daily schedule for a person your age. For a five-year-old. For your toothbrush.
13. Make an outline of what you would like to accomplish tomorrow (next week, this year, in five years, etc.).
14. Make an outline of steps we could take as a class to improve our reading, our classroom, our school, and/or our community.
15. Make up an outline of steps to use in choosing a good book for pleasure reading. (Alternates: For research, for a Christmas present, etc.)
16. Make up an outline for what you would consider an ideal book for a person your age. (Alternate: An ideal book for teaching reading.)
17. Make an outline under three different headings for a trip you took. Heading examples: Fun, Food, Animals, etc.
18. Make an outline of the steps involved in making your favorite cookies.
19. Make up an outline that you think the author of your book used for this chapter.
20. Make an outline of some science experiment you conducted.
21. Write down the most important words in a paragraph.

MEDIA WORK-STUDY SKILLS

Sample Activities for Discussion, Task Cards, Learning Centers, and Reading Contracts

1. Plan a campaign to promote more reading in your school. Include posters, film strips, photographs, videotapes, and other media.
2. Two words that confuse a lot of people are *media* and *medium*. What are the differences between them? Make up a chart or a table to illustrate when each is used.
3. Select a filmstrip, a film, and five photographs to accompany a report you are giving on a current project. Select other audio-visual material you find appropriate.
4. Besides books and other printed matter, where can you go for information on some topic of interest to you?
5. Set up a television news program with anchor people, newscasters, etc. Have them use charts, maps, globes, etc.,

as they report happenings of interest to the class. Choose a committee to help you, if you wish.

6. Write a TV script using your book as a basis for the plot.

SELF-DIRECTION SKILLS

Sample Activities for Discussion, Task Cards, Learning Centers, or Reading Contracts

1. Make a list of all the books you read on your own last week (or month).
2. Plan and take a series of photographs or slides to illustrate your book or a book you wrote yourself.
3. What would you suggest we include in a recreational reading center where students will be working on their own? What furniture, reading materials, supplies, and the like would make the best free reading center you could hope for?
4. Make a display of things you learned to do or to make from books or other reading materials.
5. Make a graph for students who are always asking, "What can I do now?"
6. Teachers: Include several newspapers for free time reading at a learning center.
7. Teachers: Have students make a lesson plan for reading for substitute teachers that the class would enjoy doing if the teacher had to be absent.
8. Teachers: Have students draw up a plan to make themselves into better readers.
9. Teachers: Have students decide how many pages they will read for a day or a week.
10. Teachers: Have students help set up reading activities for a schedule for a week.

SELF-IMPROVEMENT SKILLS

Sample Activities for Discussion, Task Cards, Learning Centers, and Reading Contracts

1. Make out a proposed schedule of reading for self-improvement in: (a) your study habits; (b) getting information

you want to improve your school work; or (c) the kind of reader you want to be.

2. Make a list of the things you do well in reading, the things you need to improve on in reading, and the things you can't do at all in reading.

3. On what reading skill do you want to work especially hard tomorrow?

4. What goal would you like to work on in reading today? This week?

5. What kind of reader do you want to be after this year? Five years later? Ten years from now?

6. Teachers: Have a self-improvement library center; include books on personal appearances, diet, clothes, hair styles, interior decorating, and the like. Be sure to include books for boys and girls both. Primary grades can also use this center, with appropriate level books and catalogues.

7. Teachers: Ask students to write or talk about what more they would like to get out of reading.

8. Teachers: Ask students to discuss or write about the obstacles they have overcome or have to overcome to be a better reader.

9. Teachers: Ask students to discuss or write about what they would have done differently if they were learning to read all over again.

10. Teachers: Have students discuss or write about story characters they admire.

11. Teachers: Have students discuss or write about books that have changed their lives, or affected them very much, or caused them to want to change.

12. Teachers: Ask students to discuss or write about the story characters or famous people they'd like to be or be more like.

READING RATE SKILLS

Sample Activities for Discussion, Task Cards, Learning Centers, and Reading Contracts

1. Teachers: Use a tachistoscope, flash cards, or slide projector set at some comfortable rate for most of the students. Ask them to write as many letters as they can as each word is flashed, or as many words, or as many random letters as

they can. This can also be a contest between individuals or sides. Speed up the machines as the students become more proficient.

2. Teachers: Have students estimate how many minutes they need to read a page and answer correctly two of three questions on the content.
3. Teachers: Talk about the differences in time needed for reading different materials, such as science books, poetry, novels, newspapers, magazine articles.
4. Teachers: Have a tachistoscope, a speed reading machine, or controlled reader set up at a learning center where students can experiment with the equipment themselves.
5. Teachers: Have a learning center set up around a stop watch where students can time themselves as they read.
6. Teachers: Have students practice running their eyes down the middle of a page of print and try to pick up the main idea and as many other thoughts as they can.

BOOK REVIEW SKILLS

Sample Activities for Discussion, Task Cards, Learning Centers, and Reading Contracts

1. Reviewers write critiques of many other things besides books. How many can you list? (Television programs, films, special events, concerts, plays, restaurants, etc.) (Alternate: Plan a review for one of these.)
2. What would you change in the story or book? How did the book affect you, personally? Did other students feel the same way you did? Interview those students who read the book and see.
3. On a scale of ten with one being the highest rating and ten being the lowest, where would you place this book? What are your reasons?

ORAL READING SKILLS

Sample Activities for Discussion, Task Cards, Learning Centers, and Reading Contracts

1. Teachers: Have students read portions of a story into a tape recorder and play it back to them. Discuss how each per-

son's voice sounds to him/her. (Alternate: Use a videotape recorder.) (Note: The first time this is done, students may be hearing their voices for the first time. Be prepared to discuss why voices sound different on a tape from when we are listening to ourselves talk.)

2. Teachers: Use the neurological impress method to practice oral reading. (The teacher reads the passage softly from in back of the student while the student reads aloud at the same time.) (Alternate: The student reads aloud with a tape recording of the material.)

3. Teachers: Ask students to read aloud some of the story dialogue using differing voice inflections; e.g., questioning, angry, excited voices.

4. Teachers: Discuss with the students some of the reasons that people read aloud; e.g., to share something of interest from a magazine, or book, or a newspaper, to entertain; to give a presentation; to prove a point, etc.

5. Teachers: As a part of speech time, read aloud a certain number of minutes a day (or have students plan an oral reading presentation).

6. Teachers: Discuss books that students have asked others to real aloud to them more than once.

7. Teachers: Ask students to look up the answer to a question and read it aloud. (Alternate: Give each student a different book to look in for the answer.)

8. Teachers: Ask a student to read class or school announcements aloud; poems that they want to share; a narration for a film strip the class made; a narration for a pantomime or shadow show; a funny, sad, or exciting part from a story; or the directions for an assignment or for a work sheet.

9. Teachers: Have students select a story to read aloud to younger children in other classrooms.

10. Teachers: Read aloud yourself or have some student read some interesting book to the class aloud.

11. Teachers: Plan choral reading activities for the group. Use poems or stories with a lot of dialogue.

12. Teachers: Ask who would like to read a selection silently alone and who would like a chance to read it at the same time that someone else reads it aloud. Arrange the classroom accordingly.

13. Teachers: Have an older student read aloud words that students do not know during silent reading time.

14. Teachers: Have students make stories into plays and read aloud the dialogue passages, or read the dialogue passages in stories as though they were the person, using voice qualities, pronunciation, etc., that they feel would be appropriate for that character.

15. Teachers: Have an "Author's Time," when students read aloud from their own creative writing.

16. Teachers: Discuss what various punctuation marks mean for oral reading.

17. Teachers: Make up a self-evaluation checklist for oral reading for students to use. Use it also for self-evaluation of tape recordings and videotapes of oral reading by students.

18. Teachers: Have good readers read aloud to the class material written at a higher level than most students can handle.

19. Teachers: Have an oral reading sharing time once a week or so when students can present materials they think are particularly informative or interesting. Have students decide on standards for the oral reading and evaluate how well each did or evaluate themselves.

20. Teachers: Have students practice reading aloud commercial messages the students write about books, products, coming events, and the like.

21. Teachers: Have a poetry time every week or so when favorite poems are practiced beforehand to be read aloud to the entire group.

22. Teachers: Have students alternate reading minutes of class meetings.

23. Teachers: Play "Radio Announcer" and have students pretend they are auditioning for a radio announcer's job and have to read something out loud that they have never seen before. Have students write up tricky tryout scripts that use tongue twisters or names of cities or people that are hard to pronounce.

24. Teachers: Make monthly tapes of students reading aloud. Have them compare and comment on their progress.

25. Teachers: Have students record stories for a tape library for younger students or for their own age level. If there is a blind or partially sighted group in your school, share the

tapes with them. Also, ask these students who they would like to have read to them from your class and why.

26. Teachers: Give students the opportunity to select books of their choice for them to read aloud to the class. (Alternate: Have students select a book for you to read.)

27. Teachers: Have students read aloud to you passages in the book that are exciting, humorous, vivid, give the main idea, taught them something new, etc.

RESEARCH SKILLS

Sample Activities for Discussion, Task Cards, Learning Centers, and Reading Contracts

1. Conduct research to find a group of the smallest and biggest things in our classroom. Make a table for your results.

2. Make a "Whatever happened to . . . ?" bulletin board featuring once-famous people. Research your answer. Alternates: "Whatever happened to . . . (story character)?" and "Whatever happened to . . . (authors)?"

3. Where would you look to find out how to make sun tea?

4. What would be the types of shop courses taught in the time era of this story?

5. What kinds of production lines were there in the time era of the story?

6. Make a list of places, people, and references for ideas to solve problems on which you are working.

7. Make a log of a research project you carried out.

8. Make up a "report card" for yourself on your last research project.

9. Make out a plan for a schedule for some reading you have always wanted to do.

10. What would you like included in a research learning center for our classroom?

11. Look up the same topics in three different books. Which treatment seems the best to you? Why is this?

12. Research origins and differing customs for holidays in different countries or areas of the United States.

13. Organize a collection of pamphlets, magazines, slides, books, and the like around a unit or a theme. Put it on an instructional cart to use in other classrooms as part of stu-

dent learning activities, with you making a presentation showing how to use the material.

14. Research and prepare for a debate on _____ (current problem).
15. Research what the different ratings on motion pictures mean.

GROUP WORK SKILLS

Sample Activities for Discussion, Task Cards, Learning Centers, and Reading Contracts

1. Write a book with a group of friends. Choose a publisher, an editor, and the like.
2. What is the hardest part about working in a group for you? The best part?
3. Make up an ideal weekly schedule for our classroom.
4. Get a group together to make up a list of suggestions or a booklet for working in groups.
5. Give the names of class members who you feel would be interested in: learning about bicycles, making a kite, going to Australia, working on a committee to study bears, or any other topic of interest to you.
6. Make a group report about one item of interest to you in the *World Almanac* or have each person in the group choose a different item he or she finds of interest.
7. Organize or join the Library Club.
8. Teachers: Organize the class so that half work on a production line to make cookies and half work on baking cookies doing all the steps themselves. Write up the results. Discuss production, feelings, and the like.
9. Teachers: Have students research, plan a menu and cook a meal based on foods of various countries, and invite their parents to share it.
10. Have students divide up the research work necessary to solve a classroom problem such as scheduling, discipline, and the like.

A FINAL WORD ABOUT WORK-STUDY SKILLS

Helping students decide what they really want to do with their lives is one of the most exciting parts of being a teacher.

To see students begin and complete tasks that are important to them; to see their minds awaken to what they want to learn or what they don't know enough about; to see them set and achieve goals for themselves is gratifying beyond measure to us educators. Good work-study skills make these tasks easier by helping our students work quickly and efficiently, locate information, and consult current and past minds via books for needed data. In this way, we help our students understand that there is not a unitary, singular thing that we label *reading*, but that reading involves a variety of techniques and combinations of techniques to get what we want from the written page—and that's why we read—to get what we want from print.

11

Reference Skills

* * * * * * * * * * *

Where do we go to get the information we need to solve a problem, better ourselves, enrich our lives, prove a point, jog our memories, find a book, complete an assignment, locate the answer to a question that's been puzzling us, learn how-to, or learn about ourselves? If we know the answers to these questions, we will live much fuller and more comfortable lives; and knowing reference skills can give us these answers.

Be sure to help the students in your charge learn this—that reference skills aren't some diabolical continuance secretly handed down from one generation of teachers to another—but, rather, that reference skills will help them lead the types of lives they want to lead, more easily than if they had to discover or invent or deduce anew in each generation every fact now available in reference form.

SKILLS IN USING PARTS OF BOOKS: FRONTISPIECE, TABLE OF CONTENTS, PREFACE, FOREWORD, BODY OF THE BOOK, INDEX, GLOSSARY, APPENDICES, AND THE LIKE

Sample Activities for Discussion, Task Cards, Learning Centers, and Reading Contracts

1. Who drew the illustrations or took the photographs for this book? What other books has he or she illustrated?
2. Before you read a new book, look at the frontispiece. the title, the table of contents, the index, etc. What do you think the book will offer you?

3. How can these parts of a book save you time and effort? The frontispiece? The table of contents? The preface? The index? The glossary? The bibliography?

4. Look at the cover of a book. Predict what will be in the book. Check the various parts of the book, such as index, table of contents, and the like. Were your predictions accurate?

5. Make up three more good titles for your book. Put them into the format of a real frontispiece.

6. What kinds of information can you find in a table of contents?

7. What topics are covered in this book?

8. Prepare a lesson to teach younger children about the parts of a book.

9. Read the table of contents of a book. Write in three sentences what you think the book is about.

10. List characters from stories in a unit from a basal reader. Group characters in as many ways as you can.

11. List the names of stories from a unit in a reader. How many unit names can you think of for these stories?

12. If you were designing a manual for bicycling, what sections would you be sure to include?

13. Make a book showing one career possibility. What divisions will you need?

14. If you were writing a Consumer's Guide, what would be the three main headings?

15. How did each chapter or unit section in this book get its name?

16. Convert the headings within each chapter into questions. Answer three of these questions.

17. On what page(s) in your book would information on _____ be found?

18. Find an index for a newspaper. What information does it contain?

19. Write the definition for a glossary.

20. Look at the glossary of your book and list five words that especially intrigue you. Why is this?

21. What is the complete name (or complete names) of the author(s) of your book?

22. Who published the book? When? Where?

23. What is the title of a book published in 1959? In 1977?

24. What is the title of a book published in Boston?
25. If you and three friends decided to write a book and listed your names as authors in alphabetical order by last names, which would come first? Make up a sample frontispiece.
26. Teachers: Have students make books of their own with all the usual parts, from the frontispiece and the dedication to the index.
27. Teachers: Have students make a list of the parts of several kinds of books such as fiction, health, social studies, humor, reading, and the like. Compare and contrast the parts.
28. Teachers: Have students actually copyright one of their books.
29. Teachers: Preview with the students each new text you introduce, discussing what the title, table of contents, and so forth tell us about the book.
30. Teachers: Have students make their own books from discarded texts or library books.
31. Teachers: Write questions on individual cards about book contents that are answered in the table of contents. Have students select one of the cards and see who can find the answer first.
32. Teachers: Ask students questions similar to the following about books with indexes: Where will we find the information about Buffalo Bill Cody? Does this book contain anything about Navajos?

DICTIONARY AND OTHER WORD REFERENCE SKILLS

Sample Activities for Discussion, Task Cards, Learning Centers, and Reading Contracts

1. Look up a word from your story in two dictionaries. Are there differences in the way the word is defined? Look up the same word in an old and new edition of the same dictionary. Are there differences?
2. What are the guide words on the page for the word *necessary*?
3. What other information besides word meanings or definitions can you get from a dictionary?
4. Make up a list of words of things that are good to eat that

most of your classmates wouldn't know. Use the dictionary for ideas.

5. Which foreign language dictionaries would you take on a trip to Africa? To Australia?

6. Which foreign language dictionary would you select for the main story character?

7. Write a secret code message by using the pronunciation code for each word. Get the code from a dictionary.

8. Teachers: Write a word on the chalkboard. The first student or the first team that can pronounce it correctly by using a dictionary wins a point.

9. Teachers: Play *To Tell The Truth* using correct and incorrect definitions of words. Use the dictionary for reference for yourself and for students. Have students make up items for the game with one right and two wrong definitions for each word. Tell them to make their definitions sound plausible.

10. Teachers: Have a collection of picture dictionaries for an interest or learning center for young students.

11. Teachers: Make individual student dictionaries or card files of words needed for creative writing.

12. Teachers: Have students decide, as a group, which meaning of the word will make sense in the sentence they are reading.

13. Teachers: Have students make a dictionary of slang expressions.

14. Teachers: Have a contest to see who can open the dictionary closest to the word being looked for, in one try.

15. Teachers: Put the following references into a learning center called *Words, Words, Words*: (a) Books that tell word origins and histories. (b) Books that give place name origins (e.g., *California Place Names*). (c) Various different kinds of dictionaries, not just one type (e.g., technical dictionaries).

SKILLS IN USING STANDARD REFERENCES

Sample Activities for Discussion, Task Cards, Learning Centers, and Reading Contracts

1. What kinds of information would you find in these references: auto code, world record books, *Dictionary of Occupational Terms*, *Who's Who*, thesauri, dictionaries, encyclopedias, *P.D.R.*, atlases, telephone directories, mail order

catalogues, almanacs, *Books in Print*, government pamphlets, catalogues, city directories, PTA roll books, biographical dictionaries?
2. In what kinds of books would you find: The definition of a word? What water is? What water does? Information about Germany? Information about jobs? Information about bicycles? Foods of Spain? Cities of California? How far it is from Toledo, Ohio, to Memphis, Tennessee? Which is closest to Reno, Nevada—Anchorage, Alaska, or Mexico City, Mexico? What to wear in Istanbul in July? The cost of a trip by plane to Hong Kong? Who won the Indianapolis race in 1973?
3. If you were a librarian and wanted to find good library books for children, where would you look? (Ask the librarian for suggestions.)
4. Plan an ideal vacation to the city or country of your choice. Use encyclopedias, travel brochures, and the like for ideas.
5. What do you consider the five most interesting items in the *World Almanac*? Why did you make these choices?
6. Make a personal telephone directory of listings of interest to you.
7. Use reference books to fill in this table.

	E	T	O	M	P
Famous Writers					
Rivers					
Books					
Friends					

8. What was the most interesting entry to you in the encyclopedia in the *B* volume? (Teachers: You can limit this more by asking for the most interesting entry between *Au* and *Av*, etc.)
9. List the name of the encyclopedia, the volume and the page number where you found: How high and where is Mt. Everest? Where are the Atlas Mountains? Where and when was George Washington born?

10. Make up similar questions for our encyclopedia learning center.

11. How can you look up things in a magazine?

12. Where do you look if you need a plumber? How many choices would you have?

13. What is the area code for ____ county? For Orange County, California? For Los Angeles County, California? For Santa Fe, New Mexico? For Honolulu, Hawaii?

14. If you aren't getting the service you want on a bicycle you purchased, what can you do?

15. Make a list of emergency telephone numbers that you feel every teacher should have. Every student. Every parent. Are the lists the same?

16. Make up a list of geographical references you would suggest writers have in their libraries.

17. What famous journals gave geologists some concept of the geography of a place? (Lawrence, etc.)

18. What books would you want in the glove compartment of your car? Why?

19. What can you find in the *Reader's Guide*? In the *Education Index*?

20. Get a copy of the telephone directories for this year and last year. Find five names that are new this year.

21. How many Chinese restaurants are there in your neighborhood or city? Where can you look to find out?

22. Look at the yellow pages and list some entries that intrigue you. Share why with us.

23. What are some words that you could use instead of the word heavy? Fast? Said?

24. How much does it cost to call information?

25. If you were having trouble with your telephone, what number(s) should you call?

26. How many words are listed in the dictionary between *yellow* and *yesterday*?

27. What is a telephone conference call? Station to station? Person to person? Toll free? Collect calls?

28. On what TV channel, time and day could you watch: News? A sports telecast? Cartoons? A film? A musical show? A children's show?

29. Be prepared to explain how to use the index for a mail order catalogue or to make out an order form.

30. Make up two questions that can be answered by looking them up in some standard reference book.

31. Teachers: Have a catalogue center which includes many kinds; e.g., Sears, car parts, Penney's, plants, seed, furniture, commercial supply catalogues used by many businesses, etc.

32. Teachers: Have a menu center featuring menus from local and famous restaurants. (Many will send you a menu if you send a stamped, self-addressed envelope.) Practice ordering, discuss what foreign words mean, etc. Use references such as dictionaries to help understand the menus.

33. Teachers: Have a center that features book reviews for your students' grade level. Have students compare their views of a book to that of other reviewers. Include *The Horn Book*, *Saturday Review*, *Ms.*, *Children's Catalogue*, and the like.

34. Teachers: Have good readers read aloud any material in a standard reference book that the students in the classroom need but which is written on too high a level for the majority of students.

LIBRARY SKILLS

Sample Activities for Discussion, Task Cards, Learning Centers, and Reading Contracts

1. Form a committee to find out what your library needs in the way of supplies or space. Make up a plan that could solve these difficulties and share it with us.

2. Make a chart of the library showing (or write the answers to the following): Where are new books kept? Where is the card catalogue? Where are fiction books? Where are nonfiction books? Where are the reference books? Other things you located.

3. Be class librarian for a day or for a week.

4. How many books are available in the library on your favorite hobby? (Alternates: Favorite pets, historical person, period in history, means of transportation, etc.)

5. How many books written by your favorite author are available in the library?

6. What other things besides books does your library offer?

7. Interview a librarian and make a chart of his or her duties.

8. Make a chart of the meaning of the Dewey decimal classification system used in our library.
9. Where would you look in the card catalogue to locate an author whose name begins with *Mc*? *Mac*?
10. Try to read one example of each type of book featured in the library. List what you read.
11. What Dewey decimal code would you use to find a recipe? A model airplane? Space stories? Books on American Indians? A story about a giant?
12. What is the difference between a biography and an autobiography?
13. What information is given on a card in the card catalogue?
14. Give the names of the illustrators for five of your favorite books.
15. Make up an entry for a card catalogue for one of the books you have written.
16. Plan a tour of the library for parents. Plan a tour of the library for students new to the school. (Alternate: Plan a slide show on our library for parents, new students, and/or smaller students.)
17. What is there about our library that pleases you most? What is there about the library that makes it hard for you to use it?
18. Set up a plan for organizing a cassette tape collection of literature, sound effects, and/or music for our library or for improving the existing one.
19. Research and make recommendations for new magazines for the library. Justify your choices.
20. Make up a flannelboard presentation for our class on how to use the library, how to use the card catalogue, how to use the Dewey decimal system, or some other aspect of library use of interest to you.
21. Sign up to help put the books back in place on the library shelves.
22. Find out what an autobiography is. Read one or more to get the flavor, and then write and illustrate your own.
23. Find out what a biography is. Read one or more to get the feel of the genre, then interview and write and illustrate one for someone you like.
24. What are three different ways to locate a book in a library?
25. Teachers: Have students practice alphabetic order skills by

finding words that begin with each letter of the alphabet in books they are reading.

26. Teachers: Ask students to think of or look up an author whose name begins with each of the following: *S, St, Str, Stre,* and so on.

27. Teachers: Ask students to alphabetize a stack of books by author and by title.

28. Teachers: Have a library day when you take the class to the public or school library.

29. Teachers: Have students play "Alphabet Categories," where they list one item for each letter of the alphabet for authors, book titles, and the like.

30. Teachers: Have a group of students interview the librarian each month about new books or other library materials and make up a display and/or lecture to present the items to other students.

31. Teachers: Select a group of students to be responsible for looking at reviews of new children's books (Use *The Horn Book, Childhood Education* reviews, and the like) and making suggestions for purchase to the librarian.

32. Teachers: Play "What Comes Before?" and "What Comes After?" with younger children to check their skills in alphabetizing. An alphabet letter is given. The player gets one point for naming the letter before it and one point for naming the letter after it. Play with individuals or with teams. (Alternate: Give two points for naming the two letters before or after any given letter.)

33. Teachers: Dismiss the class alphabetically, either by first or last names.

34. Teachers: Discuss what to do with old magazines. Should they be sent home on a regular schedule, sent to a home for elderly patients, to juvenile hall, or where?

35. Teachers: Hold a contest between teams in which a player from each team has a contest to see who can find a given book first from the call numbers.

BIBLIOGRAPHY SKILLS
Sample Activities for Discussion, Task Cards, Learning Centers, and Reading Contracts

1. What books would you take on an archaeological dig in Mexico? In New Mexico?

2. What books do you suggest an aspiring actor/actress needs to read?
3. If you were a mechanic, what reference books would you have in your shop?
4. Make an alphabetical list of books that are important to you (either by author or title). Explain the importance of each in your life.
5. Make a list of places, people and other kinds of references for ideas to make a study you have always wanted to make.
6. Look up and recommend five film strips or films you think our class would profit from. Be sure to explain your recommendations.
7. Does our library have any material or books on a research topic you are interested in? What are they?
8. Where could you go to get books you need to study one of your interests?
9. What is the Newbery Medal given for each year? The Caldecott Medal? The Edgar Allan Poe Award? The Mildred Batchelder Award?
10. Make a display of books that won one of the various awards for children's books, or of award-winning children's books for one year.
11. Make a list of authors and titles of books you would like in your own personal library.

A FINAL WORD ABOUT REFERENCE SKILLS

There are fascinating things to be learned via good reference skills—from the lifetime batting average of a favorite baseball player to the time the sun set on your birthdate. To locate these items, students need much practice in such reading skills as skimming, scanning, and surveying, since reference materials are not generally read word for word, cover to cover. Somewhere, someplace, in some reference, that information our students need to solve a problem, answer a question, or learn about themselves is waiting for them.

12

Teaching Reading Through Visual Thinking

* * * * * * * * * * * *

Visual thinking is the spice of reading. It helps readers to see in their mind's eye the actions, characters, experiences, settings, and adventures that each author describes in print. It allows our students to create with their imaginations peoples, countries, eras, civilizations, and possibilities that are theirs, alone. At the same time, with our help, visual thinking aids our students in experiencing the flavors of actual events, discoveries, personages, time spans, and locations in the fullest way possible, short of having been eye witnesses. In every sense, visual thinking is more vivid than watching films or television (essentially visual media that present the director's, producer's, and camera person's visualizations), since it calls forth visual stimuli not limited to the imagination or viewpoint of someone else. Well done, visualization uses each reader's entire sensory spectrum, including sensations of touch, feel, warmth, cold, hearing, smell, taste, as well as vision—seeing not what someone else thought the character or setting to be, for instance, but seeing what the character is, in the depths of the imaginations of each of our students.

COMPREHENSION SKILLS

Sample Activities for Discussion, Task Cards, Learning Centers, and Reading Contracts

1. What do you think is the favorite color of one of the story characters? How does the color make him or her feel? How

does your favorite color make you feel? (Characterization)

2. You can form a clear picture in your mind of the kind of person the main character is from clues the author gives you. Make a list of character traits this person has (honest, happy, strong, etc.). (Characterization)

3. Close your eyes and pretend you are one of the story characters. See yourself having all the adventures in the story. Share with us what you did. (Characterization)

4. Close your eyes and try to see in your mind the answer to each of these questions: Who was the main character of the story? Where did this story take place? How many characters were there in the story? What form did your answers take in your mind's eye? (Recall)

5. Get an image in your mind of one scene in the story. Describe everything you can experience in this scene. Reread the scene again. Did you remember it well? (Recall)

6. Close your eyes and try to see the answer to each of these word questions about the story: Who? Where? What? When? How? Share with us what you saw. (Main Idea)

7. In your mind's eye, try to see three words that tell about this story. How were the words written? Were they in color or black and white? Describe how these words looked to you. Why do you suppose you saw these three words? (Main Idea)

8. Close your eyes and see yourself ten years (or twenty-five years) from now. How do you look? What are you doing? What are you good at? What else do you see? (Alternate: Do the same for a story character.) (Inference or Conclusion)

9. What was something foolish that one of the story characters imagined? What was something ingenious that one of the story characters imagined? Something extraordinary? Have you ever imagined something similar? (Inference or Conclusion)

10. Make a cartoon strip of your story. (Sequence)

11. After you have read your story, close your eyes and see in your mind's eye the first event that happened. Reread that part of the story. Did you remember it correctly? (Alternates: the last event, the first three events, etc.) (Sequence)

12. Try to see in your mind's eye something funny that has happened to you. See all the details clearly. Feel the same

way you felt then. Tell (or draw) what happened. Now do the same with a funny part of this story. (Understanding Humor)

13. While I read aloud a part of a story (or a poem) that other students have found to be funny, try to see what is happening in your mind's eye. (Understanding Humor)

14. Read a page (a chapter) of your book, all the time trying to see and experience with your senses all the actions, the feelings, and the impressions in the story. Be ready to write (or tell) what you experienced. (Figurative Language)

15. Pick out the words or phrases from the story that helped you see a good word picture of some story event, setting, or character. (Figurative Language)

16. Close your eyes and try to see an image of what this word means. Share with us what you saw. (Note to teachers: Use both new and old reading vocabulary words for this exercise.) (Word Meanings)

17. Picture in your mind's eye what the word *reading* means to you. Share what you saw with us. (Word Meaning)

18. Think of something you said recently to someone that may have hurt them (or something someone said to you that hurt you). Now picture in your mind's eye the same scene again, but this time imagine yourself (or the person who hurt you) saying the same thing in a kinder way. How did you change the wording? (Paraphrasing)

19. Close your eyes and listen as I read you some dialogue from this story. Does it sound right to you? How could we change it to the way people really talk? (Paraphrasing)

20. Using our box of felt or construction paper scraps, make a picture to illustrate your book without cutting or tearing any of the scraps. (Synthesis)

21. Cut a circle out of the samples of wallpaper we have in our wallpaper book. Use this circle in some way in a picture you draw about the story. Use colored chalk, tempera, watercolors, or crayons to complete the picture. (Synthesis)

22. Be ready to act out a pretend telephone call one of the story characters might make to another. Let us hear only your side of the conversation. We'll try to imagine what the other character said. If you wish, tape-record your part of the conversation beforehand, so we can replay it. (Analysis)

23. On this page, some words have been left blank. See in your mind's eye what word is missing. (Example: He drove the ____ at 60 miles per hour.) (Analysis)

24. Try to picture one of the story characters as he or she was sometime in the past before this story happened. What do you see? What do you see the character doing? Sometimes writers use such scenes in stories or movies. They are called *flashbacks*. (Identifying Literary Device)

25. Imagine two of your story characters discussing some event. When writers include what characters say as a part of their story, it is called *dialogue*. Share your imagined dialogue with us. (Identifying Literary Device)

26. Make a list of words or phrases about time, weather, houses, costumes, and the like that help you see in your imagination the setting of this story. (Recognizing Story Elements)

27. Try to visualize the story ending in a different way. What do you see? (Recognizing Story Elements)

28. Finish this sentence: Tonight I will have a dream. I will dream about _____. (Prediction)

29. Imagine the situation the story characters will be in in one year, in five years; or imagine the situation you will be in in one year, in five years. Share with us what you saw. (Prediction)

30. Be ready to share any parts of the story where you are helped to see the action by a comparison of story events to something imaginary. An example of this might be: "It was raining cats and dogs." (Reality vs. Fantasy)

31. Which actions in this story couldn't you picture yourself doing in real life? (Reality vs. Fantasy)

32. Picture in your mind an event that might have caused the author to write this book. (Cause and Effect)

33. Picture in your mind an event that might have caused one of the story characters to be the kind of person he or she is. (Cause and Effect)

34. Picture in your mind's eye all the things in this story that could be red in color. Tell us what you saw. (Classification)

35. Draw a picture of everything in the story that begins with the letter *b*. (Classification)

36. What color do you think the cover of a book containing this

story should be? Share with us why you selected this color. (Summary Skills)

37. Design a book jacket for this story that uses only three colors and three arrows. Place them in any position you want and use other effects to help a reader know what the story is about from your jacket design. (Summary Skills)

38. We're going to make tissue paper collages while listening to music. Let how you feel and what you see in your mind's eye guide you in what you do with the tissue paper. (Alternates: Read aloud a poem or a story while making tissue paper collages.) (Comparing and Contrasting)

39. While I read aloud to you this new story, close your eyes and try to imagine the way the characters look, the setting, the terrain, the costumes, and so on. Afterwards, we'll talk about (or draw) what you experienced, so we can compare and contrast what each of you thought. (Comparing and Contrasting)

40. Look again at your story to find five words that describe how one of the story characters looked. (Locating Details)

41. Try to picture in your mind the page of the story on which the main character's name was first used. Where on that page was that name first written? Check to see if you were right. (Locating Details)

42. Read this page to yourself. Now picture the page in your mind. Where on the page is the word ___ written? The picture that illustrates the page? The number of the page? (Locating Details)

CRITICAL READING SKILLS

Sample Activities for Discussion, Task Cards, Learning Centers, and Reading Contracts

1. Close your eyes and try to see a time that you were very successful in reading. See what happened as clearly as if it were happening today. Share with us the success you recalled and how it felt at the time. (Evaluating the Reading Process)

2. Close your eyes while I ask some questions and wait to see what images come to your minds. What do you need to do next to become a better reader? What book has been espe-

cially important to you? (Evaluating the Reading Process)

3. If some time machine could transport you a month ahead of time, what would you like to see yourself doing for reading time? If the time machine could transport you back six months, what would you see? (Evaluating the Reading Process)

4. Visualize the perfect reading teacher. Share with us what you see. (Evaluating the Reading Process)

5. Picture in your mind the cover of a book you read recently that you thought was well written. What was the first book cover you saw? Why do you suppose you saw this book cover? (Evaluating Authors' Skills)

6. See in your mind's eye one word that tells how well this author writes. Explain your word. (Evaluating Authors' Skills)

7. Make up a symbol of some sort to indicate whether a book is poorly written, well written, or just about average. We need these symbols for our bulletin board on new books. (Evaluating Authors' Skills)

8. Picture in your mind's eye the following scene: There is a fire in the home of this author and he or she has time only to save three things. What three things do you see the author saving? (Alternate: Same scene with the author's main character saving three things. Discuss whether the main character reflects what the author believes.) (Analyzing Authors' Values)

9. Picture in your mind one thing this author believes to be right. What did you see? How do you know this is so? (Alternates: Picture things the author believes to be beautiful, effective, good, etc.) (Analyzing Authors' Values, Biases, Points of View)

10. Draw a picture of one of the story events from the point of view of two different story characters or from the point of view of someone who would disagree with the author. (Analyzing Authors' Values, Biases, Points of View)

11. See a picture in your mind of people who might disagree with what the author said in this book. Who would these people be? Why is this? (Analyzing Authors' Values, Biases, Points of View)

12. Picture in your mind one thing this author believes to be true about males. What did you see? Do you agree with the

author on this? Would everyone? (Analyzing Authors'
Hidden Assumptions)

13. Draw a picture of what this author means by the word
    family. Share why you think your drawing shows what the
    author believes a family to be. Are all families like this?
    (Analyzing Authors' Hidden Assumptions)

14. Draw a cover of a book you could write that would make
    you feel better (or successful or smart or richer). Find and
    share a book that you feel was written by an author for this
    same reason. (Discovering Authors' Purposes)

15. Why do you think this author wrote this book? Draw the
    cover of a book you could write for the same reason. (Dis-
    covering Authors' Purposes)

16. See in your mind's eye a picture of the author at work
    writing your story. What do you see him or her doing first?
    Second? Next? Describe all the steps you see the author
    taking in writing this. (Analyzing Authors' Organizational
    Patterns)

17. See in your mind's eye the place where the author might
    have sat as he or she wrote this book. What materials do
    you see? What references do you see? What time is it? What
    else do you see? (Analyzing Authors' Organizational Pat-
    terns)

18. As I read a part of this story aloud, see how hard or difficult
    it is for you to get a mental picture of the story. What did
    the author do that helped you? Hindered you? (Analyzing
    Authors' Organizational Patterns)

19. Make a chart of fact vs. opinion in your story. (Separating
    Fact from Opinion)

20. Make a list of at least three of the author's opinions from
    this reading selection. From your list, try to get a mental
    picture of what the author looks like. If you can, find a
    picture of this author to compare with your mental image.
    If not, be ready to tell how you think the author looks.
    (Separating Fact from Opinion)

21. Make an exhibit of propaganda techniques you find in
    newspapers, books, magazines, television, or advertise-
    ments. Choose some friends to help you, if you wish. (Rec-
    ognizing Propaganda)

22. Find an ad in a newspaper or magazine that appeals to you
    and one that does not. What differences do you see be-

tween the two ads? What propaganda techniques are used in each? Can you picture yourself using the product advertised? (Recognizing Propaganda)

23. Find an illustration in a book, magazine, or newsaper that gives a stereotyped view of males or females, of a certain group of people by race.

24. Here are five pictures of people along with a list of their occupations. Try to match occupations with faces. How successful were you? (Identifying Stereotypes)

25. Find a film or a picture in the library that pictures the location of this story. How close was the author's description of the setting of this story to the picture or the film? (Determining the Reliability and Validity of Written Materials)

26. Find a book written about the place where you live. How well did the author describe your area? Does his or her description ring true to you? (Determining the Reliability and Validity of Written Material)

27. Draw a picture of some scene, event, or person in your story. Make one part or detail of your drawing inaccurate or an error. See if the people in our class who have read your story can find the error. Think hard so you will stump them or really make them think. (Evaluating Content and Format of Written Material)

28. Does the book cover fit the book that you just read? Why or why not? (Evaluating Content and Format of Written Material)

29. Find two descriptions of the same event, person, or location in two different books. Which description helps you see best what is described? (Comparing Two or More Sources)

30. Compare the illustrations in two similar books written about the same subject, person, or event. Which book's illustrations did you feel were the best? Why is this? (Alternate: Compare covers of books written on the same subject.) (Comparing Two or More Sources)

31. Picture yourself doing the same things the main character in this story did. Would you be a better person if you acted as he or she did? (Analyzing Self Through Critical Reading)

32. Read the story through a second time. Did you see anything new or differently the second time? (Analyzing Self Through Critical Reading)

CREATIVE READING SKILLS

Sample Activities for Discussion, Task Cards, Learning Centers, and Reading Contracts

1. We all daydream. Let your mind daydream for a few moments, then write a story about one of the daydreams you had (or draw a picture of it). (Developing Author Skills)
2. Write a pretend interview with one of the story characters about upcoming holiday plans or a new adventure. (Developing Author Skills)
3. See yourself as an author or a writer. What kinds of things are you writing? What does your writing area look like? How old are you? Share with us the kind of writer you saw yourself being. (Developing Author Skills)
4. Write a message that could be put in a bottle and set loose in a river or the ocean. Imagine who will find the bottle, under what circumstances, and what the person will do about the message. (Creating Original Materials)
5. Draw, paint, write, or tell about your own secret place in your mind where you can go when you want or need to. What is there? Who is there? What can you do? What else can you share about your secret place? (Creating Original Materials)
6. Design a maze based on the story (or design a maze that has nothing to do with the story.) If you don't know what a maze is, study the books of mazes in the library. (Designing Games, Puzzles, Anagrams, etc.)
7. Design a toy or an imaginary tool that the main character would like or could use. (Designing Games, Puzzles, Anagrams, etc.)
8. How many objects or people from your story can you draw that include this shape? (Creative Thinking – Divergent)

9. See the main character in your mind's eye. Make the character's clothes green. Red. Blue. Purple. Now see the

character with a pink face. Orange. Brown. Now open your eyes and tell us how you were able to do this. (Creative Thinking – Convergent)

10. Daydream about adventures in which you solve a problem for someone. For instance, a rowboat springs a leak, a fire breaks out in the classroom, or the like. Share with us (either by writing or by talking) how you saved the day. Use a story you have read as the basis for your daydream, if you wish (Problem-Solving)

11. Sometimes the solutions to problems we have can come to us in the middle of the night while we're dreaming or half awake. Share with us a time when this happened to you. (Problem-Solving)

12. Tonight, before you go to sleep, think of a problem you have and ask your mind to solve it for you while you sleep. We'll talk tomorrow about what happened or what solution came to you. (Problem-Solving)

13. Draw a plan of the ideal classroom for learning to be a good reader. (Planning)

14. Daydream for a few moments about an ideal vacation. After you have had a few minutes to think about yourself experiencing this ideal vacation, think of the first step you would have to take to make it a reality. (Planning)

15. Play *Twenty Questions* with some friends about a story you have all read. (Formulating Questions)

16. What questions would you like to ask the author that would help you see the setting, a character, or a story event more clearly? (Formulating Questions)

17. Play one of the story records or tapes from our library and then read the same story for yourself. Which way did you enjoy the story most? (Relation of Reading to Other Media)

18. Design a stage setting for a puppet play, a film, or a TV show about this story. (Relation of Reading to Other Media)

19. Write a story, a description of something that happened to you, or a description of a friend. Put it aside for one week. One week later, look at the story as if it had been written by someone else. What do you like about it? What did you leave out? What do you want to add to the writing? What should you take out? What could you do to make the work better? Does your work seem better or worse to you than it

did a week ago? What do you need to do to make it what you want it to be? (Evaluating One's Own Written Work)

20. Write a description of a place you enjoy being. Describe it so well that we can see it in our mind's eye. (Evaluating One's Own Written Work)

21. Write a letter to yourself about all the things you would like to do better in reading. We'll put these letters away and look at them in a month to see how we are doing. (Improving Self-Concept and Self-Development)

22. Decide on one thing that one of the story characters did that you would like to do (or perhaps one of the ways a story character was that you'd like to be). Close your eyes and see yourself doing (or being) what the story character did (or was). What do you see yourself doing (or being)? (Improving Self-Concept and Self-Development)

23. What is something you could do today to make yourself more like your favorite story character? (Improving Self-Concept and Self-Development)

24. What things in this story could help you have a better life? Close your eyes and imagine yourself doing this. Share with us what you see. (Reader Purpose Skills)

25. Imagine yourself being a better reader. Close your eyes and see yourself being this better reader. What did you see yourself doing? (Reader Purpose Skills)

26. Design an ideal library for yourself. What would you include to help you enjoy the library more? (Recreational Reading)

27. Imagine yourself as your favorite story character. What do you see yourself doing? (Recreational Reading)

28. Did you ever read about something that you wish you had done or you wish you had said? Write a story (or tell us) about it. (Emotional Response)

29. I'm going to read a passage from this book to you while you have your eyes closed, then again while you have your eyes open. Tell which way you enjoy the most. (Emotional Response)

LITERATURE APPRECIATION SKILLS

1. Picture yourself in your mind's eye as a good reader. See yourself doing the things a good reader does, acting as a

good reader does, getting a report card that shows you are a good reader. What would that report card look like? What do you see yourself doing as a good reader? How would your life be better if you were a good reader? (Value of Reading)

2. Share with us a book that was helpful to you in developing a picture of yourself as a better person. (Value of Reading)
3. Review in your mind's eye the actions of one story character. What parts of this story character are like you and which parts are not? (Recognizing Story Elements)
4. Close your eyes and "flashback" in your mind to a time in your life that was similar to something in this story. Experience again all the feelings you had at that time. Share with us what you saw in your "flashback." (Recognizing Story Elements)
5. Make a cartoon strip of this story or book. (Recognizing Story Elements)
6. Can you see in your mind's eye another setting in which this story could take place? (Recognizing Story Elements)
7. What kinds of stories do you most enjoy having read aloud to you? Share with us some of the reasons this is so. (Recognizing Literary Forms)
8. Look in the TV section for this week to find a program based on a book in our library or a book you have read. Watch the show and share your reactions with us. What kind of book (fairy tale, fiction, etc.) was the basis for the television show? (Recognizing Literary Forms)
9. What are three different kinds of books that make good television programs or good movies? Why is this so? (Recognizing Literary Forms)
10. Draw a map of the setting of your story. How did this setting affect the lives of the story characters? (Cultural Analysis Through Literature)
11. Make a display of books on the culture of one part of your ancestry. Did you learn anything new about this culture from these books? (Cultural Analysis Through Literature)
12. See in your mind's eye a picture of your favorite character in the story. See yourself. In which ways do you and the story character look alike? Think alike? Act alike? (Bibliotherapy)

13. What story character could you see yourself being in real life? Why is this? (Bibliotherapy)
14. Close your eyes and picture yourself and one of the story characters walking toward each other on a lonely road. Picture yourself meeting. Watch the meeting for a few moments. (Pause.) What did you do? What did the lonely road look like? (Bibliotherapy)
15. Design an award to present to your favorite author. (Identifying Famous Authors and Writings)
16. Select a book that won an award for illustration or for writing. List at least three reasons why you believe the book won this award. (Identifying Famous Authors and Writings)
17. Picture yourself walking into a bookstore. You have enough money to buy three books for yourself. In your mind, see yourself walking around and selecting the three books. What books did you buy? Any guesses as to why you bought those three books? (Selecting Appropriate Material)
18. Picture in your mind a member of your family or a friend receiving a book as a birthday present that made him or her very happy. See the person opening the gift package and being happy. Who was the person? What was the book? What did the person do on unwrapping the book? (Selecting Appropriate Material)

VOCABULARY DEVELOPMENT SKILLS

1. Imagine yourself meeting one of the story characters for the first time. What do you hear yourself saying? What would the story character say? What would you do? (Vocabulary Patterning)
2. Picture in your mind a good friend of yours (or your teacher or someone in your family.) Hear them saying something that they often say. Share with us what they said. (Vocabulary Patterning)
3. Picture to yourself one ending to this sentence: Red is _____. Now picture another ending. Now picture a third. Share with us what you saw. (Vocabulary Patterning)
4. Using our tinker toys, erector set, or building logs, make a

representation or creation to explain what one of the new vocabulary words in your story means. (New Vocabulary)

5. Think of two new words you have learned this week. Picture yourself using these two words in some situation. See in your mind's eye all that might happen at the time you use these two words. Share the scene you saw in your imagination with us. (New Vocabulary)

6. While we watch a film about an occupation, write down all the words you hear that are special to that occupation. (Alternate: Listen to a story that contains occupational vocabulary.) (New Vocabulary)

7. Listen to a police channel broadcast for a few minutes and try to get a picture of the action or of what is happening. (Alternate: Listen to control tower instructions.) Remember any words you don't know and we'll talk about them. (New Vocabulary)

8. Animals are sometimes used to help us understand something about a person, an object, or an event in a story; for instance, "swift as a deer," or "busy as a bee." See if you can think of three of these sayings or find three in the book you are reading. (Figurative Language – Similes)

9. If you were an animal, what animal would you be? What word? (Special Word Relationships – Synonyms)

10. Draw a picture of the meaning of two words that sound the same but mean different things, that are written the same but mean different things, that mean the opposite from each other, or that mean the same thing. (Special Word Relationships – Synonyms, Antonyms, Homonyms, Homographs)

11. While you listen to the sound of a person's voice on a tape recorder, picture in your mind what the person looks like. Later, I'll show you a picture of this person to see how accurate a mental picture you got from her or his voice. (Variations of Vocabulary)

12. Tape-record the voice of someone you know. Play it back for the class to see if we can picture the person from his or her voice. (Variations of Vocabulary)

13. What person in our room would you choose to be the voice for each character in this story on a tape-recorded dramatization we'll make this afternoon?

14. If you were to write the script for a film or a television special based on this story, what are some words or phrases you'd be sure to have the main character say so he or she would sound authentic or "right" in his or her speech? (Appropriateness of Vocabulary)

15. Listen to yourself carefully all day today. At the end of the day we'll talk about any words you wished you hadn't used or words you wish you had used instead. (Appropriateness of Vocabulary)

16. Who in our classroom do you think uses words well? (Appropriatenss of Vocabulary)

17. Picture yourself as having some other name. What name did you give yourself? How would you be different if you had that name? Look up what this name means in a book that gives the meanings of different names. (Etymology)

18. Draw a picture of the meaning of your name, of a friend's name, or of the name of someone in your family. We'll try to guess from the picture which name you drew. (Etymology)

19. Pretend you are ready to take a picture with your camera of something very special; something of which you want a good picture, but you find you have run out of film. Describe the picture so well in words that listeners could see the picture in their minds from your word description alone. (Figurative or Idiomatic Vocabulary)

20. As clearly and as thoroughly as you can, tell us how you picture one of the main story characters. (Alternate: Describe a room in a character's house.) (Figurative or Idiomatic Vocabulary)

21. Close your eyes and see what different images you get when I stress each word of this sentence. (Example: *That's* not all. That's *not* all. That's not *all*?) Share with us what you saw. (Relating Word Stress, Pitch, and Intonation to Meaning)

22. The color for uncertainty is ____. (Alternates: Failure, success, good intentions, etc.) (Word Meanings; Figurative Language – Analogies)

23. Be ready to write (or tell) what you see in your mind when you see or hear the words *trees, night, slink, powerful,* or *white.* List five other words and be ready to write (or tell)

what they cause you to see in your mind's eye. (Word Meanings)

24. Describe how to play a certain sport without using words. (Nonverbal Vocabulary)

25. Use pantomime to show the meaning of each of these words: *run, sticky, upset, quick, lazy, banana*, etc. (Nonverbal Vocabulary)

26. What interesting words did the author use that helped you see pictures in your mind? (Word Enrichment)

27. See in your mind the most beautiful person you know. Use five words to describe that person. (Word Enrichment)

WORD PERCEPTION SKILLS

Sample Activities for Discussion, Task Cards, Learning Centers, and Reading Contracts

1. Draw a chart or a picture of the origins of your first, middle, and last names. (Etymological Cues)

2. Draw a map of the routes three different groups of peoples took in settling your area. List three different words each group contributed to your language. (Etymological Cues)

3. Play a game of *Hangman* with three other friends. (Configuration Cues)

4. Make a design by cutting out or drawing one of our new vocabulary words on a folded piece of paper. (Configuration Cues)

5. Cut out of cardboard or tagboard the shape of three words from our story. Choose a friend to play with who has also cut out the shape of three words. Close your eyes and see if you can guess the words by feeling the shape of the words your friend cut out. See if your friend can identify the three you cut out. (Configuration Cues)

6. Choose five words from our reader that you do not yet know. Make flashcards for the five. Practice by yourself until you know the five by sight. When you're ready, ask a friend or the teacher to check how well you know the words. (Sight Cues)

7. See if you can see an image of each word in your mind while I pronounce five words from the story. How did each

word look? What kind of writing did you see? What colors were the letters? The background? (Sight Cues)

8. Select three objects from our odds and ends box (or learning center). Look at them carefully. Name at least three ways the three objects are alike and three ways they are different. (Word Similarities and Differences)

9. Select three words from our story. Look at them carefully. Name at least three ways they are alike and three ways they are different. (Word Similarities and Differences)

10. Cut out from sandpaper or velvet scraps the letters needed to form three words from your story. Close your eyes. Put the words together correctly by touch alone. (Alternate: Use letter shapes the teacher provides.) (Kinesthetic Cues)

11. Write five of our new vocabulary words using the letter stencils at the stencil table. Make a poster or a design from the five words if you wish. (Kinesthetic Cues)

12. Close your eyes and see a word that fits the consonant-vowel-consonant (CVC) pattern. What word did you see? See another word that fits the same pattern. What was the second word? Can you see or imagine any other words that use the CVC pattern? (Linguistic Cues)

13. List as many words as you can see in your mind that have the letters *at* somewhere in the word. (Linguistic Cues)

14. Close your eyes and try to get a picture in your mind of what each of these three new reading words mean to you. We'll compare images when we've finished. (Semantic Cues)

15. Draw at least four pictures that show different meanings for the word *run*. (Alternates: The words *bill, saw,* etc.) (Semantic Cues)

16. Make up a description of one person in our room. Every time you come to his or her name while writing (or telling) the description, leave a blank. We'll try to guess who you are describing. (Context Cues)

17. Choose one paragraph from our story to read aloud. Skip every fifth word while you read it aloud to us. We'll try to see the missing words in our minds every time you come to them. (Context Cues)

18. See in your mind an image for each of these words as I read them aloud to you. We'll talk about the image you see after

I read each word: car–cars, boy–boys, tree–trees, etc. (Structural Analysis)

19. Make a word family chart or draw a word family tree for all the words you can think of that contain the suffix *ful* or *full*. (Note to teachers: Similarly assign other common suffixes, roots, or prefixes.) (Structural Analysis)

20. Close your eyes and listen while I clap out a syllable pattern. (Example: clap–CLAP–clap.) What words do you know that fit that syllable rhythm pattern? (Syllable Analysis)

21. Make a list of as many words as you can that have the syllable __ (Examples: *on, lot, mi*, etc.) in them. (Syllable Analysis)

22. Close your eyes and listen while I read the same sentence in different ways stressing different words each time. What kind of emotion does each stress pattern suggest? (Accent Analysis)

23. Tape-record one sentence from your story four times, using a different type of voice each time such as an angry voice, a happy voice, etc. We'll try to guess the type of voice you were using. (Accent Analysis)

24. Make a connect-the-letters puzzle by using letters from the alphabet or by using the letters of new vocabulary words. (Encoding-Decoding, or Phonics Cues)

25. Make up a four-line poem about someone, some thing, or some event ffrom your story. (Encoding-Decoding, or Phonics Cues)

26. Make a collage of five or more words that begin with the same sound (or contain the same medial or ending sound). (Encoding-Decoding, or Phonics Cues)

27. Write each word from a sentence in your story on a separate card. Rearrange the cards as many ways as you can to form other sentences that make sense. (Syntax Cues)

28. Write down on separate cards five words that describe something (adjectives). Put these words in a pile. Write down on separate cards five words that name a person, place, or thing (nouns). Use interesting nouns and adjectives. Have a friend choose a card from each pile and draw (or describe) what he or she chose. (Alternate: Use the two words in three sentences.) (Syntax Cues)

AUDITORY PERCEPTION SKILLS

Sample Activities for Discussion, Task Cards, Learning Centers, and Reading Contracts

1. Tape-record an imaginary dialogue passage that describes a few moments in the life of a waiter or waitress, a short order cook, or a secretary. Choose friends to help if you wish. (Auditory Figure-Ground)

2. Make a tape-recording of the sounds in our classroom during some five minute period today. We'll play it back and discuss what we hear on it during reading time. (Auditory Figure-Ground)

3. Shut your eyes and pay attention only to what I am saying. Shut out all other sounds. Think of your favorite person. See his or her face. Think of things that make this person feel good. Think of this person wearing his or her favorite clothes. See this person eating his or her favorite food. Think of other things this person likes to do. Doesn't like to do. Write a story (or tell us) about what you saw. (Auditory Figure-Ground)

4. Choose your favorite character from the story to impersonate when we play *What's My Line?* today at _____ . We'll have fun listening to and remembering all the clues we get as other students do the same. (Auditory Memory)

5. Close your eyes and see these things in your mind's eye: a flower opening, a cat stretching, a boy playing, a woman working, a car racing, a ball bouncing. Open your eyes and tell us the details of what you saw in the order I gave them to you. (Auditory Memory)

6. Close your eyes and try to hear in your imagination endings for each of these sentences: See me _____. Hear _____ (story character) say _____. Come and _____. Blue is _____. (Auditory Closure)

7. Close your eyes and listen while I play the opening notes of a familiar song one at a time. Raise your hand when you know the song. (Alternate: Teachers: Give only the first three notes of a song. Have students close their eyes and listen, then tell you the name of the song.) (Auditory Closure)

8. Listen while I (or a student) read(s) a paragraph from to-day's story using different emotions in our voice. See if you can hear what emotion we feel by the way we read. (Auditory Pitch, Timbre, Stress, and Intonation Skills)

9. Tape record some of the dialogue from your story trying to sound as much as possible like one of the characters. (Auditory Pitch, Timbre, Stress, and Intonation)

10. Close your eyes and try to hear in your mind exactly what was said during one of the dialogue passages in your story. Hear the first thing that was said, and so on. Check how well you remember by rereading that part of your story again. Could you do it? (Auditory Sequence)

11. Listen carefully while I read aloud to you a new, interesting story. After I finish, we'll talk about the sequence of the story, or what happened first, second, and the like. (Auditory Sequence)

12. Close your eyes and listen to the first three sounds you hear. Make up a story using those three sounds. (Auditory Sequence)

13. Draw a rebus sentence using one sentence from your story. (Auditory Blending)

14. I'm going to give you three sounds that make up a word. The sounds may not be in order. Try to guess what the word is. (Example: *t, a, c.*) (Auditory Blending)

15. Close your eyes and try to hear with your mind's eye words that have the syllable *sol* in them. The syllable *al*, etc. (Auditory Blending)

16. Tape-record one paragraph from your story trying to sound as if you were some famous film or TV star. We'll try to guess who you are by the way you sound. (Auditory Discrimination)

17. Tape-record three common sounds around school or the home. We'll try to guess what you recorded. (Auditory Discrimination)

18. Listen with your eyes closed and tell me the differences you hear between these words: came–come, sing–sang, ran–tan, etc. (Auditory Discrimination)

19. Are any words used in the story that help you hear what was happening; for example, "the whistling teakettle"? (Auditory Comprehension)

20. I'm going to read a poem aloud to you. Close your eyes and

imagine what the setting looks like. We'll discuss what each of you imagined when I'm finished. (Auditory Comprehension)

21. I'm going to play some music and I'll turn the lights off so you'll be listening to it in the dark. While you're listening, use the fingerpaints (crayons, tempera, colored chalk, clay, etc.) to express what you feel. (Auditory Comprehension)

22. Find a picture or illustration that you particularly like in your book. Close your eyes and try to hear all the sounds that it would be possible to hear on an imaginary walk through this setting. (Auditory Tracking)

23. Close your eyes and pretend you are in a forest or a jungle. Hear a bird above your head. Hear an animal behind you. Hear a limb fall from a tree to your left. Hear an animal run from left to right in front of you. When you open your eyes, tell us (or draw) what you saw. (Auditory Tracking)

24. Write up or tape-record five cues to some setting or place in the school or in the neighborhood. During game time we'll try to guess the place you are describing. (Listening)

25. Choose a good story for me to read aloud to our class tomorrow. (Listening)

26. Write a story or a poem that tells about your favorite sounds. (Listening)

27. Make a list of five words that you enjoy hearing. (Listening)

28. Be ready to tell us briefly about a beautiful sight you have seen. Be ready to tell us so clearly that we can see in our mind's eye just what you saw. (Oral Language)

29. Practice reading aloud a poem you like until you can read it aloud to us so well that we can see in our mind's eye what the writer meant. (Oral Language)

30. To whose voices do you enjoy listening while they talk or read a story aloud? Why is this? (Oral Langauge)

VISUAL PERCEPTION SKILLS

Sample Activities for Discussion, Task Cards, Learning Centers, and Reading Contracts

1. Write down the names of five friends. What color do you feel best represents each one? Why is this? (Visual Comprehension)

2. What color do you feel represents you best? Tell us why. (Visual Comprehension)
3. Draw a picture of some object or person in the story. Draw your picture in such a way that it is clear to anyone who looks at it that the object or person is moving in some type of action. What did you have to do in your drawing to indicate this motion? (Visual Comprehension)
4. Choose one of the scraps of plywood in our art center. Look carefully at your scrap in a sort of dreamy way until you begin to see forms, shapes, or people emerge from the wood grain pattern. Paint what you see right on the plywood, using the wood grain pattern as part of your picture. (Alternate: Use driftwood.)
5. Use this squiggle in a drawing you make of something about the story: (Visual Figure-Ground)

6. Find an illustration from the story in which you can find either a circle, a triangle, or a square hidden somewhere in the picture. (Visual Figure-Ground)
7. Each of these photographs has been cut in half. Choose one and tell us what you think is on the part that is cut away. We'll compare your thoughts with the actual picture when you finish. Maybe what you "see" in your mind's eye will be more exciting than the actual picture. (Visual Closure)
8. Think of an object from your story. Draw one detail at a time until the students in the class can guess what it is. (Visual Closure) Example:

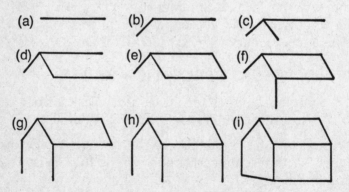

9. Select five objects from this box. Put them on a sheet of paper. Look at them for a moment. Have a friend take one away while you hide your eyes. See if you can guess which one is missing. If you can, play the game again using more objects. How many can you remember at a time? (Visual Memory)

10. Look carefully at the front page of this newspaper for a few seconds. Good. Now I'll put it away. Draw a quick sketch of what was on that page. Look at it again. I'll put it away again. Add to your sketch anything you forgot. We'll do that again. Now compare what you remembered with the original. (Note to teachers: Use pages in a book or magazine, transparencies, or material on opaque projectors in a similar fashion.) (Visual Memory)

11. Draw a cartoon strip (or make up a chart) that shows how to do something. (Alternate: Draw a cartoon strip of some action from your story.) (Visual Sequence)

12. Make a word scramble for our new vocabulary words for us to figure out. Put your list of scrambled words in the puzzle center. (Visual Sequence)

13. See one of a pair of dice in your mind's eye. See one dot on the top and two dots on the side facing you. How many dots are on the bottom? How many dots are on the side away from you opposite the two dots facing you? Roll the dice over in your mind so that it tips one roll away from you so the side with two dots is on top. How many dots are on the side facing you now? How many dots are on the bottom? (Alternate: Picture two dice moving in similar ways.) (Form Constancy)

14. Draw an object, a person, or an event from the story as seen by a bird, an ant, a person from an airplane, or a person from Mars. (Form Constancy)

15. In your mind, picture a cylindrical package of cookie dough, covered with nuts, lying on its side. Cut the dough in half so the pieces are still cylinders. How many pieces do you have now? (Two) Cut these pieces in half again. How many pieces do you have now? (Four)

16. Make a design for a small paper box from one sheet of paper. Make a pattern of your box for our design center. Compare your pattern with those other students design. (Form Perception)

17. Draw a design. Repeat it five times in all. On one of the designs, leave out one part. Put your design in our puzzle center to see who can find the design with the missing part. (Visual Discrimination) Example:

18. Find a picture of the outside of some building. Draw a floor plan for that building based on the picture. (Visual Discrimination)

19. Read any page of the story. Put it down and try to see the happenings you read about on the page in your mind's eye. Write (or be ready to tell) what you saw. (Visualization)

20. We're going to listen to musical selections in two ways, with the classroom lights on and with them off (or with eyes open or closed). Some of you will enjoy the music more while listening in the dark; some will enjoy it more with the lights on. We'll discover which *after* you have a chance to hear the music both ways. Some of you may like listening both ways. (Visualization)

21. Close your eyes and wait for an image of something in your mind. Share with us what you saw. (Visualization)

22. See in your mind an object from the story in some type of action. Watch it move. Describe (or draw) what you see. (Visual Tracking)

23. Watch while I draw an object (a letter or a word) in the air. Can you guess what it is? (Visual Tracking)

24. How many times can you find the word ____ on this page? (Eye Movements)

25. How many places can you see the color ____ in our room? (Alternate: in this picture or illustration?) (Eye Movements)

26. Work with the controlled reader today during choice time. How fast do you want it to be set? Why? (Left-to-Right Eye Movements)

27. Arrange with the school nurse to give us a talk on eye movements during reading or prepare a report on this subject yourself. (Left-to-Right Eye Movements)

PERCEPTION SKILLS

1. Were any words used in the story that helped you "smell" what was happening? (Olfactory Perception)
2. Find or draw pictures of smells you enjoy. (Olfactory Perception)
3. What do you see in your mind when you smell each of the following? (Note to teachers: Provide several things for the students to smell.) (Olfactory Perception)
4. See if you can really experience an imaginary smell. Close your eyes and try to smell: a fire burning, bacon cooking, the first raindrops on a summer day, apples, etc. Tell us what you experienced. (Olfactory Perception)
5. Pretend you are eating one of your favorite foods. Describe to us in words how it tastes without using the name of the food. Let us see if we can guess what you are describing. (Taste Perception)
6. Close your eyes and imagine that you are at a dinner where some of your favorite foods are being served. Savor the aroma for a few moments. Tell us what you smelled. (Taste Perception)
7. If you were a castaway on a desert island, what foods do you think you would dream about? (Taste Perception)
8. Imagine you are touching something that one of the characters touched. How does it feel? What is its temperature? Is it rough or smooth or what? Describe it to us. (Tactile Perception)
9. We'll all close our eyes while someone describes how something feels to the touch without telling us what it is. We'll try to guess what they are describing. (Tactile Perception)
10. Close your eyes and try to feel: a sunny day, warm sand at the beach, cold water, raindrops on your face. (Tactile Perception)
11. Make a list of words in this story which helped you to see, hear, smell, or feel something from the story. (Maybe all at once!) (Multisensory Perception)
12. Choose a partner for a sensory awareness walk where one leads the other for a walk while the one being led has his or her eyes closed. The one doing the leading should try to

find interesting things for the one being led to feel, smell, etc. Reverse roles after a while so you both get a chance at leading and being led. What did you enjoy most? What did you learn about each other? (Multisensory Perception)

13. Listen with your eyes closed while I read you a poem or story. Imagine what it would feel like to be in this setting. We'll share afterwards. (Multisensory Perception)

14. Close your eyes and pretend you are somewhere else away from the classroom. Select a spot you truly enjoy. Write a story about your spot. (Position in Space)

15. Many of us have imaginary secret hideaways where we go to rest or relax. Imagine one for yourself. What is your secret place like? (Position in Space)

16. Draw a sketch or describe your ideal home (school, classroom, etc.). (Position in Space)

17. Close your eyes and see the animal you would be if you were an animal. Now see the animal you wish you were. Have them meet. Describe to us (or draw a picture of) what they did. (Position in Space)

18. Using the tinker toys or the erector set, make a representation of some scene or some object in the story. (Alternates: Use playing cards, spaghetti, macaroni, rice, or the like.) (Hand-Eye Coordination)

19. Work one of the dot-to-dot pictures in the puzzle learning center. (Hand-Eye Coordination)

20. Close your eyes and play a pretend game of jacks (tetherball, dodgeball, etc.). Describe to us what you felt. (Hand-Eye Coordination)

21. Design a class yell using pompoms, balloons, or flags. (General Coordination)

22. Pantomime some event from your story. We'll try to guess which. (General Coordination)

23. Prepare a good item for *Charades* for our game tomorrow. Use your story or book for inspection. (General Coordination)

24. Design a dance (or a game) based on the story. (Motor Coordination)

25. Visualize in your mind's eye how one of the story characters would run. Show us how they would do it. (Motor Coordination)

26. Visualize yourself dancing to a slow tune, a fast song. What did you see yourself doing? (Motor Coordination)
27. Close your eyes and stand quietly while you listen to this music. Make sure there is enough room so you won't touch anyone else. With your eyes closed and without talking, move your arms in some way to the music. Now open your eyes and move your whole body in some way to the music. Don't watch what others are doing. (Body Awareness)
28. Close your eyes and follow these directions. Wave your right hand. Hold up your left thumb. Touch your left shoulder with your right hand. (Etc.) (Laterality)
29. Cut out three pictures of people using their right hands. (Laterality)
30. Make a list without looking of all the left-handed students in our class. (Laterality)
31. Close your eyes and pretend you are a dancer in a chorus line. Watch yourself dance. Show (or tell) us what you did. (Alternates: Skaters, swimmers.) (Directionality)
32. Design a dance featuring balls, fans, flags, balloons, or other objects. Be ready to teach us your dance. (Directionality)
33. Here is a list of students in our classroom. From memory, list them in order of height, with 1 the tallest and ＿＿ the smallest. Check your memory at ＿＿ o'clock when we'll line up by height to see where everyone fits. (Spatial Relationships)
34. What comes next in this pattern? (Spatial Relationships)

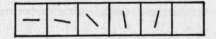

35. Picture a square piece of paper. In your mind's eye, picture yourself folding it in half. What shape is each half? Now picture yourself folding another identical square piece of paper in half a different way. What shape is each half now? (Answers: Rectangle, triangle, etc.) (Spatial Relationships)
36. Teachers: To give a rest break during particularly long or intensive or repetitive work assignments, have students

take time out to pretend that they are rag dolls or stuffed toys and move their bodies accordingly. (Body Awareness)

WORK-STUDY SKILLS

Sample Activities for Discussion, Task Cards, Learning Centers, and Reading Contracts

1. From a map or a globe, pick out a place you have never been to but think you would like to go to. Imagine yourself living there. See in your mind's eye how your life would change. Use books, magazines, or study films about this.
2. Make an imaginary map of the type of location you would consider ideal to live in. (Map and Globe Skills)
3. Imagine how five different occupations would view the same picture; for instance, a farmer, a sports broadcaster, and the like. Choose a picture from a book, a magazine, or the picture exhibit table for this exercise. (Interpreting Pictures and Illustrations)
4. Make a diagram of some dream you have had at night or of some daydream you have had. (Interpreting Graphic Materials – Diagrams)
5. Find or draw a cartoon about daydreaming. (Interpreting Pictures and Illustrations)
6. Choose an illustration you especially like from a book in our library. Look at the picture closely and imagine yourself in the scene. Experience the sights, sounds, feels, colors, smells you would find there. Share your experience with us either with words, movement, art, or music. (Interpreting Pictures and Illustrations)
7. Look at a newspaper page. Note the first thing that catches your eye. Imagine what the headline or picture is about. Check your imagining by reading about it. (Reading Techniques – Skimming)
8. Take one of the menus from our menu center. Scan the menu to decide what foods appeal to you right now. Imagine yourself ordering those items and enjoying them. Taste, smell, eat, talk, relax in your daydream as if you were there. Share with us what you did with words, pictures, or sounds. (Reading Techniques – Scanning)
9. Listen to the following directions with your eyes closed. Try to visualize what is happening each step of the way.

Take four pretend steps forward. Take three pretend steps to the left. Take one pretend step backwards. Take three pretend steps to the right. Take three pretend steps backwards. Where are you? (Following Directions)

10. Write or tell us the steps to take to have a good daydream. (Following Directions)

11. Pretend you are a writer about to write a mystery story. List (or tell us) at least four steps you would take to create the story. (Note Taking)

12. List three things you would like to get done this week, or three things that you are glad you accomplished today. (Note Taking)

13. Imagine yourself cooking your favorite food. See yourself following each step of the recipe in order. Smell the smells, hear the sounds, feel the textures you would encounter. Now imagine yourself eating the results. Imagine all the tastes, feels, smells, sounds, and so on you would experience if you were really eating the food. If you don't know the recipe, look one up in our cooking center. Make notes of what you experienced. (Note Taking)

14. Imagine yourself accomplishing some task at school that you would like to finish this week. See the task as done. Feel how you would feel after it is finished. Outline the first three steps you would need to take to accomplish this goal. (Outlining)

15. Make an outline of the traits you have that contribute to your being a good student. (Outlining)

16. Make an outline for each of the following: 1. The things I do best are: (a) _____, (b) _____, (c) _____, etc. 2. The things I wish I could do are: (a) _____, (b) _____, (c) _____, etc. 3. Three things I'd like to learn next are: (a) _____ , (b) _____ , (c) _____ . Add other points about yourself as a worker if you wish. (Outlining)

17. Make a tissue paper collage while listening to this story (or music). (Alternates: Fingerpaints, colored chalk, tempera, crayons, or listen in the dark.) (Media Work-Study Skills)

18. Listen to this story (poem or music). We'll listen to part of it with the lights off and part of it with the lights on. Be ready to tell which you enjoyed most. Or maybe you will enjoy both ways. (Media Work-Study Skills)

19. Imagine yourself as a television or film star. What skills do

you already have that would help you become a star? What skills would you need to acquire? (Alternates: Be a writer, truck driver, mother.) (Media Work-Study Skills)

20. Make a visual representation of how you used to work on your own when you were younger and how you work on your own now. (Self-Direction)

21. Design an ideal work center for yourself at home and/or at school. (Self-Direction)

22. Tell (or write or draw) the kind of independent worker you wish you were. (Self-Direction)

23. Describe a story character whom you admire. How many character traits do you have in common? (Self-Improvement)

24. Imagine yourself as an even better reader. How would you change? (Self-Improvement)

25. Make flash cards or a list of ten words you wished described you. How fast can you read them on the controlled reader, the tachistoscope, or timed slide projector? (Reading Rate)

26. Check your reading rate on the controlled reader. Imagine yourself being able to read faster. Fully picture yourself doing this. Check your reading rate again. Any improvement? (Reading Rate)

27. Write a book review of a book that helped you see yourself more clearly or in a better light. (Book Reviewing)

28. Write a book review of a book that helped you be a better person. (Book Reviewing)

29. Imagine yourself being a famous book reviewer. What three books would you review first? Why is this? (Book Reviewing)

30. What traits do you think are necessary to be able to review a book well? (Book Reviewing)

31. Tape-record a book review for other students to listen to if they want to preview your book. (Book Reviewing)

32. Tape-record yourself reading aloud a passage from your book that you think will give the rest of the class a picture of one of the interesting parts of your story. Tell us how you chose this section. (Oral Reading)

33. Tape-record a story for younger students to listen to in the library. Use sound effects. Change your voice to suit the story happenings. Have some friends help you if you wish.

Try to use voice tones and sound effects that will help the younger students picture exactly what is going on. (Oral Reading)

34. Imagine yourself as the author of your book. What research skills would you need? (Research Skills)

35. Imagine yourself as the leader of a work group in our room. What new skills would you need? What do you already know that would help you with this job? (Group Work Skills)

36. If you were going to explore new territories on the earth or in space, what five people in our room would you want to take with you to help you with the work? Why is this? (Group Work Skills)

37. Teachers: Show movies, films, photographs, or the like about various interesting places in the world. Instructions for students: Pretend you can take a trip to this place. Write about what you might hear and experience there. Check your imaginings against books about that part of the world. (Research Skills)

REFERENCE SKILLS

Sample Activities for Discussion, Task Cards, Learning Centers, and Reading Contracts

1. Look at the table of contents in your book. Pick out a title of some story or chapter that particularly appeals to you. Close your eyes and try to imagine what is in that selection. Check your guesses by reading it. (Using Parts of Books)

2. Write the frontispiece, the table of contents, the chapter titles, and three index notations for an imaginary book about your life, some event in your life, or some person you know. (Using Parts of Books)

3. Make a sample entry for a picture dictionary using one of the new vocabulary words. (Dictionary and Other Word Reference Skills)

4. Look in your dictionary to find other words that mean the same or almost the same as *dream, vision, imagery,* and *imagination*. (Dictionary and Other Word Reference Skills)

5. Look in your dictionary until you find a new word that appeals to you. Close your eyes to see if you can remember how to spell it. Look at the meaning. Close your eyes and

see what kinds of things the definition causes you to see in your mind's eye. (Dictionary and Other Word Reference Skills)

6. Suppose you had always dreamed of going to _____. (Examples: Hawaii, the moon, the country fair.) What books would help you with your dream? Show us which ones. (Using Standard References)

7. Use the reference center to plan one of the following: your ideal garden, a wardrobe for a trip to a cold country, a menu for a special picnic, a menu for a restaurant you'd like to own, an ideal vacation, mountain peaks you'd like to climb, or some other dream of your own. (Using Standard References)

8. Close your eyes and imagine yourself as a writer. What kinds of books would you like to write? If you wrote those books, what would be their Dewey decimal code? Where would they be located in our library? (Library Skills)

9. Find three books in our library that are about dreaming or imagining a better life. (Library Skills)

10. Make a bibliography of at least ten books that you consider well illustrated. Be sure to include author, book title, publisher, and date of publication. Tell us why you chose each book. (Bibliography Skills)

11. What are the dates of publication of three books that tell about someone's dreams coming true? What are the books? (Bibliography Skills)

12. What are the authors, titles, publishers, and dates of publication of three books that give information about something you have always dreamed of doing? (Bibliography Skills)

A FINAL WORD ABOUT TEACHING READING THROUGH VISUAL THINKING

Using visual thinking skills while reading is analogous to having one's own private motion picture theater or television receiver, only better because the programmer is ourselves. If students visualize in this fashion, they can use the literature they need for hours of pleasure at the same time they are learning reading academics. To be able to think visually, to see the relationships between objects and people in space, to be able to manipulate symbols visually in the mind's eye are abilities that are basic to all thinking skills as well as to those abilities involved in reading. The whole wisdom of many civilizations is available in print, enabling our students to share the visions and dreams of others who have gone before as well as to find fuel to spark their own thinking and dreaming.

13

Teaching Reading
Through Interpersonal Process

* * * * * * * * * * * *

Meaning is what reading is all about; and when students are aware that what they read relates to their own lives, this has powerful meaning, indeed. To learn that story characters and authors face situations identical to their own; that reading can show one how to live a better, more satisfying life by introducing new behaviors and interpersonal solutions never experienced before, as well as new possibilities for the self never imagined possible, brings the concept of meaning right into the innermost part of our students' lives.

COMPREHENSION SKILLS

Sample Activities for Discussion, Task Cards,
Learning Centers, and Reading Contracts

1. Name one mood each story character felt, then list the things that make you feel the same way. (Characterization)
2. Some things that happened in this reading selection that make me angry (sad, anxious, feel good, laugh, etc.) are _____ (Characterization)
3. Choose one event from the story. How do you think each character felt about that event? (Characterization)
4. If we were to produce a class play based on this story, which character do you think you would be best suited to play? Give reasons for your choice. (Characterization)

251

5. Of which of your friends does each story character remind you? Which of these story characters do you think your best friends would say you resemble? (Characterization)
6. If you were to take the name of any character or person you have ever read about, which name would you choose for yourself? Why is this? (Characterization)
7. Which character in the story would you most like for a friend? Which character in the story do you believe would most like to have you for a friend? Share your reasons. (Characterization)
8. Which of the story characters had goals that you also share? (Characterization)
9. If you had the chance to spend a day with a character from the story, which would you choose? What would you want to happen during that day? (Characterization)
10. Make a list of the characters in your story. Beside each character's name, write the name of someone in our class who you feel would like that character if the character were in our classroom. (Characterization)
11. Choose one of the main characters who gets into trouble. Recall all the reasons why he or she is in this trouble. Have you ever gotten into trouble for the same reasons? (Recall)
12. Find a classmate who has read the same book you have. Ask him or her four questions about the story. Try to answer four questions he or she asks about the story. Make up questions to ask that will show whether he or she really read the story carefully. (Recall)
13. From memory, retell or rewrite the part of the story that interested you most. Reread that part. Did you remember it well? (Recall)
14. Cut out three pictures of people showing emotions. Think of a one-word caption that captures the main idea for each picture. (Main Idea)
15. Select a sentence from your story. Eliminate all but three words in this sentence, leaving the three words you feel to be the most important words in understanding the sentence. See if other students agree with you. (Main Idea)
16. Name as many times in the story as you can when story characters felt one way inside and showed a different feeling on the outside. (Making Inferences or Conclusions)
17. How would some of the people in your family feel if you

acted the way one of the story characters acted? (Making Inferences or Conclusions)

18. Are there places in the story where you would have acted differently from the way the characters did? Why do you suppose you would act one way while the characters acted another way? Do you have any information that the character didn't have? (Making Inferences or Conclusions)

19. If you lived at the time of this story, what problems might you have? How would your life change? What would you need to know? (Making Inferences or Conclusions)

20. Why is life in the book's setting different from your own? Think of at least three good reasons. (Making Inferences or Conclusions)

21. What did ____ (story character) do that showed he or she was feeling ____ (some emotion)? (Making Inferences or Conclusions)

22. Where in the story did the characters use good judgment? Poor judgment? (Making Inferences or Conclusions)

23. What do you think the teacher reads? (Making Inferences or Conclusions)

24. What is the birth order of the main character in the story? What is yours? Does this difference or similarity in the order in which you were born make a difference in your understanding of the character? (Sequence)

25. Make a comic strip about a time you felt successful. (Sequence)

26. Choose one of the characters in the story. Tell how he or she felt at the beginning, the middle, and the end of the story. (Sequence)

27. Write about the important events or landmarks, both good and bad, that have happened to you in your life. (Sequence)

28. Explain (or write about) the steps you took to solve a problem in your life. (Sequence)

29. Explain the steps that you feel one of the story characters should take to solve a problem he or she has. (Alternate: Do the same for a problem one of your friends has.) (Sequence)

30. Make up a list of words or phrases from the story that caused you to smile, laugh, chuckle, or otherwise enjoy the humor you read. (Understanding Humor)

31. A group of students in our class is setting up an exhibit on humor in books. What books do you recommend they look at in choosing some for the display? (Understanding Humor)
32. Be ready to read aloud a section from the story that you found to be funny or humorous. Be ready to tell us why you chose that selection. (Understanding Humor)
33. Sometimes a reader enjoys the way an author says things as much as what the author says. Find examples of this in your story, if possible. (Figurative Language)
34. Write or tape-record a word description of one of your best friends. Share the description with that friend. (Figurative Language)
35. Write ten descriptive words about a character in the story. See if classmates can guess which character you are describing. Or do the same thing about someone in our class. (Figurative Language)
36. Make up a list of "happy" words from the story. Of "exciting" words, etc. (Figurative Language)
37. Choose and be prepared to read aloud a part of the story that you find to be vivid or picturesque. Be prepared to tell why you think so. (Figurative Language)
38. List the ten words that you feel describe one character in the story. (Word Meanings)
39. List five words the author used that you particularly like. Give the meanings for each word and tell why you enjoy each one. (Word Meanings)
40. Which words from the book were new to you? (Word Meanings)
41. Tell briefly in your own words why you think each character did the things he or she did in the story. (Paraphrasing)
42. What would you want to tell a friend about this story? (Paraphrasing)
43. Take one sentence that one of the story characters said. Restate it, using other words but keeping the same meaning. (Paraphrasing)
44. Which traits do you most admire in each of the characters featured in this story? Which traits do you least admire? (Synthesis)

45. Did the author deal with anything that applies to all people in this book? (Synthesis)
46. Did this book give you anything new to think about? (Synthesis)
47. Did this book cause you to want to find out more about something or someone or some idea? (Synthesis)
48. Did you think of a way to use any ideas in this book in your own life? (Synthesis)
49. Did you get anything new from this book to add to your own personal philosophy? (Synthesis)
50. If it were within your power to change one part of this book, what would you change and why? (Analysis)
51. Choose a character from the book. Was this character good or bad? Why do you think so? What percent of the time was the character good? Bad? (Analysis)
52. Think about your three favorite story characters. Do these three have any characteristics in common? Does this tell you anything about yourself? (Analysis)
53. Find a story that is written in the first person. Does this literary device help you enjoy the story more, or less? Do you have a feeling the narrator sometimes sounds like you or some person you know? (Understanding Literary Device)
54. Could the story have ended differently? Write an ending that you would have preferred to the one the author chose. (Understanding Literary Device)
55. Cut out or draw pictures of people feeling different moods in the story, such as sadness, anxiety, or anticipation. (Understanding Story Elements)
56. Does the story ending leave you feeling satisfied or dissatisfied? What does this tell about you? (Understanding Story Elements)
57. What is the mood or tone of this story? (Understanding Story Elements)
58. Write a one-page flashback scene that explains why one of the characters acts the way he or she does. Insert the flashback scene in the spot it best fits into the story. (Understanding Story Elements)
59. Be ready to discuss the development of friendship between

two story characters. How did it develop? (Understanding Story Elements)

60. Cut out five pictures of people showing emotion. Predict what the people in the pictures will say (or do) next. (Prediction)

61. What five words would you use to predict the future of each of the story characters? (Prediction)

62. What do you predict that you would do if you had to solve the problem that one of the characters in the story had to solve? (Prediction)

63. Make up a predicted family tree of the future for one story character. Did family patterns change? (Prediction)

64. Give two realistic and two unrealistic solutions to a problem that one of the story characters faced. (Reality vs. Fantasy)

65. Was the main character of the story real or make-believe? How do you know? (Reality vs. Fantasy)

66. Find and prepare to read aloud examples from the story that you feel could not possibly happen in real life. (Reality vs. Fantasy)

67. In real life, how many things can you think of that might cause a person to feel the way one of the story characters did? (Cause and Effect)

68. Write some endings to these sentences: If the sky were green, then _____. If I could fly, then _____. If I were kinder, then _____. Make up some If-Then sentences of your own about yourself, a friend, or a story event or character. (Cause and Effect)

69. Give at least three answers for each of the following: During reading I feel happy when _____; I feel slightly happy when _____; I feel extremely happy when _____. (Classification)

70. In what areas in reading do you feel you have improved this last month (week, day, etc.)? In what areas of reading do you feel our class has improved? We'll compare ideas on this during discussion time today at __ o'clock. (Classification)

71. Be ready to share a collection of something you made. If you haven't made a collection of anything, share with us what you would like to collect. (Classification)

72. A name is a way of summing up a person. Do you feel the

names the author chose for the characters in this story summed up the character's personalities well? Does your name fit you? What other name, if any, do you wish you had? (Summary)

73. Ask someone who has recently finished reading a book that you are going to read to give you a short summary of the book (two or three sentences). Read the book. Would you have summarized the plot in the same way? (Summary)

74. How are you and the main character alike in the way you feel about yourselves? How do you differ? (Comparing and Contrasting)

75. Has anyone ever treated you the way the main character in the story was treated? (Comparing and Contrasting)

76. Look at the title of an unfamiliar book or story. Guess what the story is about using only the title as a clue. Check the story to see if you are right. (Comparing and Contrasting)

77. If one of the story characters had three wishes, what do you think he or she would wish for? Compare and contrast those wishes with what you would wish for if you were given three wishes. (Comparing and Contrasting)

78. Compare one character in the story to a real person you know. How are they alike? Different? (Comparing and Contrasting)

79. Take a good look at your friends. What do they have in common? (Comparing and Contrasting)

80. Here are three key words about an incident in today's story. (Give students three key words.) Locate the event in the story and be ready to read it aloud to us. (Locating Details)

81. Look back through the reader and choose the story you liked best. Tell why you chose this particular story. (Locating Details)

82. Locate a place in the story where a character was feeling strong emotion. (Locating Details)

83. Teachers: Divide the class into small groups for this exercise. Instructions: Let's spend some time giving pretend gifts to each other, something we feel the other person would truly like or need and something that fits that person. As each person in your group volunteers to be *It*, the rest of you think for a moment, then when you're all ready,

share one by one the gifts you thought of for that person. At the end, after everyone has had a turn, you can share the gift you would give yourself. If you were going to give the main character a gift of some kind, what gift would you give her or him? (Characterization)

84. Teachers: At the first of the school year, have students make the following predictions. Share their predictions with them later in the school year. Who will do best in reading this year? What school subject will you do best in this year? How much do you think you will grow by Christmas? Who will be your best friends this year? Etc. (Prediction)

CRITICAL READING SKILLS

Sample Activities for Discussion, Task Cards, Learning Centers, and Reading Contracts

1. Do you consider yourself a good or a bad reader? When are you a good and when are you a bad reader? Have you ever been the best or the worst reader in a group? How did it feel? What is the part of reading that you feel you do best? Worst? What could we do differently in this classroom to help you be a better reader? What could you do differently in this classroom to help you be a better reader? (Evaluating the Reading Process)

2. Tape-record yourself reading aloud a page or two from a book. Listen to the tape, making a list of the errors you made. What do you want to do about this? Listen to the recording a second time and note an equal number of good things about your reading. (Evaluating the Reading Process)

3. How do you feel about reading? (Evaluating the Reading Process)

4. Which parts of reading time do you particularly enjoy? Which parts do you not enjoy? (Evaluating the Reading Process)

5. Who in our class reads the way you wish you could read? (Or who in your family?) (Evaluating the Reading Process)

6. Where is your favorite reading spot? Why is this? (Evaluating the Reading Process)

7. Whom do you find it most comfortable to be near when

you are hard at work on some reading task? Why is this? Whom do you like to be close to when you are reading silently a particularly good book? Tell us why this is so. Who has been a good influence on you in helping you be a better reader? Tell us how they helped you. (Evaluating the Reading Process)

8. Finish these sentences: I'd read more if _____. The reasons I read well are _____. The reasons I don't read well are _____. This week in reading I learned _____. (Evaluating the Reading Process)

9. Share one success with us that you had in reading this week. (Evaluating the Reading Process)

10. Finish these sentences in as many ways as seem to show how you really feel: When I make a mistake in reading I _____. Reading means _____. During reading time I often wish _____. If the teacher left the room for 30 minutes in reading _____. In reading, I like myself best when _____; I like myself least when _____. The teacher likes me best when _____; least when _____. During reading, I wish my teacher would _____. (Evaluating the Reading Process)

11. If you could teach kindergarten students just one thing about reading, what would it be? Share your reasons with us. (Evaluating the Reading Process)

12. What is something that you are good enough at, in reading, that you could teach to someone else? (Evaluating the Reading Process)

13. What percent of the reading hour were you truly proud of yourself and your work? (Younger children: How many minutes, etc.?) Is this more or less than usual? Do you wish it were different? (Evaluating the Reading Process)

14. On a list of everyone in our classroom, with number one being the best reader, where would you fit? What number would you be? (Evaluating the Reading Process)

15. What is the first priority in becoming a good reader? Second priority? Other levels of priority. (Evaluating the Reading Process)

16. Who is the best reader in your family? How do you feel about this? (Evaluating the Reading Process)

17. What help would you like from the teacher during reading time today? (Evaluating the Reading Process)

18. Today is your turn for a conference with the teacher about

reading. Make a list of things you'd like to discuss during this time. (Evaluating the Reading Process)

19. What did the teacher help you most with during reading time today? Least? (Evaluating the Reading Process)
20. Who do you know in the class who reads better than the teacher thinks he or she does? Worse? (Evaluating the Reading Process)
21. You may arrange to bring a younger guest to school today. (Note to teachers: Occasionally have a younger brother or sister or other younger child as a classroom guest during reading. Decide with the students how long the guest will stay, who will be responsible for what, etc. Discuss with the class and the visitor if reading was what the younger child expected, and the like.) (Evaluating the Reading Process)
22. Make up five questions you would like to ask the author about her or his writing. (Evaluating Author Skills)
23. Make an exhibit of several works by the same author. List the works in order from the best book to the worst. Tell why you rated the books as you did. (Evaluating Author Skills)
24. What did this author do to help you understand some story character? (Evaluating Author Skills)
25. Rewrite the story from the point of view of either a younger or older brother or sister or of the mother or father of one of the characters, of from the point of view of some other relative or friend of one of the story characters. Be ready to tell how this made a difference in the story. (Author Bias, Point of View, Values)
26. Which culture does this author think is best? (Author Bias, Point of View, Values)
27. Does this book give you a good feeling for both boys and girls? Men and women? Old people and young? Minorities? People in different occupations? Other groups? (Author Bias, Point of View, Values)
28. Plan a talk or write a summary of this book from the point of view of two of the following: a student, a teacher, or a parent. Did the point of view change as you assumed these roles? (Author Bias, Point of View, Values)
29. How do you think this author feels about marriage and

divorce? What clues did he or she give to help you answer this question? (Alternates: Author's feelings about death, work, or war.) (Author's Hidden Assumptions)

30. What does this author imply that a reader must do to be successful? (Author's Hidden Assumptions)
31. What do you think this story meant to the author? (Author Purpose)
32. How do you think the author wanted you and other readers to feel when they read this book? (Author Purpose)
33. Be ready to discuss (or write about) one author or poet whose work you especially enjoy. Talk about (or write about) their lives and feelings and the ways this affected their writings. (Author Purpose)
34. What kind of a schedule or day do you imagine this author has when he or she is writing? (Evaluating Author Organizational Pattern)
35. Did you learn anything from the way this author writes that will help you with your own writing? (Evaluating Author Organizational Pattern)
36. Find two opinions this author gave in the story, then find two facts. (Fact vs. Opinion)
37. Make a list of words or phrases the author used that helped you know the difference in this selection between fact and opinion. (Fact vs. Opinion)
38. List three ways in which the author describes something in this book. Are these descriptions the author's opinion or are they fact? (Fact vs. Opinion)
39. What are some things the author wants you to do as a result of reading this book (newspaper, article, etc.)? (Recognizing Propaganda)
40. List all the words the author uses to describe males. Next make a list of all the words the author uses to describe females. Compare these two lists to see what they tell you about how this writer feels males and females should act. (Recognizing Stereotyping)
41. Find an example of a magazine or newspaper ad that really made you want to buy something, go somewhere, or do something. Why was it effective with you? Find an example of an ad that wasn't effective with you. (Recognizing Propaganda)

42. Choose a male and a female character in the story. Tell how the male feels about females and how the female feels about males. (Identifying Stereotyping)
43. Would you like to be treated the way the female characters in this story were treated? The way the male characters were treated? (Identifying Stereotyping)
44. Locate a book that includes no minority characters or that stereotypes by sex or in some other way. Briefly rewrite the story to get rid of the stereotyping or to include minority characters. (Identifying Stereotyping)
45. Does this story line give a bad picture of any group, such as minorities, males, females, or people in an occupation? Does the story imply that all poeple in these groups are alike? (Identifying Stereotyping)
46. What kinds of people would feel bad if they read this story? What kinds of people would feel good? (Identifying Stereotyping)
47. Do you think this book is fair to all kinds of people, such as males, females, older people, handicapped people, people from different racial or cultural groups? (Identifying Stereotyping)
48. Do you consider this author fair? Informed? Impartial? Be ready to discuss these questions. (Evaluating Reliability and Validity)
49 For what purpose would you recommend this book to your friends? (Evaluating Reliability and Validity)
50. Write a letter to the editor of a newspaper or magazine giving your opinions about the fairness and trustworthiness of some article. (Evaluating Reliability and Validity)
51. Of all the books you have read, which one would you most like to share with our class? With your parents? With a relative? With your best friend? Give reasons for each choice. (Evaluating Content and Format)
52. Plan an exhibit of the favorite books of students in this classroom. Choose people to help you set up the display, if you wish, or work alone. (Evaluating Content and Format)
53. To which of your friends would you recommend this book? Why is this? (Evaluating Content and Format)
54. Do you think most of our reading books are for boys or girls or both? How do you feel about this? (Evaluating Content and Format)

55. Find two or more books written on a common problem that students of your age might experience. Which of the books gives the most realistic look at the problem? Which seems more helpful? What other comparisons can you make between the books? (Hint: Ask your teacher or librarian for help if you have trouble locating the books.) (Alternate: Do the same with books on a common historical era, a personage, or a current dilemma.) (Comparing Two or More Sources)

56. Find a book about the reaction of some minority author to some historical event (Columbus' landing, Wounded Knee, slavery, etc.), then compare it to a white person's reaction to the same event in some other book. Ask the librarian for help if necessary. (Comparing Two or More Sources)

57. Does this book leave you feeling satisfied or dissatisfied? Happy or unhappy? What does your answer tell you about yourself? (Analyzing Self Through Critical Reading)

58. How did this story or book help you to see things to be thankful for in your life? (Alternates: things that are beautiful in your life or things you need to do in your life?) (Analyzing Self Through Critical Reading)

59. Have you ever misjudged a person because of wrong first impressions? Did you ever misjudge a book in the same way because of its cover or title or something else about it? (Analyzing Self Through Critical Reading)

60. What is your favorite book? What meaning does it have for you? (Analyzing Self Through Critical Reading)

61. Who were your storybook heroines and heroes when you were younger? Do you still admire them? Why or why not? (Analyzing Self Through Critical Reading)

62. Make a collection of poems or short excerpts from books that are especially meaningful for you. (Analyzing Self Through Critical Reading)

63. Choose an experience that the main character had. Write (or tell) a true experience you had that was similar to this experience. (Analyzing Self Through Critical Reading)

64. Write a letter to one of the advice columns in a newspaper or magazine about some question you have concerning hair, makeup, autos, sports, or the like. See if you can get it answered. (Analyzing Self Through Critical Reading)

65. Choose one statement the author makes in this story with

which you can agree. Tell us why. Choose one statement the author makes with which you disagree. Tell us why. (Analyzing Self Through Critical Reading)

66. Make a collection of articles and pictures from newspapers and magazines that would help you improve yourself. (Analyzing Self Through Critical Reading)

67. "My Ideal Self." Make a collection of ideas, words, articles, pictures, and the like, that show what your ideal self would be like. (Analyzing Self Through Critical Reading)

68. What was the impact of this book on you? (Analyzing Self Through Critical Reading)

69. What books are on your "must read" list? Why? (Analyzing Self Through Critical Reading)

CREATIVE READING SKILLS

Sample Activities for Discussion, Task Cards, Learning Centers, and Reading Contracts

1. Write a story or a poem about some time when your feelings were hurt, when you felt ignored, or when you felt inadequate. (Alternate: When you felt successful, appreciated, or when you felt good.) (Developing Authors' Skills)

2. Write a story about a time you hurt someone's feelings or a time when you helped someone feel good about themselves. (Developing Authors' Skills)

3. Write a story about what excites you most about growing up. (Developing Authors' Skills)

4. Write a poem titled, "My Life." (Developing Authors' Skills)

5. Surprise a friend by writing a story in which he or she is the main character. (Developing Authors' Skills)

6. Compliment three people on something you admire about them. Be sure you are giving honest compliments. Write about how each person reacted to your praise. (Developing Authors' Skills)

7. Keep a journal of your learnings, thoughts, and reactions for a week (two weeks, or a month). (Developing Authors' Skills)

8. Write a letter to yourself praising all the good things you did during reading time this week. (Developing Authors' Skills)

9. Write a story about something someone did to you that made you feel good this week. (Developing Authors' Skills)

10. Write a poem titled "Me" as if you were one of the characters in the story. Write one about yourself if you like. (Developing Authors' Skills)

11. Choose one of the following for the opening line for a story you write: I had never been so frightened (happy, peaceful, confident, nervous, exhausted, satisfied, curious, bored, strong, content, stupid, awed, or _____ (word of your choice)). In the next week, choose three more of these as beginning sentences for stories for a book about your emotions. (Developing Authors' Skills)

12. Many times authors write best about familiar things. What familiar things or events could you write about best? (Developing Authors' Skills)

13. If we were going to develop a class play about this story, what would you rather be: Writer? Actor? Producer? Costume designer? Set decorator? Other? Give reasons for your choice. (Creating Original Material)

14. Write a description of what it is like to learn to read in our classroom for your grandchildren to read (or to include in a capsule shot into space or in a time capsule to be dug up by students at this school thirty years from now). (Alternate: Write about learning to read to a pen pal.) (Creating Original Material)

15. Write a cinquain about a person who is especially important to you. (Creating Original Material)

16. Make a coat of arms, a personal flag, or an emblem for the main character in the story, for yourself, or for a friend. (Creating Original Material)

17. Make a collage about yourself from words, pictures, and the like that you find in newspapers or magazines. (Creating Original Material)

18. Make up an ad about yourself and reading. It can be a "help wanted" ad, a "job wanted" ad, a "sell-yourself" ad,

or any other type that appeals to you. (Creating Original Material)

19. Design and make a puppet that you feel could speak for you. (Creating Original Material)

20. Devise an ad campaign that would make students in our school want to be better readers. (Alternate: Better listeners.) (Creating Original Material)

21. Make up a new job card or task card that would help students in our class work better together. (Designing Games, Puzzles, Anagrams, etc.)

22. Arrange a bulletin board on the theme of this story. (Alternate: You may have the bulletin board space near the window for your own this week to display things of your choice.) (Designing Games, Puzzles, Anagrams, Etc.)

23. What was your favorite toy when you were little? Why do you think this was? (Designing Games, Puzzles, Anagrams, Etc.)

24. Write down six good things about yourself. (Creative Thinking – Evaluation)

25. Choose one character from the story and think up a new story about him or her, telling entirely new happenings. (Creative Thinking – Divergent)

26. What do you think causes your friends to like you? (Creative Thinking – Evaluation)

27. You find yourself alone with one of the story characters. List five interesting, but not too controversial, topics of conversation you could talk on. (Creative Thinking – Evaluation)

28. Make a list of every opportunity you have had to use your creative imagination since awakening this morning. (Creative Thinking – Convergent)

29. If a Martian came to our school, what would you want to show him or her?

30. Which character do you feel did the best job of solving his or her problems? Why do you think this? Have you ever solved a problem similar to the one in the story? What did you do? How did you feel after solving it? (Problem-Solving)

31. If you had a problem similar to one in the story, where or to whom would you go for help in solving it? (Problem-Solving)

32. Did this reading selection help you in any way with a problem you have to solve? (Problem-Solving)
33. How would some of the story characters solve your problems? (Problem-Solving)
34. It's your turn to be featured on the "Student of the Week" bulletin board. Plan what you want to put on that board. (Pictures, favorite poems, special colors, papers you are proud of, and the like.) (Planning)
35. Set a goal for yourself in reading that you feel you could reach today (or this week). Let us know when you have achieved your goal. (Planning)
36. We are going to have a fashion show where everyone wears his or her favorite clothes. What will you wear? (Planning)
37. Suppose one of the story characters called you for advice about solving a problem he or she had. Choose the character, the problem, and make up three to five questions you would ask him or her to help with solving this problem. (Formulating Questions)
38. What three questions would you like to ask one of the story characters about his or her feelings? (Formulating Questions)
39. Select an advertisement from the lost and found (older students: personal ads) classified advertisements in the newspaper or in a magazine. Write or tape-record a story you made up based on that ad. (Relating Reading to Other Media)
40. Make up and produce a puppet show about some interesting event in your life or some exciting event that occurred in our classroom. Invite as many classmates as you need to help you with the production. (Relating Reading to Other Media)
41. Design a mural about our class reading time. (Relating Reading to Other Media)
42. In the "TV Commercial Recap Center," repeat one of the commercials that compare products (soap, shampoo, pop, etc.). (Relating Reading to Other Media)
43. When we start our class newspaper, for what position do you think yourself best suited? List your reasons. (Evaluating Own Written Work)
44. We are going to make a class journal of the events that

happened during the year. For which job on this project are you best suited? Share your reasons with us. (Evaluating Own Written Work)

45. Share with us the best story you have written this week (or month). (Evaluating Own Written Work)

46. Complete this sentence: Some behaviors I found in this story that I should use in my own life are _____. (Improving Self-Concept and Self-Development Through Reading)

47. What were two successes you had during reading time today? (Improving Self-Concept and Self-Development Through Reading)

48. How did you help someone in reading today? (Improving Self-Concept and Self-Development Through Reading)

49. What kinds of books make you feel proud that you can read them? Why is this so? (Improving Self-Concept and Self-Development Through Reading)

50. What are the roles you play in life (for example, son, brother, sister, and the like). Write a story about one of your roles. Find a story or book about the roles someone else plays. (Improving Self-Concept and Self-Development Through Reading)

51. We have many new books and reading activities in our "Self Improvement Learning Center" for you to choose from today. (Note to teachers: Set up a center that includes books on clothing, hair styles, personal hygiene, manners, advice columns, and the like. Be sure to include books for both boys and girls.) (Improving Self-Concept and Self-Development Through Reading)

52. Choose an activity today from the grooming center. (Note to teachers: Set up a grooming center entitled, "Hey, Look Me Over!" Include shoe shining, hair styling, and the like.) (Improving Self-Concept and Self-Development Through Reading)

53. Make a collection of pictures, words, and thoughts that show how you want to be when you grow up. (Improving Self-Concept and Self-Development Through Reading)

54. There are books that deal with many happenings in our lives. Think of something that happened recently in your life (a new baby, a move to a new house, for example). Find a book or ask the librarian for help in locating a book that is written about the same topic. Read the book to see if the

characters reacted in the same way or differently from the way you reacted to a similar event. (Reader Purpose)

55. Interview three adults about how they use reading in their work. Share their answers with us. (Reader Purpose)

56. Interview three adults about what they would do differently if they could learn to read again. Share their answers with us. (Reader Purpose)

57. Who, do you feel, is the most proud of you when you read well? (Reader Purpose)

58. To whom do you like to read aloud? (Reader Purpose)

59. Why did you choose your present recreational reading book? (Recreational Reading)

60. Outside of required reading in school, when do you like to read? (Recreational Reading)

61. Set up a display of one of your hobbies including books you found helpful. (Recreational Reading)

62. When you remember this story, what will you always remember about it? Will this be a story you will always remember? Why or why not? (Emotional Response)

63. Does this book make you feel good about yourself? Why or why not? (Emotional Response)

64. Be ready to tell about or read aloud an embarrassing or other emotional moment described in the story. (Emotional Response)

65. Draw or make some kind of representation of a "monster" that frightens you. This monster can be one from a story or one from your imagination. (Emotional Response)

66. What was the most exciting thing that happened to you during reading time this week? The most surprising? The most embarrassing? The most worthwhile? Think of some more "most" experiences you had in reading this week and share them with us. (Emotional Response)

67. How do different kinds of weather make you feel? Check the weather forecast for tomorrow. How do you think you will feel? What can you do to change your feelings? (Emotional Response)

68. Keep a diary of your day at school for a week. (Emotional Response)

69. Is there anything a story character did in this story that you wish you had done? (Emotional Response)

70. Share a book that really made a difference in your life.

Interview classmates or your family about books that really made a difference in their lives. (Emotional Response)

LITERATURE APPRECIATION SKILLS

Sample Activities for Discussion, Task Cards, Learning Centers, or Reading Contracts

1. Finish these sentences after taking some time to think carefully about how you truly feel: I believe reading is valuable to me because _____. The grownup I know who most values reading is ____ because _____. (Value of Reading)

2. Here is a typical utility bill that a family might receive. How much is due? What period is covered by the bill? How much of the bill is tax? What is the account number? What other things can you find out from the bill? (Value of Reading)

3. Here are some typical labels from bottles of medication. How often should the dosage be repeated? Is the medicine to be used internally or externally? What should be done if a child gets an accidental overdose? Is there a warning? (Alternate: Have students examine over-the-counter medications for similar information.) (Value of Reading)

4. Here are some typical clothing labels. Choose one and find out: the name of the manufacturer; the size of the garment; the country of manufacture; the material; and the instructions for cleaning. (Value of Reading)

5. Do all people from the same race as the main story character live in the same setting as the one used in this book? Can you give any examples of other books that give a different setting for leading characters of the same race? (Recognizing Story Elements)

6. In what setting for which book would you most like to live? (Recognizing Story Elements)

7. If you went to a costume party as some story character, who would you be? (Recognizing Story Elements)

8. Find an example of writing that describes the physical setting of the story in such a way that you would really like to drive or walk through it. (Recognizing Story Elements)

9. If a story were written about your learning to read, what would be five sections of it? (Recognizing Story Elements)

10. If we were to stage a play based on this book and you were

cast as the main character, what would be the hardest part for you of striving to give a good performance in that role? (Recognizing Story Elements)

11. What character in literature would you want to portray in your Broadway debut and/or your first film role? (Recognizing Story Elements)

12. Choose a book in the autobiography or biography section that looks interesting to you. After you finish reading it, make a list of at least five ways you are like and five ways you are unlike the main character. (Recognizing Literary Forms)

13. What types of books do you enjoy most? Tell us why. (Recognizing Literary Forms)

14. Put these types of books in the order that you enjoy them: fiction, non-fiction, poetry, science fiction, adventure, mystery, history, science, biography, autobiography, and add any other kinds you can think of to the list. (Recognizing Literary Forms)

15. What has happened in your family that has become a family legend? (Recognizing Literary Forms)

16. Write a short biography of yourself but do not use your name. Include anything that seems important to you. We'll collect the cards to read them aloud to see who can guess what person each biography describes. (Recognizing Literary Forms)

17. If someone wrote a book about you, what kind of book would they write (science, fiction, poetry, etc.)? (Recognizing Literary Forms)

18. Finish this sentence after you have given it some careful thought: If I had to spend all my time during reading with only one type of book, that type would be _____. (Recognizing Literary Forms)

19. What would be your chief satisfactions if you lived in the time and setting of the story? Your chief dissatisfactions? (Cultural Analysis Through Literature)

20. We are going to give a play called *You Are There* based on the reading selection we just finished. What should we keep in mind about this culture? (Cultural Analysis Through Literature)

21. How does the culture in which these characters live differ from your own? Are they expected to do different things?

Would something they consider a success be a success for you? (Cultural Analysis Through Literature)

22. Be ready to retell this story from the point of view of a minority person or that of a male or female in this culture or in your own culture. (Cultural Analysis Through Literature)

23. In what ways is the home life in this story different from or similar to yours? (Cultural Analysis Through Literature)

24. Would you want to be an older person in the setting of this story? Why is this? (Alternates: Would you want to be a grownup or a child in this story setting?) (Cultural Analysis Through Literature)

25. If a visitor from outer space read only this book, what would he or she or it conclude about the way people on Earth get along together? (Cultural Analysis Through Literature)

26. Would you like to be a member of any of the families in this story? (Cultural Analysis Through Literature)

27. Make a display of books about the cultures of your ancestors. (Cultural Analysis Through Literature)

28. Make up a list of books about the cultures of your ancestors. (Cultural Analysis Through Literature)

29. Are most children in our reading books like you? How are they different? How are they alike? How do you feel about this? (Cultural Analysis Through Literature)

30. What foreign language do you most wish you could read? Why? (Cultural Analysis Through Literature)

31. What values for living with others does this book consider important? (Cultural Analysis Through Literature)

32. Look at the villains in three stories. Graph how they are alike and different. What does this say about our culture? (Cultural Analysis Through Literature)

33. List all the problems each of the story characters had. List all of the problems you share with any of the story characters. (Bibliotherapy)

34. What were the happiest times each story character had? What were the saddest times? What were the happiest and saddest times you ever had? (Alternates: toughest–easiest; anxious–relaxing; brave–frightened.) (Bibliotherapy)

35. Pretend that you are the main character five years before or five years after this story. Tell about your life. (Bibliotherapy)
36. We are going to set up a library club where members can discuss and recommend books to each other to help with problems they may have. Let the teacher know either a problem you would like discussed or a book you think might help students with certain problems, such as shyness, that they might have. (Bibliotherapy)
37. What did you learn that would be helpful in your life from each of the main characters in the story? (Bibliotherapy)
38. Make an exhibit of five books you have most enjoyed this year. Try to find reviews of these five books (ask the librarian for help) and compare your opinions on the book to those of the reviewers. (Recognizing Famous Writings and Authors)
39. If you could meet any famous author, which one would you choose? Share your reasons with us. (Recognizing Famous Writings and Authors)
40. What famous writer would you most want to be? Explain your reasons. (Recognizing Famous Writings and Authors)
41. For whom or for what kind of person would you recommend the book just finished? For whom or for what kind of person do you feel this book would not be valuable? (Selecting Appropriate Materials)
42. Find two or three books written for younger children on some big problem. (For instance, war, broken families, or prejudice.) Read the books out loud to younger brothers and sisters, friends, or students in younger grade levels. Which book do you feel did the best job of helping the younger students understand the problem? Give reasons for your choice. (Selecting Appropriate Materials)
43. Make a list of seven friends or relatives; Next to their names write down a book you think each would enjoy reading. Tell why. (Selecting Appropriate Materials)
44. Make a list of books that you feel would help one of the story characters with his or her problems. (Selecting Appropriate Materials)
45. If you were invited to be a weekend guest at the home of

your favorite historical character, what book would you select for a thank-you gift? Why? (Selecting Appropriate Materials)

46. Look through magazines for five pictures you think your teacher would like. Share them with her or him. (Selecting Appropriate Materials)

47. Select a partner. Silently watch him or her while you leaf through a magazine and choose pictures you think he or she would like. (Examples: ideal home, clothing, people, etc.) Share, then have your partner do the same for you. (Selecting Appropriate Materials)

48. Make a list of books you would recommend for someone who works too hard. Explain your choices. (Alternate: For someone who doesn't work hard enough.) (Selecting Appropriate Materials)

49. Select three stories you could read aloud to one of your younger brothers or sisters or other relative. (Selecting Appropriate Materials)

50. What books would you suggest for a very shy ten-year-old to read? Why? (Selecting Appropriate Materials)

VOCABULARY DEVELOPMENT SKILLS

Sample Activities for Discussion, Task Cards, Learning Centers, or Reading Contracts

1. Give at least five answers to one of the following: I feel energetic when _____; I feel frightened when _____; I feel helpless when _____; I feel strong when _____. (Vocabulary Patterning)

2. Write or tell at least one ending for these sentences: I don't like _____ especially _____. I don't like _____ even if _____. I don't like _____ under _____. (Vocabulary Patterning)

3. Make up a limerick about yourself, a friend, or a story character. (Vocabulary Patterning)

4. Make up five sentences using this pattern: I'd like to be a _____ because _____. (Vocabulary Patterning)

5. What new words and phrases do you wish your teacher would learn? (New Vocabulary)

6. What one new word from this story gave you the most pleasure to read? (Alternates: What new word from the story do you want to add to your own speech? What new word that you heard someone use recently do you especially like?) (New Vocabulary)

7. Make a list of five words that your parents use in their work that are used only in that work. (Technical and Specialized Vocabulary)

8. Interview someone who works in a field involving human relations, such as a psychologist or teacher. Find out five words and their meanings that are used in that field. (Technical and Specialized Vocabulary)

9. List as many different ways as you can to greet someone. (Specialized Word Relationships – Synonyms)

10. Think of a word that you use too much. If you can't think of one, ask a classmate or the teacher to suggest one. Make up a list of at least four other ways to say the same word. (Special Word Relationships – Synonyms)

11. List three words that are antonyms for you; that is, they do not describe you at all. (Special Word Relationships – Antonyms)

12. Write a list of words or expressions that students your age use that adults do not. (Variation of Vocabulary)

13. Find words or expressions in the story that are examples of speech used in the region where the story is set. (Variation of Vocabulary)

14. Find words or expressions in the story that are examples of the age of the story characters; words that children might use, or teenagers, or older people, for example. (Variation of Vocabulary)

15. Choose a favorite fairy story. Rewrite it in modern language, using a modern setting. (Variation of Vocabulary)

16. Find an older book and look for samples of the use of the words *man, mankind, he*, etc. Find a more modern book on the same subject and see if you can find examples of less sexist wordings. (Appropriateness of Vocabulary)

17. Look for examples of sexist wordings in your daily newspaper. Be prepared to tell why you consider each example sexist. Rewrite the examples to eliminate the sexism. (Appropriateness of Vocabulary)

18. Ask two friends of yours to write down or tell you words or phrases that you use often when you are speaking. Were you surprised at what you found out? (Appropriateness of Vocabulary)

19. List five students in our class. Beside each name, list the words or expressions that person often uses. You may have to listen carefully all day today to find out this information. (Appropriateness of Vocabulary)

20. Choose a set of alliterative initials for yourself. Choose letters that have a pleasing sound to you. Make up nicknames for yourself using the same sound as a beginning for a two-word nickname, then a three-word nickname (L. L. or L. L. L., for instance). Do the same thing for a story character or for a friend. (Etymology)

21. Did you have a nickname when you were younger? How did you get it? How do you feel about it now? Do you have a nickname now? How did you get it? How do you feel about it? (Etymology)

22. Write down three words that describe you. Look up the names that mean the same as each of the three words you have chosen in a book that explains what different names mean. Would you like to have any of the three for a real name? (Etymology)

23. What words can make you sleepy? Happy? Tired? Energetic? Puzzled? (Figurative or Idiomatic Language)

24. If you were going to characterize the type of day you had today, what name would you name it? (Hint: Hard Luck Day, Breezy Day, Oh! My Achin' Head Day, etc.) (Figurative or Idiomatic Language)

25. Proverbs often give us a clue as to how to live our lives. From what you have learned through living your life, so far, finish these beginnings of old proverbs with new endings: You can lead a horse to water but _____; A stitch in time _____; People who live in glass houses _____; A penny saved _____; Look before you _____; A rolling stone _____; Eat, drink, and _____; and The bigger they come _____. (Note to teacher: If the students don't know the proverbs they are working on, wait until they have had a chance to make up their own endings before telling them

the rest of the proverb.) (Figurative or Idiomatic Language)

26. Write down a word or two that describes you that begins with each letter of your name. Do the same for a friend. (Figurative or Idiomatic Language)

27. Think about what I am like as a teacher during reading time. If I were an animal during reading time, what would I be? What kind of food? Weather? Word? Color? Time of day? Can you compare me to anything else the way I am as a teacher at reading time? Make some comparisons of yourself as you are as a student during reading. (Figurative or Idiomatic Language)

28. Choose one line that one of the characters said in the story. Think up at least five different ways to stress different words in the sentence so that the meaning is changed even though the words stay the same. (Relating Word Stress, Pitch, and Intonation to Meaning)

29. What do the punctuation marks such as question marks, exclamation points, commas, periods, quotation marks, and the like tell you your voice should do when you read this story aloud? (Relating Word Stress, Pitch, and Intonation to Meaning)

30. Say aloud some words or sentences your parents and your teacher use when they want you to do something. Use the exact tone they use to you. (Relating Word Stress, Pitch, and Intonation to Meaning)

31. List the story characters and the words that describe the feelings each experienced in the story. (Word Meaning)

32. List any "loaded" words the author uses to describe a group, a sex, an age, or an occupation. (Words that seem insulting or cause the reader to feel a certain way.) (Word Meanings)

33. List the ten words that you feel best describe you. (Word Meanings)

34. Are there words or phrases that make you feel especially bad when they are spoken to you? (Word Meanings)

35. Are there words or phrases that cause you to feel as if you want to stop trying or working when they are spoken to you? (Word Meanings)

36. Write down five words that describe you and five more

words that you wish described you. What are some things you could begin doing this week to turn your "wish" list into reality? We'll talk about all these meanings and more during discussion time this afternoon at 2:15. (Word Meanings)

37. What does the word *reading* mean to you? (Word Meanings)

38. Cut out three pictures from newspapers or magazines of people showing emotions. Write down (or be ready to tell) what you believe the people in each picture are feeling. (Nonverbal Vocabulary)

39. We give clues about how we feel in the way we move and our expressions. Without talking, show us how a story character felt. We'll try to guess who it is and how he or she felt. (Nonverbal Vocabulary)

40. Use body language to show one of the following: "I know the answer," "I hope the teacher doesn't call on me," "I'm confused," "It's OK." Make up body language for a sentence of your own. (Nonverbal Vocabulary)

41. Act out an example where body language and oral language do not agree. (Nonverbal Vocabulary)

42. Make a list of words you meet in your reading that you want to remember. During discussion time on Tuesday we'll discuss our choices and reasons for the choices. (Word Enrichment)

43. Give your own definitions for the following words: loyalty, jealousy, honesty, anger. We'll compare thoughts on these words during discussion time today. (Word Enrichment)

44. Make a list of fifteen descriptive words from this story. How many apply to you? (Word Enrichment)

45. What do you hope the students in this class will say about you in ten years? (Word Enrichment)

46. We're going to take turns describing a friend in this classroom in ten words that tell something about him or her. We'll try to guess who each person is. (Alternate: Describe a story character in ten words and see who can guess the character.) (Word Enrichment)

47. Describe each of these things in your own words: something beautiful, happiness, curiosity, etc. (Word Enrichment)

WORD PERCEPTION SKILLS

Sample Activities for Discussion, Task Cards, Learning Centers, and Reading Contracts

1. Look up the word for *happy* in several languages. Do you find any similarities? Do the same for one other word that describes feelings or emotions. (Etymological Cues)
2. Look up information on where names come from. What are the meanings of some of the names in your family? Why were they chosen? Who named you? (Etymological Cues)
3. Sometimes words can come from names of people. There are words in our language that were originally someone's name; for instance, *sandwich* and *lynch*. If your name were used as a noun, what would be the definition? What about the name of a friend—what would it mean? (Etymological Cues)
4. Draw from memory the outlines of names of four classmates. (Configuration Cues)
5. Draw one outline (or configuration) of a shape that would fit the written-out name of at least two students in our room. (Configuration Cues)
6. Draw or write the name of someone in the class in such a way that it looks like the person whose name it is. (Configuration Cues)
7. Use the controlled reader, the tachistoscope, or the timed slide projector to see how fast you can learn to identify each name of students in our class. Practice to better your time in a week. (Sight Cues)
8. Use the shape of the name of a special friend to make a design or a picture. (Sight Cues)
9. Make an alliterative sentence about a friend. Use the sound of the beginning of his or her name as many times as you can in the sentence in words that truly describe your friend. (Example: Supple Sally sat swiftly in the swing.) (Word Similarities and Differences)
10. List as many words as you can that begin with *ch* and describe feelings. (Word Similarities and Differences)
11. Make a word chain of a group of ten words that describe you. (Kinesthetic Cues)

12 Design a birthday cake for yourself in our cake-decorating center using at least four words that describe you. (Kinesthetic Cues)

13. Paste small stars into the shape of a word that describes one of your better qualities or traits. (Kinesthetic Cues)

14. List ten words that describe you (or a friend) that follow the CVC pattern. (Alternates: Words that follow the CVCV or CVVC pattern.) (Linguistic Cues)

15. List five words that you had trouble reading in this story. Think up ways that you would be able to recognize them the next time you see them. (Linguistic Cues)

16. Make up a crossword puzzle using the names of at least seven class members. Your clues for each word should be based on something each person that you choose can do well. (Semantic Cues)

17. Write down a list o five words that describe you. Opposite each word, write down the name of a friend who has the opposite (or same) characteristic. (Semantic Cues)

18. Use three new words from the story in sentences that describe yourself (or a friend). (Context Cues)

19. Write a paragraph about a friend in this room, leaving out the friend's name. Draw a line for the name each time it comes up in the paragraph. See if we can guess whom you wrote about. (Context Cues)

20. Look up or think up a word or words that describe you that begin with the following prefixes: *tri, un, in, de,* and *re.* That end with the suffixes *feel, ness, like,* or *ish.* That contain the roots *calm* or *come.* (Structural Analysis)

21. Write down or tape record an imaginary conversation between you and some story character or some author; first using no contractions at all, then again using contractions. Which sounds best to you? More natural? (Or read aloud some dialogue from the story; first use contractions, then omit them. Any differences?) (Structural Analysis)

22. Make up a haiku poem about yourself, a friend, or a story character. Be sure you know the syllable pattern before you begin. (Syllable Analysis)

23. Find a haiku book you particularly like. Read several until you can tell us the syllable pattern usually used to write haiku poetry. (Alternate: Limericks.) (Syllable Analysis)

24. Which student in our classroom has the name with the most syllables? The least? (Syllable Analysis)
25. Which of these words describes an emotion: *con´tent* or *con tent´*? (Accent Analysis)
26. Choose a sentence from the story. Read it aloud in a whiny way, a belligerent way, a timid way, and a sarcastic way. Think of three other ways to stress the words so that the sentence meaning changes. (Accent Analysis)
27. Make a list of at least twenty-five words that begin with the same sound as your name. (Encoding-Decoding, or Phonics)
28. Did you ever talk in a secret language to a friend? Give us some examples of that language. (Alternate: Write or tell about that experience.) (Encoding-Decoding, or Phonics)
29. Rewrite one paragraph you especially enjoyed from this story in some secret code. Put it in our Secret Code learning center. Be sure to include the key to the code. (Encoding-Decoding, or Phonics)
30. Make an alphabetical list of things that are important to you. (Encoding-Decoding, or Phonics)
31. Mix up the letters in the names of five classmates for us to use as an activity in our scrambled words center. (Encoding-Decoding, or Phonics)

AUDITORY PERCEPTION SKILLS

Sample Activities for Discussion, Task Cards, Learning Centers, and Reading Contracts

1. Listen to this recording of a song and pick out three words from the lyrics that describe you (or a friend). (Auditory Figure-Ground)
2. Here is a recording of five minutes of our room during reading time. We'll play it back to hear all the different kinds of sounds we can hear. (Alternate: have the students record the sounds.) (Auditory Figure-Ground)
3. Make a recording of the sounds that annoy you most during reading time. (Auditory Figure-Ground)
4. Make a list of things you should know by memory, such as your phone number, etc. (Auditory Memory)
5. Today is your day to be the helper who remembers all the

important things to tell students who are absent. Choose someone to help you if you wish. (Auditory Memory)

6. Think of a sentence that gives people good advice about themselves or getting along with other people. Give us the first half and we'll try to think of the second half. (Auditory Closure)

7. Act out a pretend telephone conversation where you show good telephone manners. Act out only your side of it. We'll try to guess what the other person said. (Auditory Closure)

8. I'm going to say the first parts of words that are about feelings. What are the endings? Con ___? Ha ___? Sa ___? Anx ___? (Alternate: Teachers: Do the same with the endings of feeling words.) (Auditory Closure)

9. Whose voice do you enjoy listening to? Give three reasons for your choice. (Auditory Pitch, Stress, Timbre, and Intonation)

10. Write down five words that you feel describe your voice. Have a friend write down five words that he or she feels describe your voice. What differences and similarities did you find in your lists? (Auditory Pitch, Stress, Timbre, and Intonation)

11. Tape-record your voice while in a conversation with a friend or reading aloud a selection from a book. How does your voice sound to you? Any surprises? (Auditory Pitch, Stress, Timbre, and Intonation)

12. Tell us the first thing you have to do to make your favorite recipe. (Auditory Sequence)

13. What was the very first sentence your teacher said to the class this morning? (Auditory Sequence)

14. Think of a sentence that gives young people good advice about themselves or about getting along with each other. Make a rebus of your sentence and put it in our puzzle center for others to solve. (Auditory Blending)

15. We're going to use our favorite songs to play "Name That Song." Think of your favorite song. Play it on the tone bells (or piano or hum it) one note at a time until we guess the song. (Auditory Blending)

16. We have been recording some of our activities this week. Listen to see how many of your classmates' voices you can identify on this tape. (Auditory Discrimination)

17. Tape-record a tongue twister. During puzzle time today

we'll play it back to see how many of the words in it we can identify. (Auditory Discrimination)

18. What do you believe are the favorite sounds of your favorite character in the story? What are your favorite sounds? Your least favorite sounds? (Auditory Comprehension)

19. Finish this sentence: Some sounds that make me nervous (happy, confused, tired, excited) _____. (Auditory Comprehension)

20. Listen while I read aloud this poem about getting along with people. I'm going to be moving around, so listen carefully. Let me know afterwards if there were any parts of the room from which you had trouble hearing me. (Auditory Tracking)

21. Listen while I play this stereo tape recording of part of our reading time activities yesterday. See if you can identify from the recording where in the room various people were. (Auditory Tracking)

22. Make a list of rules that you feel are necessary for good listeners. (Listening)

23. Give five reasons why you feel good listening is important. (Listening)

24. Make a list of five stories you would like to have read aloud to you. Give your reasons for including each. Whom do you like (or would you like) to have read aloud to you? Why did you choose this person (or these persons)? (Listening)

25. Who is the best listener in this room? Give reasons for your choice. (Listening)

26. What do you feel you need to do to make yourself into a better listener? (Listening)

27. Were there any examples of someone really listening to what someone else said in the book you just finished? In our classroom today during reading time? (Listening)

28. We're going to talk about things we've imagined that are foolish at discussion time today. Be ready to share some of the things you've imagined that later turned out to be foolish. (Oral Language)

29. Be ready for a discussion on what things about our reading time are meaningful to you. (Oral Language)

30. Be ready to discuss things you like to do (things you need to learn, things that are important to you, etc.) during discussion time today. (Oral Language)

31. Teachers: Read, tape-record, or have students tape-record some dialogue passages from unfamiliar reading materials. Ask students to listen and respond to these questions. What was the first thing that was said by ____ (story character)? What were the exact words ____ (story character) used to reply? What was said first? Second? What is the rest of the order of the dialogue? (Auditory Sequence)

VISUAL PERCEPTION SKILLS

Sample Activities for Discussion, Task Cards, Learning Centers, and Reading Contracts

1. I'm going to read you a scene from a story. Close your eyes while you listen and try to see the action just as clearly as if you were watching television or a film. We'll share the different things each of you sees when I'm through. (Visual Comprehension)

2. What comes to your mind when you hear the word *house? jump? wonder? become?* (Note to teachers: Use new words from reading materials in similar ways to teach differences in perception.) (Visual Comprehension)

3. Make up a word search containing as many names of the students in our classroom as you can fit in. Cover your work with clear plastic to protect it and put it in our word search center for other students to solve when you're done. (Visual Figure–Ground)

4. Make pinhole cameras. Use two pieces of construction paper, one of which has a pinhole in it, or look up the instructions for a more complicated design and build one with a group of friends. Use it to look at the sun safely or look at things around the classroom. What do you see that would make a good picture? (Visual Figure–Ground)

5. We're going to play a game that will depend on how much you remember of what you see. One person will be *It*. He or she will stand in front of the class for 30 seconds, then go outside the room. We'll try to remember such things as hair color, the side of the part in the hair, number of buttons on clothing, and so on. The one who remembers the most gets to be *It* next time. (Note to teachers: Students can write or give their answers verbally.) (Visual Memory)

6. I'm going to have you look carefully at one student for

thirty seconds, then that student will leave the room. Your job is to draw (or describe in writing) as many details as you can remember about the person's appearance. (Visual Memory)

7. Here are some photographs of different people in our room. I've covered up all but a small part of each face or figure. How many can you recognize from these partial pictures? (Visual Closure)

8. We're going to play "Who Is It?" Three students are standing behind this curtain. You can see only their hands (or eyes, mouth, etc.) Who are they? (Visual Closure)

9. Here are parts of words that describe different emotions. Fill in the missing parts. Ang--, ---ror, --ppi----, ho--. Make up five partial words of your own. (Visual Closure)

10. Choose a partner to play *Name Scrabble*. Only the names of people in this class can be used. (Visual Sequence)

11. Unscramble these feeling words: yoj, papyh, ragne, revsoun, siouxan. (Visual Sequence)

12. Find different pictures of the same model in magazines or in a catalogue. Notice what the changes in clothing or hairstyle do to the model's looks. (Form Constancy)

13. Have a photograph of you or of a friend Xeroxed so you have three copies (or put a photograph under a sheet of plastic). Draw different disguises for the face. (Form Constancy)

14. Use an identikit to reproduce a friend's face without looking at that friend until you are through. (Form Constancy)

15. Make a silhouette of one of your classmates, using the lighting set up in our silhouette corner. Paste the silhouette on a folder. Inside the folder put a list of ten words that describe your friend. We'll have a guessing game to see who can identify the most people from their silhouettes when we've all finished. (Note to teachers: You or an aide may need to make the silhouettes for lower grade levels.) (Form Perception)

16. Draw from memory the floor plan of your home. (Form Perception)

17. Using paint sample cards or chips, identify the color of your eyes or the color of those of a friend. (Visual Discrimination)

18. Look carefully at pictures in the stereo view center. Be ready to tell about or show the differences between one pair that makes them appear three-dimensional when viewed together. (Visual Discrimination)

19. I'm going to read you a new story (or part of a story). Listen carefully and try to visualize the action as clearly as if you were there. We'll share our different views when I've finished. (Visualization)

20. Here is a description of a character in the story. Close your eyes and try to see the story character as I read aloud the description. When I've finished, draw (or tell) what you saw. (Visualization)

.21. During this discussion, keep your eyes on the person who is talking, looking from person to person as each one has something to add to the discussion. (Visual Tracking)

22. We're going to read this story aloud, with a different person reading aloud each page (or dialogue part). Keep your eyes on the person reading. (Visual Tracking)

23. Find and be ready to read aloud the sentence that tells how _____ (story character) felt. (Eye Movement Skills)

24. How many "feeling" words, or words that express feelings, can you find on this page? (Eye Movement Skills)

25. Make a sampler using textile paints (or stitchery, if you'd rather) to copy a saying or a proverb that you would like to hang in your room. (Left-to-Right Eye Movements)

26. Teachers: Before assigning this exercise, make a grid of "feeling" words, using only left-to-right patterns: How many feeling words can you find on this grid?

PERCEPTION SKILLS

Sample Activities for Discussion, Task Cards, Learning Centers, or Reading Contracts

1. Make up a riddle about smells you like. (Olfactory Perception)

2. Make or draw a face that shows how you feel about these kinds of smells: burning leaves, wet clothing, summer rain, vinegar. (Olfactory Perception)

3. Choose a restaurant menu from our menu learning center and answer the following questions: How many different sandwiches (types of potatoes, kinds of salad dressing) are

on the menu? What different kinds of desserts can you order? Can you make substitutions on the menu? If you were to order a meal for yourself, what would you order? How much would it cost you (be sure to include tax and tip)? (Taste Perception)

4. Sometimes it feels good to feel things. What things make you feel better or work better if you can feel them? (Tactile Perception)

5. If the climate of the story setting were changed (from hot to cold, for instance), how would that change the way the story characters lived? (Tactile Perception)

6. Using the frosting tubes and a plain cupcake, create a miniature birthday cake for a story character, yourself, or a friend. Be ready to explain how the cake decoration fits the person for whom you are designing the cake. (Taste Perception)

7. Choose three students to help you to plan snacks for next week. Choose snacks that are good for us, but that you truly enjoy. (Taste Perception)

8. Some families have a custom of allowing the "birthday girl or boy" to choose all the meals on their birthday. What would you choose for your birthday meals? (Taste Perception)

9. We are going to plan a menu to serve to our parents that would be suitable for the story we just finished reading. At the same time, we're going to share the story with them. What suggestions do you have for what to serve? How can we share the story with them? What helpers do we need to have a successful treat and story telling session for our parents? What would you like to do to help make the parents' visit to our classroom a success? Be ready to share your ideas during planning time at __ o'clock. (Taste Perception)

10. Write a poem or a short description of yourself enjoying something using a different sense from the usual. (Hint: The smell of a sunset or the feel of the color brown.) (Multisensory Perception)

11. Choose someone you'd like to know better and take turns leading each other while the person being led has his or her eyes closed. Try to provide interesting experiences for your partner while leading him or her—interesting things to

smell, touch, feel, hear, and the like. Don't talk to each other any more than is absolutely necessary for safety reasons. Explore the room and outside. (Note to teachers: Limit the area any way you wish. Be sure to give lots of time for the partners to talk to each other about the experience, whether they enjoyed leading or following more, the best part, etc.) (Multisensory Perception)

12. List all the feelings, smells, tastes, and other sensory feelings that you can recall from the best day you ever had in your life. (Multisensory Perception)

13. Make up a dot-to-dot picture about your story for our puzzle center. (Hand-Eye Coordination)

14. Make a clay representation of something in your story. (Hand-Eye Coordination)

15. Be ready to act out an emotion described in this story. Be so good that everyone who watches can guess just exactly which emotion you are demonstrating. (General Coordination)

16. Plan a "Book Day" where each student dresses as his or her favorite story character. Choose friends to help you if you wish. (General Coordination)

17. Choose three words that describe you. Move your body in such a way that you illustrate those words for us. (For teachers: These instructions can be used during movement time, motor skills education, or creative dance.) (General Coordination)

18. Make an origami project that relates to your feelings about your story. (Motor Coordination)

19. Decide which story character or author you'll be when you're *It* when we play *Charades* this afternoon. Get your gestures and props ready. (Motor Coordination)

20. Draw a birds-eye view of one emotional scene in your story or in your life. (Position in Space)

21. Draw one story character from the point of view of a very young child. (Position in Space)

22. Pantomime a series of emotions from the story. Be so good that everyone will know what you are demonstrating. (Alternate: Be ready to act out how both sides of some conflict in the story must have felt about the conflict.) (Body Awareness)

23. Make a list of the physical characteristics for the "bad guys" in a series of books. Do they have similar physical traits? How would you feel if you looked like this? (Alternates: Do the same for people pictured as wise, as happy, as powerful, as the hero or heroine.) (Body Awareness)
24. What three things do you like best about your body? What three things do you like least? (Body Awareness)
25. What is the most tiring part physically of our reading program? (Body Awareness)
26. Choose a partner. Each of you takes a turn lying down on the big sheets of butcher paper while the other draws your outline on the paper with a crayon. Cut out two of each of the shapes and color one as the front and one as the back view. Staple them together and stuff the finished lifesize dolls of yourself with tissue paper. Write a list of ten words that you feel describe what kind of person you are and pin it to the figurine you stuffed. (Body Awareness)
27. Write how you will look in twenty years. (Body Awareness)
28. Today we're going to see how people feel who work mostly with a different hand from the one they usually use. During reading time, if you are left-handed, use your right hand for everything. If you are right-handed, use your left. When reading time is over, we'll talk about what you discovered. (Laterality)
29. Name as many situations as you can in which it is best to be left-handed. Right-handed. (Laterality)
30. Play "Director." Write down one action from the story. Decide what motions make up this action. Tell your friends who are the actors to move their arms, legs, bodies in these motions, a step at a time. See if they can guess the action you are having them do in slow motion. (Directionality)
31. Make up a dance based on your story. Use balloons, balls, fans, tambourines with streamers, or the like as part of the dance. (Directionality)
32. Take a walk, especially to watch things move. Make notes to help you describe what you see when you get back from the walk. (Spacial Relationships)
33. Look at an object first with both eyes, then with your right, next with your left eye. Look at the object again with both

eyes. Keep your head still while doing this. Be ready to draw or tell the differences in what you saw. (Spatial Relationships)

WORK-STUDY SKILLS

Sample Activities for Discussion, Task Cards, Learning Centers, and Reading Contracts

1. Draw a map of what you would consider to be an ideal community. (Map and Globe Skills)
2. Mark on a map or a globe five places you would very much like to visit. Be ready to tell us why you chose those places. (Map and Globe skills)
3. Interview the students in the classroom to find out their favorite authors. Mark the location of the birthplace of each on a map or a globe. (Map and Globe Skills)
4. What would you have named the streets in your neighborhood if you had been in charge of street names? Draw a map using these names. (Map and Globe Skills)
5. List all the books you can find for students at your age level that took place in our locality. (Map and Globe Skills)
6. Make a diagram of your dream house. (Interpreting Graphic Material)
7. Make a diagram of your ideal school or classroom. (Interpreting Graphic Material)
8. Make a chart or a graph of your progress in some human relations skill or of your progress in accepting yourself. (Interpreting Graphic Material)
9. Compare a diagram of your house with a diagram of the home of the main character in the story. (Interpreting Graphic Material)
10. Make a time line of the ten most important events that have happened in your life to date. (Interpreting Graphic Material)
11. Make a graph of the number of people in the families of students in our classroom. (Interpreting Graphic Material)
12. Make an ideal schedule for yourself for a week. (Alternate: Compare your ideal weekly schedule with your actual one.) (Interpreting Graphic Material)
13. Look over the illustrations in this book. How do they por-

tray minorities? Females? Males? Old people? Are all people in these groups like the people in the illustrations? Does this book imply they are? (Interpreting Pictures and Illustrations)

14. Look at a series of pictures of people's faces from magazines or from newspapers. Choose five and make up names for the people pictured. Write (or tell) a brief explanation of why you choose each name. (Interpreting Pictures and Illustrations)

15. Select a picture from a book, a magazine, or a newspaper that particularly appeals to you. Tell (or write) the feelings you would have if you were there. (Interpreting Pictures and Illustrations)

16. Scan the weekly television log to see if any of your favorite books are being dramatized. Plan to watch and share your feelings about the television production with us. (Alternate: Check movie programs.) (Reading Techniques)

17. Scan the help wanted section of the newspaper until you find a job you might like to have. What schooling would you need? What salary would you earn? What traits would you need? (Reading Techniques)

18. You are assigned to the Sewing Learning Center today. Look through the pattern books and choose three outfits you like. Perhaps the books and articles on clothing for different body types will help you choose. Choose one simple design (maybe a scarf or a shirt) and make one for yourself out of the materials and directions available. (Note to teachers: Have pattern books, clothing references, scissors, material, and the like, available in this center. Alternate: Set up a sewing center for story doll clothes.) (Following Directions)

19. Write out (or tell) the directions a story book character should follow to solve one of his or her problems. (Following Directions)

20. Plan a dinner for yourself and three friends. Interview your friends and take notes about their favorite foods. Plan a menu that will please all of you. (Note Taking)

21. Make a note each day for a week of one thing you did well in reading that day. Share your notes with us at the end of that time. (Note Taking)

22. Make a list of how many times you used sight, hearing,

touch, taste, and smell since you woke up this morning. (Note Taking)

23. Interview an older resident on the changes that have taken place in the neighborhood of your school. Keep notes to remind yourself of what he or she said. (Note Taking)

24. Interview five students to see what would make them happier at reading time. Keep notes of what they say. (Note Taking)

25. Make up an outline for a substitute teacher to use during reading time. Plan reading activities you feel you and the other students would enjoy and learn from. (Outlining)

26. List the qualities you think every good reading teacher should have. (Outlining)

27. If you and a friend could watch television all night tonight, which programs would you watch? Use a TV guide to help you answer this. (Media Work-Study Skills)

28. Take notes of the scenes you felt were particularly well photographed in the film we'll see this afternoon. (Media Work-Study Skills)

29. In what kind of setting do you do your best work in reading? Is there a particular place in one classroom where you do reading work best? What else could we do in our classroom to make this a better place for you to work? (Self-Direction)

30. If you were the teacher, how would you schedule reading time for one day? Write out or make a diagram of the schedule you would follow. Be ready to share with us your reasons. (Self-Direction)

31. Make a road map of the ways you took to becoming a better reader. Be sure to put in all the "road blocks," "highways," "detours," and the like. (Self-Improvement)

32. Make a list of three things in reading you'd like to work on next week. (Self-Improvement)

33. Make a chart of your reading improvement in the tachistoscope center for a week. (Reading Rate)

34. List three reasons you might want to read a selection rapidly and three reasons you might want to read the same selection (or another) slowly. (Reading Rate)

35. Thomas Gordon has written a book, *Parent Effectiveness Training*, on how to be a better parent. (*Parent Effective-*

ness Training: The Tested New Way to Raise Responsible Children. New York: Wyden Books, 1970.) From the viewpoint of a son or daughter, what do you think of this book? (Alternate: Review Gordon's book on how to be a better teacher (*Teacher Effectiveness Training*) from a student's viewpoint.) (Book Reviewing)

36. Write a critique of your books as if you were a psychologist reviewing it. (Book Reviewing)

37. Write (or give orally) a review of your book from the viewpoint of one story character. (Book Reviewing)

38. Who reads aloud the best of any person you know? What does this person do that makes him or her such a successful oral reader? (Oral Reading)

39. Select a part of the story you especially like. Practice reading it aloud until you sound as if you were just talking. Be ready to read it to us. (Oral Reading)

40. Find an interesting dialogue or conversational section in your story. Practice with some classmates until you can read these parts aloud as if you were really talking to each other. Let us know when you are ready to read them to us. (Oral Reading)

41. Do you like to have someone read aloud to you? Anyone special? Any special stories? (Oral Reading)

42. Find passages from your book that analyze a character from the book; prepare to read these aloud orally to the teacher. (Alternates: Setting of the book; most interesting page of the book.) (Oral Reading)

43. Be prepared to read aloud several parts of the story that show how a character changed his or her attitude or behavior. (Alternate: Selections that show traits or emotions of a character.) (Oral Reading)

44. Be ready to read aloud a conversation between two story characters that shows something about the characters of these two people. If there is no suitable passage in the book, make one up. (Oral Reading)

45. Pick a story that you feel younger students would enjoy hearing. You can choose the story from one you remember enjoying when you were younger, from some of the newer stories, or from the recommendation of a friend. Practice reading the story aloud in our oral reading center in front of

the full length mirror. Let me know when you're ready to read it aloud to younger students. Be ready to tell if your selection was a good one. (Oral Reading)

46. Where would you go to find good books on a problem you might have in human relationships? (Research Skills)
47. Make an exhibit of three books about the same subject. Write questions or comments about the books so that people who look at the exhibit will be more interested or better informed. (Research Skills)
48. Read books on three different kinds of animals. On the basis of what you read, tell why these animals would or would not make a good pet for you. (Research Skills)
49. Compare what living in two different areas would mean to you. How would your life be different in each? (Research Skills)
50. Do you usually prefer to work alone or in a group on a reading job? (Group Work Skills)
51. What size group do you feel is best for a reading group? Tell us your reasons for your choice. (Group Work Skills)
52. List three people you were proud of during reading time today. Beside each name briefly tell why you are proud of that person. Include yourself if you wish. (Group Work Skills)
53. We're setting up a "Working Together" reading learning center. You can choose to work with someone on one of your reading tasks (or assignments) today. (Group Work Skills)

REFERENCE SKILLS

Sample Activities for Discussion, Task Cards, Learning Centers, and Reading Contracts

1. What is the date of copyright for this book? How do you think this date of publication affected the contents? Give specific examples from the book to prove your point. What was happening in your life when this book was written? (Using Parts of Books)
2. Look at the table of contents of a new book. Which parts of the book do you think you will like best? Read the book and see if you were right. (Alternate: Do the same thing, trying to predict, from the table of contents, which parts of the

book will teach you the most.) (Using Parts of a Book)

3. Choose one word that you feel best describes you. Look this word up in a dictionary or thesaurus. Find at least three other words that mean the same that also describe you. (Using Dictionaries and Other Word Reference Skills)

4. Select three words from your reading today that you'd like to add to your own vocabulary. Write three sentences using each word correctly. (Using Dictionaries and Other Word Reference Skills)

5. Make a personal telephone directory of telephone numbers that are important to you. (Using Standard References)

6. Look up information about the place where you were born. Be ready to tell us three things about it that were of interest to you. (Using Standard References)

7. Make an alphabetical list of the emotions the characters in this story experienced. (Library Skills)

8. Make an alphabetical list of the emotions you felt as you read the story. (Library Skills)

9. What do you like about going to the library? Dislike? (Library Skills)

10. List a problem one story character had and give a place in our library that character could go to find help with it. (Library Skills)

11. Make a list of books that you feel do a good job of telling students your age about their bodies (their emotions, their problems, etc.). Briefly (in a sentence or so) tell why you included each book. (Using Bibliographies)

12. What books do you especially recommend for students two years younger than you? Give brief reasons for why you included each book. (Using Bibliographies)

13. Make a list of books on sex that you would recommend for seven-year-olds. Discuss briefly your reasons for including each. (Alternates: Books for seven-year-olds on war, friendship, American Indians.) (Using Bibliographies)

14. Make a list of books you would recommend that students your age need to read if they want to take up one of your hobbies or special interests. Why did you recommend each book? (Using Bibliographies)

15. Make a list of three to five books or stories you have read that made you feel good about yourself. Share with us the reasons each made you feel good about yourself. (Alter-

nate: Do the same with books that made you feel bad about yourself.) (Using Bibliographies)
16. What books would you like for your home library? (Using Bibliographies)

A FINAL WORD ABOUT TEACHING READING THROUGH INTERPERSONAL PROCESS

Reading provides our students with insights on how to handle more adequately the interpersonal aspects of their lives. No matter what interpersonal problems they may meet, there are poems, novels, or how-to books they can read that were written by others who were trying to deal with the same dilemmas. Reading helps our students have infinitely more possibilities of action available to them in their lifelong quest to learn about themselves and others—all the possibilities ever conceived by ingenious writers throughout the ages. Reading helps students learn that no one—neither themselves, the authors they read, nor their teachers—has an option on truth or accuracy.

From reading comes words that help our students describe what is happening to them emotionally as they wrestle with their human relations interactions; words that mirror and define their own feelings, dilemmas, hopes, aspirations, and plans; words that reassure them that others have experienced similarly; words that are in themselves often the causes of human relations problems, since no one person can ever understand the depths of meaning any other person assigns to any word. From reading, too, students gain an understanding of the power of words; words used as weapons, as balm, as offerings; wounding or soothing or healing or intensifying; drawing closer or holding off—the power of words given or withheld.

14

New Ways
With Book Reviews

****

Although many ways to develop reading skills through the medium of book reviews are included in this chapter, teachers will also want children to have opportunities to read for pleasure without obligation to analyze, report, interpret, dissect. Reading time for solitary enjoyment is an important part of learning about literature.

For those other times when it is appropriate to teach more analytic reading skills, the variety of book review techniques suggested in this chapter are designed to fit various student learning styles. Each suggested technique, although listed under one skill subhead, actually develops many more reading skills; a bonus for student and teacher, alike. These skills were defined in further detail in chapters 1 through 11. The following ideas may be written on task cards, may be used for individual or group assignments, or may be a part of a student learning contract. Allowing students a choice of several methods of reporting is another way to use these suggestions.

COMPREHENSION SKILLS

Activities for Discussion, Task Cards, Learning Centers, and Reading Contracts

1. Write a character in the story a letter suggesting: What might have happened if he had acted in a different way, or what you think might happen in his future if he continues to act as he presently does. (Prediction)

2. Choose a character from the story and one from another story. Write a conversation between the two as if they had met. (Prediction)

3. Switch characteristics of two main characters. How would this change the outcome of the story? Or add a character or take out a character. How would that change the book? (Prediction)

4. Write part of the story, pass it on to someone else to write a page, then to someone else. See if they came out with a story similar to the original. (Prediction)

5. Pretend that your favorite story character is going to be interviewed on your favorite talk show. Write what you think would happen. (Prediction)

6. Choose five different occupations. Write why the main character would or would not be qualified for these jobs. (Prediction)

7. Place the main character in another setting (Mars, for example). List how you predict he or she would act. (Prediction)

8. If the setting of the story is in the past, take some modern day appliance (TV, pocket calculator, etc.) and insert it in the story. What would happen? (Prediction)

9. Look at the book jacket and first page of a book you haven't read. Write down the date and a prediction of whether you will like it. Read the book. See if you predicted correctly. (Prediction)

10. Read one chapter in a book. Predict what will happen in the story. Sign your prediction in the presence of a witness. Read the book. How accurate were your predictions? (Prediction)

11. List the following values in the right order for two characters in the book: Self-respect, happiness, money, family, wisdom, friendship, peace, work, cleanliness, cheerfulness. Give reasons for your rankings. (Prediction)

12. Place the story in a different time setting. How would it differ? (Prediction)

13. If you were to give this book to people you know, who do you predict would enjoy it most? Why? What other acquaintances or family members would enjoy it? Explain. (Prediction)

14. How do you feel about a character in the story? Give some

sentences, words, or phrases that caused you to feel as you do. (Characterization)

15. Write some sentences from the story to show some character was pleased. Angry. Surprised. Anxious. Rewrite the sentences in a different way to give the same feeling. (Characterization)

16. Choose a story character. Pretend he or she needs a job. Write a job resumé for him or her. What jobs do you think the character is suited for? (Characterization)

17. Act like the main character for an hour; for a day. (Characterization)

18. Design a wardrobe for a favorite character in the book. Make the wardrobe appropriate to that character. (Characterization)

19. Design a sports car for a main character. (Characterization)

20. Pretend a character gets a mysterious box. What are his or her reactions? (Characterization)

21. Would favorite characters of yours from other books like the characters in this book? (Characterization)

22. Make a "Happiness is _____" list for four main characters. (Characterization)

23. Make up a "Favorite" list for the main character (favorite actor, song, book, color, food, sports, etc.). (Characterization)

24. If this book were made into a movie, which actors and actresses would you like to see play the main characters? (Characterization)

25. Choose a birthday for your favorite character. Look up the Zodiac sign. Would he or she be compatible with you? (Characterization)

26. Would you like the main character to live with you? What about him/her/it would you change before? (Characterization)

27. What character did you not want to be like? In what ways? (Characterization)

28. Write a letter to yourself from a story character, offering you advice. (Characterization)

29. Write a short biography of a story character, filling in unknown details by using your imagination. (Characterization)

30. Pretend a character from your book meets a character from

another book you have read in a different time era. Write or record their conversation when they first meet. (Characterization)

31. How many sentences can you find where the writer did not mean exactly what he/she said and you had to read between the lines? What did he or she really mean? (Making Inferences and Conclusions)

32. What ten presents would your favorite character want for his birthday? Explain. (Making Inferences and Conclusions)

33. Tell what happened to two of the characters before the events in this story. (Making Inferences and Conclusions)

34. Find sentences in the story that tell: How something works, how someone behaves, and how someone sounds. (Locating Details)

35. Make up five questions that can only be answered by reading the book. Answer the questions. (Locating Details)

36. Draw a picture of a scene in the story that really impressed you. Make the picture detailed enough so that someone who had never read the book could visualize the scene. (Recall)

37. Make up a series of questions that you feel a person who has read the book should be able to answer (discussion questions, true-false, short answer, essay, multiple choice). Make an answer sheet. (Recall)

38. Select a person you know who is similar to a character in the story. Select another real person who is different. How are they alike? How are they different? (Comparing and Contrasting)

39. In what ways are you similar to your favorite character? In what ways are you different? (Comparing and Contrasting)

40. Name three good friends of yours. Which characters in the book do you think each would like? Which characters would they dislike? (Comparing and Contrasting)

41. If you were the main character, would you have acted any differently? (Comparing and Contrasting)

42. Find five pictures that fit a character in the story. Write why you chose each picture. (Making Inferences and Conclusions)

43. Pretend you are a feminist or "women's libber" who read

the story. Write a review of the book as this person might. (Making Inferences and Conclusions)

44. Make an advertisement for the book. (Main Idea)

45. Write a short paragraph about each of five characters. Tell the good and bad parts you see in each personality. (Making Inferences and Conclusions)

46. Draw a picture for a book jacket. (Main Idea)

47. Tell the high points of the story in five brief sentences. Then summarize the story in only one short sentence. (Summary)

48. Choose a place mentioned in the story. Write a legend about it. (Making Inferences and Conclusions)

49. Make scenery to go with the story. Act out the story. (Alternates: Make puppets to illustrate the story or make a collage, a diorama, a poem, or a poster about the story.) (Summary)

50. What would you have to do to make the book into a play? A musical? A motion picture? (Main Idea)

51. Pretend you are a newspaper reporter. Write two articles that could have appeared in the local paper about the story or a story character. (Main Idea)

52. Make a comic book of the story. (Sequence)

53. If this book were to be made into a television series, what would be five episodes? (Sequence)

54. Report the middle of the story. See if the class or a friend can give an ending and a beginning. (Sequence)

55. Make a filmstrip of classmates acting out the story. Record dialogue, sound effects, and background music. (Alternate: Become a movie producer. Make a videotape recording or a motion picture of classmates acting out the story. Record dialogue, sound effects, and background music.) (Sequence)

56. Pretend you are a photographer on an assignment to illustrate the story. Use an instant or other camera and take and share appropriate shots. (Sequence)

57. Write five characters from the story across the top of your paper. List voice, attitude, expression, height, eye color down the left-hand side. Fill in the chart for each character. (Classification)

58. Make a *Book Categories* chart. Fill in the names of the types

of books as you read them (mysteries, science fiction, detective, adventure, sport, etc.). (Classification)

59. Write, in alphabetical order, ten words of a certain type that you found in the story; e.g., mysterious words, fantasy words, etc. (Figurative Language)

CRITICAL READING SKILLS

Sample Activities for Discussion, Task Cards, Learning Centers, and Reading Contracts

1. What assumptions does this author make about life? (Author's Assumptions)

2. What assumptions does this author make about the reader? (Author's Assumptions)

3. Pretend that you are the author of this book. Plan a speech about it as if you had written it. (Analyzing Author's Organization)

4. What did the author say that you especially agreed with? Disagreed with? In what ways are both of you right? Wrong? Who do you know who would argue with you? With the author? (Analyzing Author Bias, Point of View)

5. Write a letter to the author about his book. (Evaluating Authors' Skills)

6. Have a mock trial to judge whether the author wrote an exciting or dull book. (Evaluating Authors' Skills)

7. What phrases did the author write that you wish you had said first? (Evaluating Authors' Skills)

8. What did the author write that you've always wanted to write yourself? (Evaluating Authors' Skills)

9. A good author is one who can write in such a way that you say, "I've thought of that a million times. Why didn't I write that?" What made you feel this way in this book? (Analyzing Authors' Skills)

10. Is this a book you would like to have authored? Explain. (Analyzing Authors' Skills)

11. Compare this book to others written by the same author. (Analyzing Authors' Skills)

12. Some people choose new books mostly because they were written by an author whose works they usually enjoy. Is this an author whose books you would choose again on this basis? Explain. (Analyzing Authors' Skills)

13. Which do you think this author prefers, boys or girls, men or women? Support your view. (Identifying Stereotyping)
14. Write another story using this author's style. (Analyzing Authors' Skills)
15. What inaccuracies, if any, did you find in the book? (Analyzing Reliability and Validity)
16. How does what this author has to say about events, characters, setting, and the like compare with other authors?
17. In the library, find a review of the book you read. Compare the reviewer's opinion to yours. (Evaluating Content and Format)
18. Evaluate your book carefully: What were its strengths? What were its weaknesses? (Evaluating Content and Format)
19. Of all the books you have ever read, where would you place this book? One of the three best? One of the ten best? Better than most books? Not as good as most? Other? Explain. (Evaluating Content and Format)
20. Make a list of the ten best books that you have read. Tell how you made your choices. (Evaluating Content and Format)
21. Create your own rating scale for books, using numbers, letters, symbols, or other means. (Evaluating Content and Format)

CREATIVE READING SKILLS

Sample Activities for Discussion, Task Cards, Learning Centers, and Reading Contracts

1. What do you know a lot about that the author probably doesn't? Maybe it's something that doesn't even come up in the book. (Developing Self-Concepts and Self-Development Through Reading)
2. Record a telephone conversation between two main characters. (Relationship of Reading to Other Media)
3. Draw an illustration of each of the main characters. (Relationship of Reading to Other Media)
4. Dramatize a scene from the book. (Alternate: Write the story as a play.) (Relationship of Reading to Other Media)
5. If you were going to film the book: Who would you select for leading roles? Where would you go for location shots?

Would you change the story in any way? Explain. (Relationship of Reading to Other Media)

6. If the book you read has been made into a movie, explain the similarities and differences between the two. (Relationship of Reading to Other Media)

7. Use some type of creative dramatics to interpret your book (pantomime, character sketch, scenes, etc.). (Relationship of Reading to Other Media)

8. Write newspaper features related to your book; e.g., headlines, news stories, want ads, editorials, comics, etc. (Developing Authors' Skills)

9. Make a book containing all classmates' telephone numbers, addresses, shoe sizes. (Developing Authors' Skills)

10. Make a book of photographs or drawings of children's homes. (Creating Original Materials)

11. Make a book of baby photos of all students. Have the captions for the pictures in the back. See who can identify the most pictures correctly. (Creating Original Material)

12. Prepare a travel brochure for tourists who might visit the story location. (Creating Games, Puzzles, Anagrams, etc.)

13. Make either a word search or crossword puzzle of 20 new words. (Creating Games, Puzzles, Anagrams, etc.)

14. Make an electric board that can be used with interchangeable sets of questions and answers about the book. (Alternate: Make up a game board that can be used for many games. Design one game on it that relates to this book.) (Creating Games, Puzzles, Anagrams, etc.)

15. Create a new way to report on a book. (Creating Original Materials)

16. Write anything you want to about your book. (Creating Original Materials)

17. State real, honest, sincere reasons for liking or disliking the book. (Creative Thinking – Evaluation)

18. What do you really wish had been different about the book? (Creative Thinking – Evaluation)

19. What do you think would have made the story better? (Creative Thinking – Evaluation)

20. Teachers: Other media for book reviews include: Mobiles, comic strips, posters, clay, soap carving, wood carving, plaster models, dioramas, peep shows, book marks, dolls, stick figures, puppets (stick, paper bag), collage, accordion

books, water colors, book jackets, booklets, bulletin board, string stories, murals, flannelboards, movies (roller, flip pictures, motion picture camera, filmstrip, videotape recorder), pipe cleaners, papier maché, riddles, displays, transparencies, bookends. (Relating Reading to Other Media)

21. Teachers: Keep a class journal from the beginning to the end of the school term. Sample entries: birthdays, important events, visitors, the best papers, photographs of activities, records of trips, charts of class progress (spelling, behavior, etc.). (Developing Authors' Skills)

22. Teachers: Make an anthology of students' work. Examples: poetry, stories, art work. (Developing Authors' Skills)

23. Teachers: Keep a book including all work done the first day of school (handwriting, math, etc.). Compare the progress of the class and of individual children periodically. (Creative Thinking – Evaluation)

LITERATURE APPRECIATION SKILLS

Sample Activities for Discussion, Task Cards, Learning Centers, and Reading Contracts

1. Write an analysis of the book by a person from the future. (Cultural Analysis Through Literature)

2. If a person from a distant planet had only this book to use to learn about life on earth, what would you think of his chances of getting an accurate understanding? (Cultural Analysis Through Literature)

3. Make a categories chart. Fill in the names of the types of books as you read them (mysteries, science fiction, detective, adventure, sports, etc.). (Identifying Literary Forms)

4. Report on a travel book by compiling a series of pictures (slides, photographs, magazine illustrations) for a talk. (Identifying Literary Forms)

5. Make a diary for a main character about the experiences in the story. (Alternate: Compare diaries of two characters.) (Identifying Literary Forms)

6. Rewrite the book ending. If the story ended happily, change it to an unhappy ending, etc. (Identifying Literary Devices)

7. Write a sequel, or write an epilogue to your book. (Identifying Literary Devices)

8. Perform a science experiment that relates to the subject of a science or nature book. (Identifying Literary Forms)

9. Perform a magic trick or two from books on magic. (Identifying Literary Forms)

10. Is this story about the present, past, or future? Make a list of items that give a clue to the setting. Let the class try to guess the time from your clues. (Identifying Story Elements)

11. Make a costume that a character in the book might wear. Wear it to explain the story setting and the particular character. (Identifying Story Elements)

12. Construct a miniature stage setting for the story (or part of the story) using a shoe box, or the like. (Identifying Story Elements)

13. In what ways did this book prove valuable to you? Did it make any difference in your life? (Value of Reading)

14. What do you know now that you wouldn't if you hadn't read this book? (Value of Reading)

15. At the end of the year, make a recommended bibliography for next year's class. (Selecting Appropriate Material)

16. For whom would you recommend this book? Age levels, backgrounds, etc. (Selecting Appropriate Materials)

17. Find out information about the author and/or illustrator of the book you read. (Recognizing Famous Authors and Writings)

18. Play "Who wrote _____?" Use the entire class, select teams, or choose a panel. Have class members design the questions. (Recognizing Famous Authors and Writings)

19. Some book critics are especially well known. Make a list of five nationally known book critics. (Recognizing Famous Authors and Writings)

20. Describe one part of the story that is similar to or different from your own life. (Alternate: Compare episodes, friends, family setting, etc., of the story to your own life.) (Bibliotherapy)

21. Give personal reactions to one of the characters. (Alternate: To the book.) (Bibliotherapy)

VOCABULARY DEVELOPMENT

Sample Activities for Discussion, Task Cards,
Learning Centers, and Reading Contracts

1. *Synonyms and Antonyms.* Make a chart of opposite characteristics. Place your story character on the chart at the appropriate places. Example:

Hot	/____/____/____/____/	Cold
Strong	/____/____/____/____/	Weak
Sour	/____/____/____/____/	Sweet
Fast	/____/____/____/____/	Slow
Friendly	/____/____/____/____/	Unfriendly
Curious	/____/____/____/____/	Uninterested

Make up a similar rating scale of your own. (Special Word
Relationships)
2. Make a chart of specialized and technical words used in the
story (technical terms, ordinary words used in a specialized
sense, occupational words, etc.). (Technical and
Specialized Vocabulary)
3. Make a list of technical or specialized words the author
could have included to make the story more authentic.
(Technical and Specialized Vocabulary)
4. Make a list of new words you found in the story. (New
Vocabulary)
5. Choose ten words from the story that you think anyone
should know before they can enjoy the book to the fullest.
Give reasons for your choices. (New Vocabulary)
6. Guess at the definition of words in the story that are new to
you. Try to figure out their meaning from the story; then
look them up in the dictionary. (New Vocabulary)
7. Record a phone conversation between two main characters. Categorize and use their unique speech patternings
(including vocabulary, voice patterns, and the like) and use
this patterning in the recording. (Vocabulary Patterning)
8. List the different ways you think various characters would
phrase the following sentences: (a) "Please pass the
potatoes." (b) "What a beautiful day." (Alternate: Make up

a sentence of your own and phrase it in the vocabulary style of several story characters.) (Vocabulary Patterning)

9. Write, in alphabetical order, 20 words from the story that intrigue. Why do these words intrigue? (Appropriateness of Vocabulary)

10. What phrases did the author use that you especially like and want to use in your own vocabulary? (Appropriateness of Vocabulary)

11. Make a list of unusual words in the book from geographic regions, professions, or from the time period indicated. (Variations of Vocabulary)

12. Place the story in a different setting. Write a conversation between two characters using different regional dialects (Southern, Western, space, etc.). (Variations of Vocabulary)

13. Take an actual conversation from the book and change it to a different dialect (Southern, Western, Ghetto, etc.). (Variations of Vocabulary)

14. Did the story characters of different ages use different vocabularies? Explain. (Variations of Vocabulary)

WORD PERCEPTION SKILLS

Sample Activities for Discussion, Task Cards, Learning Centers, and Reading Contracts

1. Write ten sentences about the story that are not complete and that can be completed only by someone who has read the story. (Linguistic Cues – Syntax)

2. Were any of the sentences in the book worded differently from the way you and the people you know talk? Explain. (Note to teachers: If you feel that the language of the book is unnecessarily stilted due to vocabulary, restrictions or the like, discuss with the class other, less labored, ways to say the same thing. Say something as honest as, "When authors write for primary grades, sometimes their wording sounds funny because we don't know how to read many words yet. If we could read every word in the world, how could the writer have written this sentence to sound the way people really talk?") (Linguistic Cues – Syntax)

AUDITORY PERCEPTION SKILLS

Sample Activities for Discussion, Task Cards, Learning Centers, and Reading Contracts

1. Describe how you think the voice of your favorite character in the story would sound. What clues did you get from the story that would verify your conclusions about his or her speech? (Relating Auditory Pitch, Stress, Timbre, and Intonation to Meaning)

2. Practice reading aloud and tape-recording interesting passages from the book, stressing certain words and changing the pitch and rhythm of your voice until you feel you have caught the real meaning of that section of the story. (Relating Auditory Pitch, Stress, Timbre, and Intonation to Meaning)

3. Play a book title memory game with classmates. Give the first word (or, for book titles that are one word long, the first letter or syllable) of the title. See who gets a point by completing the title. (Alternates: Give the author; see who can say the title. Give the title; see who can say the author.) (Auditory Closure)

4. Select a passage in this book that you would like to be able to recite from memory. Why did you choose this passage? (Auditory Memory)

5. Use three or four tape recorders, placed in various corners of the room, to give realistic sound effects as you present your book in a speech to the class. (Auditory Tracking)

6. Tape-record some dialogue from a specific character in the story. Use his or her speech patterns. (Oral Language)

7. Have a trial as to whether or not the book is worth reading. (Oral Language)

8. Conduct "Person-on-the-Street" interviews where other students respond as would story characters. (Or act out, using a videotape recorder, or a tape recorder.) (Oral Language)

9. Plan a panel discussion on the book that you think classmates would enjoy. Prepare an interesting evaluation sheet to check their reactions to the discussion. (Oral Language)

10. Role-play a character. (Oral Language)

11. Pretend you are a radio or TV interviewer and record an interview with a story character. (Oral Language)
12. Give a chalk-talk on the book. (Oral Language)
13. Start a listening center for literature. Tape-record a series of stories for other class members to enjoy. Include realistic dialogue, sound effects, etc. Alternates: (a) Create a series of tapes of stories suitable for young children. (b) Plan and make a tape recording of a favorite story as a gift. (Listening)

VISUAL PERCEPTION SKILLS

Sample Activities for Discussion, Task Cards, Learning Centers, and Reading Contracts

1. Make a flip book of a series of action pictures from the story. Bind it together so that pages can be flipped to show the action and sequence of the story. (Visual Sequence)
2. Draw some illustrations for the story. Use printing or lettering as part of the design. (Visual Figure-Ground)
3. Find book posters or book jackets that include words as part of their design. (Visual Figure-Ground)
4. Describe how you see the main characters. (Alternate: Draw the characters.) (Visualization)
5. If your book has been made into a film or a television program, describe the similarities and differences in how you expected the characters (setting, props, etc.) to look. (Visualization)
6. Design a seal for a story character to use in sealing letters. (Alternate: Make a stamp out of it from a potato and make a print pattern.) (Form Constancy)
7. Make a design by repeating the names of story characters over and over on a sheet of paper. (Form Constancy)
8. Write and draw a rebus for your story. (Visual Comprehension)
9. Use at least three slide projectors simultaneously to illustrate your talk on the book. (Visual Tracking)
10. Give a group book report. Station each of the group of reviewers in different parts of the room. Toss the conversation "ball" back and forth among the reviewers. (Visual Tracking)

PERCEPTION SKILLS

Sample Activities for Discussion, Task Cards, Learning Centers, and Reading Contracts

1. Find sentences in the story that tell about sense impressions; e.g., how something sounds, looks, feels, smells, tastes, etc. (Multisensory Perception)
2. Use at least three of the following to accompany your presentation on your book: films, tape recordings, pictures, smells, sounds, foods, etc. (Multisensory Perception)
3. Plan your book review so the audience will have a chance to do all of the following: Taste, smell, feel, hear, see, move. (Multisensory Perception)
4. Select fabrics for costumes for a play made from the story. (Tactile Perception)
5. Make clay figures representing story characters. (Alternates: Dolls, stick figures.) (Tactile Perception)
6. Make a clay plaque representing the story, the action, or a character. (Tactile Perception)
7. Prepare a typical meal that the story characters would be accustomed to eating. (Taste Perception)
8. Make a recipe book for the setting and era of the story. (Taste Perception)
9. Make a three-dimensional map of the story setting, or of a character's home. (Motor Coordination)
10. Present your review of the book by using pantomime to show how you think each character moved. (General Coordination)
11. Hold an audition for a pantomime of the story. Select the performer who you think moves the most like the story character. (General Coordination)

WORK-STUDY SKILLS

Sample Activities for Discussion, Task Cards, Learning Centers, and Reading Contracts

1. Make a diagram of the emotions of a story character. (Alternate: Diagram changes in a character's attitudes. (Interpreting Graphic Materials)

2. Make a diagram of the house where a favorite character lived. (Interpreting Graphic Materials)

3. Make a diagram of the action in the story. (Interpreting Graphic Materials)

4. Write the names of five characters across the top of your paper. List voice, attitude, expression, height, eye color down the left-hand side. Fill in the chart for each character. (Interpreting Graphic Materials)

5. Make a chart of the reviews of this story from book review books, magazines, and/or newspapers. Show similarities and differences in the kinds of things included in the review (reviewer liked the book, wrote about the same character, ratings, format of book review, and the like). (Interpreting Graphic Materials)

6. Make a map of the action in the book, of the travels of a character, of the setting, of the town where a favorite character lived. (Map and Globe Skills)

7. Locate the place(s) where your story took place on a map or globe. Write a description of that setting. (Map and Globe Skills)

8. Make a booklet containing photographs, illustrations, and/or pictures that illustrate the book you read. Put captions under each. Either make the pictures or illustrations yourself or choose them from magazines. (Interpreting Pictures and Illustrations)

9. Find pictures that fit the main character in the story. Explain. (Interpreting Pictures and Illustrations)

10. Make a table showing the time line of the book. (Alternate: Make a pictorial time line.) (Interpreting Graphic Materials)

11. Review several articles on censorship of books. Make a list of effective points you find pro and con. (Note Taking)

12. Act as secretary for the Book Review Club. (Note Taking)

13. Read a book on how to make or do something. Review it by sharing directions or steps of what you did or made as a result of reading the book. (Following Directions)

14. Write directions for presenting an exciting book review. (Following Directions)

15. List four characters from the book across the top of your paper. Write five characteristics of each person under each name. (Outlining)

16. List and analyze historical facts used in the book. (Outlining)

17. Prepare an outline for a talk on the book. Include photographs, slides, pictures from magazines, artifacts, etc., to make your presentation more interesting. (Outlining)

18. Make an original reference book on a subject of interest to you. Use materials you develop as a result of your own research and/or library research. (Research Skills)

19. What items, actions, phrases, sentences, episodes in the book cause you to think the author did research before writing? (Research Skills)

20. Be prepared to read a short selection from the book that might interest your audience. (Oral Reading)

21. Read an exciting part of the book out loud, stopping at an exciting place that will encourage others to finish reading it. (Oral Reading)

22. Practice reading aloud a library book suitable for younger children. Read it to them, then critique yourself. (Oral Reading)

23. Write a book review for the school (or classroom) newspaper. (Alternate: For a class collection of book reviews) (Book Reviewing)

24. Make a display of book reviews about your book from magazines and newspapers. Include your review, too. (Book Reviewing)

25. Compare your opinion of this book to that of other class members in our *Classroom Review of Books* file. (Book Reviewing)

26. Keep a record of your speed of reading for several hundred words of this book. Continue to do this with the next five books you read. What happens to your rate of reading. Does this have anything to do with the type of reading material? (Reading Rate)

27. Sometimes readers like to read a book slowly. List books you have read that you wanted to read more slowly than usual. Why? (Reading Rate)

28. Get together with a few people who have read the same book and design and construct a mural illustrating the sequence of the story. (Group Work Skills)

29. Plan a group book review. (Group Work Skills)

REFERENCE SKILLS

Sample Activities for Discussion, Task Cards, Learning Centers, and Reading Contracts

1. Make an outline for an autobiography. Include possible titles, table of contents, etc. (Using Parts of Books)
2. Write a table of contents for a book on a trip you would like to make. (Using Parts of Books)
3. To whom would you dedicate a book if you wrote one? Write a sample dedication. (Using Parts of Books)
4. What are book titles you especially like? (Using Parts of Books)
5. Take one letter of the alphabet. Develop an index from the book for that one letter. (Using Parts of Books)
6. In the library, find a review of the book you read. Compare the reviewer's opinion to yours. (Library Skills)
7. Write an introduction to your book. (Using Parts of Books)
8. What do the names of each of the story characters really mean? What kind of book would you use to find out? (Using Dictionaries and Other Word Reference Books)
9. Authors often have a list of pet words or phrases they use again and again. Did you find this author using words over and over? Did you find this helpful or distracting in furthering the story? What are some other words the author would use again and again? What other words could he/she use? Use your thesaurus. (Using Standard References)
10. If you wanted to find a word that rhymed, where would you look? Can you think of a word that cannot be rhymed? (Using Standard References)
11. Look up story place names, episodes, inventions, geographical locations, historical characters in the encyclopedia. Report on the information you found. (Using Standard References)

A FINAL WORD ABOUT NEW WAYS WITH BOOK REVIEWS

The best book reviewing is that which inspires the reviewer to creative efforts of his or her own. As students review the writing of others, it is natural for them to turn to their own creating. As students learn to review and critique from such a creative stance, they come to realize that literature consists not only of great classics, but also of much written material that can help them live better lives, solve their problems, and increase their creativity.

Index

DATE DUE			

DEMCO 38-297